Know My Name
A Novel

Michael Carley

Copyright © 2016 Michael Carley

All rights reserved.

ISBN: 151949761X
ISBN-13: 978-1519479761

"Castaway" words and music by Kris Kristofferson. Copyright © 2013 Jody Ray Publishing. Used by permission.

DEDICATION

For Beckie, who has always known mine.

iv

CONTENTS

Acknowledgments	vii
Epigraph	1
Andrew and Lucy	3
Names	9
Missing	40
Books	75
Prayers	124
Dreams	164
Discovery	188
Ripples	202
Epilogue	229
About the Author	232

ACKNOWLEDGMENTS

First, and most importantly, I would like to thank my wife Rebecca and son Lucas for their continual support, confidence, and encouragement. You are my inspiration and this book would not have been possible without you.

Many people have contributed to this novel after the first draft. Ann Marie Wagstaff, Beverly Richardson, Catherine Hodges, Neal Blakie, and Laurie Buchholz provided comments and suggestions that helped me correct many errors, from structure to small details. One evening discussion with Rebecca, Ann Marie, and Laurie was one of my best memories of this process. It meant a great deal to me to not only know that you liked what I was doing, but that you understood it.

I also appreciated the input of Greg Miller, a writing coach who can improve anyone's work. Jenny Kanevsky provided great copy-editing support. Both of you improved this book far more than you likely know.

For all of you who made suggestions that I did not take, please chalk it up to my stubbornness and inexperience. Your help is ever appreciated.

'Cause like a ship without a rudder
I'm just drifting with the tide
And each day I'm drawing closer to the brink
Just a speck upon the waters
Of an ocean deep and wide
I won't even make a ripple when I sink

Kris Kristofferson

Ain't one soul in the whole world knows my name...

Gillian Welch & David Rawlings

ANDREW AND LUCY

Andrew Grey was *not* suicidal.

That is to say, he'd never been diagnosed with depression, or any mental illness. In fact, he'd never even consulted a mental health professional for any reason.

It wasn't that he had anything against psychologists, psychiatrists, or therapists. To the extent that he'd considered the idea at all, he was sure they performed a valuable service for those who needed it. Andrew had just never considered himself among that group.

So, as he drove his Honda Civic up the Alameda, his mind was on more practical matters. Andrew was nothing if not practical. His choice of car had been as sensible as his choice of apartments. It was one of the few things he took real pride in, and as he turned off the Alameda onto Emory, he recalled the criteria he'd used.

The Bay Bridge Apartments weren't on the Bay and they weren't near any of the bridges. But that was just marketing, which Andrew could forgive. He'd pulled out his checklist at each of the nine places he'd visited. This one had all the things he needed: laundry facilities in the apartment, not down the hall (using a shared laundry room was something he associates with college students, not to be mixed with the world of adults), not too many kids or pets running around, and close enough to work were just the last three items on his two-page list. The Bay Bridge complex wasn't luxurious, but it met most of his criteria.

As for work, the complex was only a mile and a half from the

Maitland & Mason firm. On sunny days, he could, and often did, ride his bike to work. His boss, G-dub (God did Andrew hate that nickname, but at G-dub's insistence, he'd gotten used to it) teased him about the bike. "Don't we pay you enough to get yourself a real ve-hicle?" he'd niggled. Andrew never responded. It didn't really matter to G-dub whether Andrew biked or drove. He'd tease him about the Civic as well. G-dub himself drove a new Miata convertible, purchased, he'd said with last year's bonus. Andrew suspected the bonus had supplied little more than the down payment. But he didn't worry about G-dub's bragging or his teasing. He was immune to his boss's opinions on his choice of vehicle. His bike was practical, as was his Civic.

When he'd gotten his own bonus, a full month after G-dub's, the money had gone into the bank. He'd ignored the not-so-gentle suggestion that he upgrade his car. The Civic was only six years old. It had been two years old when he'd bought it, prime value for the money, and he hoped to keep it until it was at least ten, maybe twelve or fourteen. That would really be nice.

He did concede that he might need to trade the car in sooner if he had G-dub's job. His boss had to interact with clients on a more regular and personal basis. Wining and dining was part of the job. Andrew had no interest in schmoozing, but if he had to someday, he'd do it. A sense of duty had long since been ingrained in him.

Still, such impracticality rankled. Of course, a promotion would come with a raise, but what's the point of a raise if you have to waste it on a new, and completely unnecessary and overpriced, car every two years? He'd take it if it was offered, but hopefully, promotions were far into his future.

Right now, he was thinking of the one thing he'd forgotten to include on his apartment search list four years ago. He should have considered the orientation of the sun. On his drive to work in the morning, half his trip was to the east, meaning he was driving right into the sun's glare. On the return home, the westerly drive had the same problem. If the car's windshield had any dust (which was admittedly a rare problem for Andrew) the glare could be blinding, especially in the winter, which would be coming in a few weeks.

Andrew mentally chastised himself for the oversight. This was something he should definitely have considered. But, it wasn't worth moving either. He'd already done a mental cost-benefit analysis and until he had more compelling reasons to upgrade, the Bay Bridge Apartments would do.

But today, his mind was on other things. It was Friday, and his weekend was fully planned. He'd sort the laundry tonight and wash it on Saturday. While the clothes were washing, he'd plan out his meals for the week, including lunches to take to work, in preparation for grocery shopping on Sunday. It was almost the end of the month, so it was also time to pay the bills. Thus prepared, he stepped carefully down the hallway and inserted his key into the door of apartment 2F.

Yes, it would be a full weekend indeed.

**

Lucinda Fuentes had never been suicidal. No one in her life would have considered her so, not even her mother who worried about her often. Lucinda wasn't depressed, nor did she have big highs and lows. While Lucy's mother would have preferred that she was married by now, or at least dated more often, she'd never worried about her daughter harming herself in any way.

And, her lack of worry on that front was justified. Lucinda was quite content with the direction of her life, which might have seemed to others rather directionless indeed. If someone could read her internal emotional state, she might have even seemed happy-go-lucky.

The weekend was special to Lucinda as well and she turned her mail truck out of the Bay Bridge apartment complex just minutes after Andrew turned in. Once she dropped off the vehicle, she was free to run her own errands. Friday was time to do her weekly shopping, leaving the weekend free. Lunardi's was a bit out of the way, but she liked the small market where she could shop in peace without being disturbed by workmates or others she knew.

Lucy passed by the tortillas. She was supposed to make fresh ones with her mother on Sunday, but she was hoping there might be some way out of it. Not that she didn't like spending time with family, she just valued her alone time more. Reading was her passion and she was excited about the new Tolkien biography she'd picked up at lunchtime. Normally, she didn't read much non-fiction, but after all, this was Tolkien.

She'd already picked up enough yogurt for the week and the makings for sandwiches. Taking her lunch to work didn't just save money. It allowed her to spend most of the lunch break reading in the park. She hadn't been able to do that today, not only because she was out of sandwich supplies and had to go to a restaurant, but also because the bookstore stop had taken up her time. With the need for groceries adding another delay, Lucinda was getting antsy. The day had involved far too much human interaction and far too little solitude for her tastes.

As she made her way through the soup aisle, that same bagboy she'd seen before was making his way from the other direction, but Lucy hardly noticed him. The piped-in sound system was playing James McMurtry's "Walk Between the Raindrops" and she was absentmindedly dancing along the aisle as she examined the various soup choices. *So many different variations of the same things*, she thought.

"...raindrops . . . smooth as a pearl" a voice sang next to her.

"Excuse me," Lucinda had been startled out of her soup/Tolkien daydream.

"The song," the bagboy said, stopping for a moment and leaning on his wide broom. His name badge identified him as Alex. "Weren't you listening?"

"Sorry, wasn't paying attention." Lucy turned away and grabbed a can of "Grilled Chicken Italiano" and another of "Vegetable Medley" and made her way back toward the tortillas at the end of the aisle, Surely she could put her mother off for another week, she thought as she picked up the smallest package of corn ones she could find.

"McMurtry," Alex called out. "You should check him out. That's a great song".

"Thanks" Lucinda intoned, giving him a brief smile. He seemed like a nice guy, but it had always seemed bizarre to her when someone opened a conversation with a perfect stranger. It was something that would never occur to her.

Having decided to put her mother off for at least one more week, Lucinda headed to the produce section. If she was going to avoid making tortillas and salsa, she'd of course be hearing a lecture about her eating habits. Less canned food, more fruits and vegetables, that was Ramira Fuentes' mantra. Lucy was determined to at least have a few fresh things in the refrigerator to stifle the argument a bit. She half-heartedly grabbed a couple of bell peppers, some cabbage, and then her favorite, plums. She liked all kinds, but now they had the best ones, the Avalons.

With both real food needs and responses to potential arguments supplied for the upcoming week, she headed for the checkout, with Tolkien back on her mind. The new biography was a tome, over eight hundred pages, but she still thought she could knock it out in a weekend if she started tonight. She'd once read the entire *Lord of the Rings* trilogy in just a week, though to be fair, it was her fourth time through.

It wasn't just Tolkien of course; Lucinda liked to think she had a wide variety of tastes in books. But for pure escapism, you couldn't beat fantasy. Tolkien was everyone's yardstick, though there were many others: Martin, Pullman, Brooks and a whole trove of wannabes and copiers. She liked most of them, but Tolkien was. . . literature. Though she wasn't opposed to reading literary fiction on occasion, she didn't often use the word. Something about it was too academic, but some word was needed to recognize Tolkien's place in the canon. After reading every piece of the legendarium and anything else she could get her hands on, this new biography was the first new thing she'd seen in some time. She hoped it would give her some new insights rather than just rehash what she already knew.

With any luck, she'd be home soon with the groceries out of sight and mind and the book in her hand. Lucy planned on getting through the first couple of chapters before falling asleep tonight.

For the second time, she didn't notice Alex, but he noticed her and traded places with one of his fellow bagboys, who moved a bit reluctantly when he saw what had attracted Alex's attention, to bag up Lucy's purchases. "Need help out?"

She tried again to give him a smile, but demurred. "Just two bags" she said, holding them up as she stepped around the counter.

Lucinda didn't notice the hopeful grin on Alex's face or its fall into disappointment. So again she was startled as he called after her in an exaggerated melody, "Don't be a stranger!"

"I'm sorry?" she turned back toward him.

"The song" he repeated. "You need to listen to that song."

"OK, maybe I will."

Then Lucinda turned, stepped out of the store and into her car and pointed it toward home and her book.

NAMES

Gerold Walker knew that names were important and his parents had done him no favors with his. He still shook his head at the idea, Gerold, really?

It could have been worse. His parents pretended to old money and his mother had really wanted him named Gerhold. Gerold was the compromise, for which he constantly thanked his father. Willard Walker had faced the same problem and knew something about how merciless kids could be. At school, his name quickly turned to Gerry. Not long after he could spell, he even changed it to Jerry, further obscuring the pretentiousness of his mother's selection.

It was in college when it he became G-dub. It seemed like half the guys in Sigma Alpha had nicknames, and most of them were ridiculous, ranging from the tried and trite (T-Bone and The Beast) to the stupid and embarrassing for their futures (Gravekicker and Boobsqueezer). When it came to pledge time and the name Gerold Walker was called out, he could see on their faces that the ribbing was about to start. That name hadn't crossed his mind in years except when filling out forms. He prided himself in thinking on his feet, so, quick as a whip, he'd put the long-forgotten G with his surname initial and called out "G-dub," I go by "G-dub." It had been one of his luckier moments to be sure. The guy just before him was going by his initials, but J.R. was boring and never made it past pledge week.

College was indeed where G-dub had found his way. His mother had been appalled at both his choice of college and his fraternity. San Jose State was several tiers below what she'd expected from her son and worse, to have him join that Sigma Alpha party frat just added insult to vicarious injury. But young Gerry was smarter than they realized. Sigma Alpha may have had a reputation for partying, but it was also the frat most of the business majors joined. It was how connections were made and that's where G-dub shone.

Partying helped create the connections G-dub would need in the business world. While his grades were adequate, his contacts within Sigma Alpha, with their former members, with other frats, and increasingly with sororities, would provide the network for a career trajectory that consistently moved upward. If Maitland and Mason didn't work out, he had a half-dozen people ready to give him an equal or even better job.

Not that this was especially likely. He'd be at this firm for some time. Within a couple of years, it would be Maitland and Walker. Old Man Mason was coasting toward retirement and although G-dub wasn't first up for the partnership, he expected that by the time the choice was made, he'd be perfectly positioned. There were only a couple of guys, Chaplan and Rucker, ahead of him, and Chaplan was a blooming idiot.

He'd built his own team along the same philosophy. He'd selected every member from his own alma mater, where his connections were strongest. Although others might not understand his criteria, G-dub was, in his own way, meticulous. He actively avoided the 4.0 graduates with the perfect résumés. Even if they were good, they'd be looking to move up too quickly. G-dub went after the high middle, those who could balance an active social life, especially if it included the Greek life, and classwork. If someone could come in at 8:00 AM with a hangover and still put in a good day's work, he was a good candidate for team Walker.

Women were OK too. G-dub wasn't into discrimination; he was happy to have a woman or two on board as long as they were of the same mindset as the guys. These days, sororities were churning out party girls almost as prodigiously as the frats did party guys, and that was a good development as far as G-dub was concerned.

The one he still wondered about was Grey. Of the five team members he'd hired since becoming an account manager, Andrew Grey was the only misfit. He'd come with high recommendations from the B-school faculty he trusted, but didn't socialize with the team. Yet his favorite professor, Rinehardt, who'd been as close to a mentor as G-dub had ever had, had said it would be good strategy to hire Andrew. "You have enough frat boys on your team Gerold. You need a steady man to pick up the slack when the rest of your guys are home worshipping the porcelain goddess."

G-dub had bristled at the suggestion at first, but he knew solid advice when he heard it. Grey had been the third of his five hires, so his middling tenure was perfect for his role and his middling personality.

This morning, G-dub wasn't having to recover from any kind of bender. His weekend had been uncharacteristically sober. The SJU contract was starting today and he knew the importance of getting off to a good start. Alcohol was for loosening up corporate clients and to get new ones, for project-wrap parties, and just for breaking the tension during the middle of tax season. It was not a part of project kickoff meetings. Better that everyone has a clear head for those.

Thirty seconds after the MX-5 was safely parked under the carport, G-dub was inside the building and greeting his team. Coming in twenty minutes late was not just a perk; it allowed him to touch base with every member of his staff. The first thing he did, especially on a Monday, was count heads. "Massey, how was the weekend," he boomed, not waiting for an answer after patting Pete Massey on the back. "Sykes, Ballard . . . . ." G-dub tapped each man's cubicle before stopping to rub Ellie Davenport's shoulders for a moment. "How was the old weekend, Elsie?"

"Ugh" Davenport gave an exaggerated groan.

"That good, huh?"

Davenport smiled, but G-dub was already on his way to his windowed office. He didn't feel the need to stop at Grey's desk. Andrew never missed work or came in late and he seemed to bristle a bit when G-dub slapped his back or even tapped the side of his cubicle. Just as G-dub didn't enjoy the hassle of a boring staffer, Grey didn't really need any monitoring. These things had a way of balancing themselves out.

"Morning Lily" he called out to his assistant.

"It's Lillian!" she replied affably, with the voice that reminded the whole team that this game had been played before and would be played again as long as she was the organizing force in Gerold Walker's professional life.

"Got it Lily," he repeated, stepping through the glass door, leaving it open as it had been propped for the past six months.

"Kickoff meeting in fifteen!" he shouted to his squad, ignoring the good natured rejoinders that sailed his way.

Great coaches do make great teams, he thought as he settled down to his email.

**

Lillian Jacobs noticed things.

It was a trait she'd developed early in life and it was crucial to making sure G-dub stayed on track. The man would be lost completely if not for her little nudges. She was subtle when should could be, more forceful when necessary, but her main job was corralling his passions and stray idiocies. Because that man noticed next to nothing.

Like this morning. He did his usual Monday routine, the folksy back-slapping of his staff. It didn't surprise her that he didn't stop by Andrew's cubicle. Though she had a soft spot for Andrew, it was no secret that he was a bit of a loner. She'd been pleasantly surprised when G-dub hired him. He provided a nice balance to the raucous personalities of the rest of the group. Lillian took his kindness and sincerity for sweetness and, though it was nothing more than a mild irritation to Andrew, she had almost informally adopted him. If she and her husband had been able to have kids, they'd be almost his age by now, she often thought.

But what struck her today wasn't just that G-dub hadn't stopped by his cube, but that G-dub hadn't noticed that Andrew wasn't occupying it. Andrew was often the first to arrive, usually about five minutes before starting time, and yet today, at nearly 9:10 when the rest of the team was already gathered for the kickoff meeting, there was still no Andrew.

Lillian was surprised, but not truly worried yet. Worry would come in the late afternoon when she realized Andrew had missed the entire day without a call. That was unprecedented. For now, she decided to make a game of it.

When G-dub arrived in the conference room to meet with his team, each of the audit packets were on the table in front of each staffer. Andrew's packet was at his spot at the far end of the table from G-dub and to the left. The others already had their packets open and were guessing what each of their assignments might be.

"All right," the boss started things off. "We all know the importance of this project. Second biggest account since I've been here. This is our first go round with San Jose Unified. This is the public sector, so we shouldn't have many of those shenanigans we see with some of those start-up techies. Still, you have to make sure everything is in line. Line A needs to match line B, yadda, yadda, yadda. They've also got unions over there that get pretty sensitive when you step on their turf. Do your job, but watch what you say and who you say it to."

G-dub glanced only briefly in the direction of each team member when addressing them. Now he began tossing them their assignment sheets; how quickly they picked them up was taken as an informal sign of their alertness and readiness for work. "Ballard, you've been around the longest, so you'll be with me, interviewing the key players. They've already done their internal audit and the state's given them the once over; now it's our turn. The internal auditor's an old buddy of mine, so I'm not expecting any major problems and he'll give me a heads up about any issues. The new superintendent is kind of an asshole, so let me deal with him, but watch how I do it. You might be in this chair before you know it."

"Sykes, your job is to check out the comparables. It's not really part of the audit, but they want to know if they're overpaying on their health care. They'll use it as a weapon with the unions if they can, so see what we can give them." Sykes' assignment sheet was caught in a nanosecond with his left hand. G-dub liked sports metaphors and Duane had scored at least a triple.

"We want this contract for next year, so let's do it right and not piss anyone off. Grey, you're on accounts receivable, Elsie, you got the payables."

At this point, the snickers started around the room as Andrew's assignment sheet flew across the table and down into his black leather chair. G-dub didn't notice, but he did see that Ellie Davenport had caught hers as quickly as always.

"Massey, you knew one of the accounting specialists in college, didn't you?"

"Yeah," Pete spoke up, "Danny McDowell. He's a stiff, but he'll talk to me."

"OK, your first job is to take this McDowell out to breakfast, kiss his ass, whatever. Find out what's really going on, who's doing shady stuff, who to avoid. You've got this morning to get the lay of the land from your old pal, then check in with Grey and Davenport to see where they need help. If they don't need you, you can meet up with me and Gil and learn a bit about project leadership."

There were more chuckles around the table, but G-dub was on a roll. "They have a conference room downtown where we'll meet up at 4:15, no later. That's when we reconnoiter. We'll have the rest of the week for the boring stuff."

"Your contact sheets." Once more, papers began sailing down the table, one at a time, very precisely. Again, Andrew's slid down to his chair, and now the chuckles turned to giggles.

"What? Did I miss something?"

"Nah."

"Nope."

"Don't think so." Around the table, there was team solidarity.

Lillian had impeccable timing, mostly gained by eavesdropping. She stepped into the room, silently gathered up the unclaimed assignment sheet and contact sheet and sat down in Andrew's chair. She knew her place and she wasn't an accountant, but she did her best Andrew Grey impersonation, putting on her reading glasses, sitting up as straight as possible in her chair with her hand under her chin and an over serious, slightly disdainful look on her face as she stared toward the still oblivious G-dub. To complete the Andrew Grey look, just as G-dub glanced her direction, she raised her left

KNOW MY NAME

eyebrow questioningly.

The chuckles around the table now turned to guffaws, just as G-dub was preparing his big finish.

"OK, to wrap up, this project is going to figure big into this year's bonuses, and next year's are . . . what the hell is so damn funny?"

The laughter only escalated and though the entire team tried to avoid it, eventually both Sykes and Davenport looked toward Lillian in Andrew's chair enough to finally catch G-dub's attention. "Lily, what are you . . . where the heck is Grey?"

Finally, the bottled up laughter completely exploded and G-dub finally gave in. "No one's seen Andrew Grey?" he asked again. Heads shook around the room as the mirth gradually subsided.

"All right, you've had your fun. Lily, give Grey a call and find out why he's missing the biggest project launch we've had in the past year. Maybe he's finally getting some action. It's about time."

"Not likely," said Massey as they gathered up their belongings and started for the door.

"Aw, give him a break," Ballard broke in. The guy's due for a long weekend. What's it been, six months since that FedEx chick broke up with him?"

"Yeah, well, he just picked a hellacious time for it. And Pete, you're going to have to cover for him this morning. You'll have to get the scoop from your dumbass friend quick, then join Elsie."

"So much for you showing me the ropes, huh?"

"Blame that on Grey, when you see him. But just remember, he's covered for you about half a dozen times already."

**

Lillian made her call, but Andrew's familiar voice mail came was all she got, "Hello, this is Andrew Grey. Please leave a message with the date and time you called and I will return your call at my earliest convenience."

"Andrew, where the heck are you? This is Lillian. You've never missed a day, much less a project launch meeting. Give me a call back and let me know you're OK. Then get your butt down to San Jose Unified. Everybody else is already there."

She was sure there was no need to worry. Andrew Grey was as

reliable as clockwork, probably more so if such a thing could be measured. He was her favorite staffer, and not just because he was reliable and didn't engage in the nonsense of the rest of the team. She'd always been drawn to the quiet types, and she liked his name.

Lillian was fascinated with names, but not just with singular ones. She liked how two names fit together, and she knew when they didn't. Two people who belong together should have names that flow well orally. They shouldn't rhyme, that's too cutesy, and they shouldn't start or end with the same letter or sound. Like Massey's last two girlfriends. She knew they wouldn't work out. That first one was named Jocelyn, but when she brought her friends by to visit the office, they all called her Skeeter. "Peter and Skeeter?" That wasn't going to last, and it didn't.

After that it was Cassie. She was perfectly nice, but if they got married, she'd have been Cassie Massey. There was no way around that since no woman was going to marry Pete Massey and keep her birth name. Not that Lillian disapproved of that, though she hated the hyphenated thing (just commit already ladies!) but Pete would never have put up with it. No, Cassie Massey would have driven Lillian nuts and she was secretly pleased when Pete broke it off.

Sykes' last boyfriend had the same problem, though it wasn't a perfect rhyme. Mike was a nice guy, though a bit flamboyant, but Mike Sykes? To be fair, Lillian didn't know if gay men took each other's last names when they married, and she'd never learned Mike's last name, but why chance it?

Lillian believed that relationships worked best when the names flowed well. Like her husband of almost twenty years. David and Lillian, Lillian and David. It flows well either direction. Some couples names flowed well one way, but not the other. Lillian had no evidence, but she suspected that led to an imbalance in their relationships.

It had been Lillian who'd set Andrew up with Tina Gamble, known to everyone else in the office as "the FedEx girl." Lillian had struck up conversations with Tina and had commiserated with her after Tina had broken up with her boyfriend. Apparently, Andre was not to be trusted and though Tina never had hard evidence, she was sure he'd been cheating.

After Tina had left that particular day, Andrew stopped by her desk to ask a question. He'd always seemed so solitary, if not necessarily lonely, though Lillian didn't make much distinction. Almost immediately, it clicked in her mind. Andrew and Tina, Tina and Andrew. It worked. These names flowed as well as any two names she'd ever matched up. And one started with a vowel, the other with a consonant. That was important too, especially if the man's name started with the vowel. A couple whose names both started with vowels were a weak match and if they both had consonants, particularly hard ones (her own L didn't count, thankfully) they were likely to clash.

The surnames were what appealed to her most. In this case, they provided a perfect contrast. Grey was such a bland last name, and some would say it described Andrew's personality as well, but combining that with one like Gamble, pure genius.

She was aware that Andrew was awfully close to Andre, at least on paper. But they sounded different and it was the sound that mattered, not the spelling. She hoped Tina wouldn't notice.

The next time Tina came in, Lillian asked if she was ready to meet someone new. Tina was hesitant, but Lillian Jacobs was persistent yet tactful. "Oh come on girl. You need to have yourself some fun so you can forget that last cheating SOB."

Tina was startled by her description of Andre, but said nothing.

Lillian pressed. "Hey, maybe it will work out, maybe it won't. It's not like you'll have to see him all the time and have it be awkward."

"I come in here at least twice a week, you know."

"Yeah, but Andrew's desk is all the way in the back. You can't even see him from here." Then she decided to get Tina's curiosity up. "But, I can," she said teasingly as she leaned her chair back to look behind Ballard's cubicle. "He's cuuute. . . ." she said, stretching the syllable as long as she dared.

"The last thing I need is cute. Cute gets me in trouble, remember? I need a guy that's stable."

Lillian couldn't keep from laughing. "They don't get more stable than Andrew Grey. Trust me." The way she said it, Tina had to know she was speaking more about Andrew's credibility than her own.

"All right, I'll meet him. But no promises."

"Of course, girl. No pressure."

She called Andrew over on the pretense of having a package he needed to sign for. She thought that she was being obvious enough because Lillian signed for all the packages herself. Plus, she'd hinted to Andrew enough times that she was going to find him a girlfriend. But Andrew looked at her questioningly as he picked up the envelope that Tina had just delivered. It had Ellie Davenport's name on it.

"Andrew, you remember Tina Gamble?"

"Hi" he said, still looking at Lillian, not Tina.

"I had been thinking that the two of you should meet."

"We've met." The way Andrew said it wasn't sarcastic. It was just a simple statement; of course he'd met the young woman who delivered FedEx packages.

"Well actually Andrew," Lillian now realized she needed to spell it out as neither of them was inclined to take the initiative. "I was thinking the two of you should perhaps go out for coffee. Like, now."

"Oh," Tina piped in, "I'd like to, but now won't work. They keep us on a pretty tight schedule."

The next move was obviously Andrew's, but Lillian was leaving nothing to chance. "Maybe you two should exchange numbers? Then, you could meet for dinner instead of just a quick coffee. Really get to know each other."

Surprisingly, they both took the bait, taking the post-its she handed each of them with pointed looks. After numbers were exchanged, it was Tina who ended the awkwardness. "It was nice to meet you Andrew. I probably should get back to my route."

"Sure. I'll call you. Tomorrow OK?"

"Sounds good," Tina said, giving Lillian a skeptical look as she started for the door.

Lillian hadn't been all that optimistic herself, but when she queried Andrew two days later, it turned out he had called. "I said I would," he replied, surprised that there was even a question.

"Well?"

"We're going out for dinner Friday night."

"Where are you taking her?"

"We're going to meet at the Olive Garden."

"That's OK I guess. You'll have to tell me all about it Monday morning."

Andrew's responses to her inquisition Monday were tight-lipped, but she gathered the date had gone reasonably well. He remained reluctant to talk for the whole of their relationship, but Lillian got enough out of Tina to know that they were a couple for at least two months. She was never clear exactly what broke them up, but all of a sudden Tina was back with Andre. Lillian could never understand it, but Tina actually seemed happy. Andrew, for his part, seemed to take the breakup in his usual stride. Which is to say, he came in to work, did his job and went home each day. Alone, if not lonely.

**

Tina didn't often think of Andrew Grey anymore, but she was thinking of him today.

Today, she had taken the day off to shop. She had so much to do with the wedding in just six weeks. Andre wanted to be married before the baby came, and his mother insisted on it, though it mattered little to Tina. She knew she'd found the right man, and in a strange way, her brief relationship with Andrew was responsible.

When she had arrived at the Olive Garden for their first date, Andrew was standing at the entryway, looking very serious. She looked down at her watch: 6:02. Well, she thought, punctuality is a good trait, but if he's mad at me for being two minutes late, this isn't a very good start.

But Andrew wasn't angry. He greeted her as she walked up and asked how she'd been. From this point on though, it had been one of the stranger first dates she'd ever been on. At the time, she'd attributed it to her own emotional state. She was worrying over her breakup with Andre, wondering if it had been the right thing to do. Her view of Andrew was as "the transition guy." She didn't go into the date expecting a relationship, but if she was going to move on from Andre, she was going to have to get out there. So, from the very start, her attitude was a bit nonchalant.

But, so it seemed was Andrew's. He responded politely when she asked questions, but revealed little. His family was from Kansas, she gathered, but she couldn't seem to learn much about his life here in San Jose. He'd been here nearly a decade, for college and several years of work, although he never brought up friends or a social life. She wondered if he was a workaholic, but when he spoke of his job at Maitland & Mason, it seemed like just a job to him. When she asked what he enjoyed about accounting, his reply had taken her off guard. "It's very precise. It has a set of rules, though not everyone understands them. Those rules are designed to keep the system ethical, and mostly do so, when followed."

Precision had never been a trait she'd looked for in a field of study, much less a career. But, she couldn't say she was doing anything better. That's when he turned the tables. "What do you like about your work for FedEx?"

"I get to meet a lot of people all day long. Some of them I only see once, but I get to know others, like Lillian at your office. It's not the most important job in the world, but it pays the bills, for now at least."

"Are you thinking of doing something else?"

"Well, this job was only supposed to get me through college, but then the hours got in the way of my college schedule and somehow it became a full-time thing."

"So, are you thinking of going back to college? What would you study?"

Tina had been expecting this. "I'm not sure yet. Maybe that's the bigger problem. I could never settle on a major."

"Why do you need to go back to college if you like your job?

"I don't know, to better myself? Get a better kind of job in the future? Shouldn't I have a good job like you?"

"My job is good for me. Do you like accounting?"

Tina had to laugh. "Not even a little bit."

Now, Andrew raised his left eyebrow in a way that she would eventually decide was curious, not judgmental. "If you like delivering packages and you don't know of another career you would like, why go to college just on the chance of finding one? Nothing wrong with working for FedEx. The world needs people to deliver things."

Tina was almost floored. Either Andrew was hiding his judgment or he was sincere, she couldn't tell which. Hopefully, he wasn't just a guy who needed his woman to be in a lesser position. Either way, she was curious enough to commit to a second date right there, whether he asked her or not.

The night had ended early after a bit more conversation, alternating between awkward and curious. Andrew Grey was like no one she'd ever met. He wasn't attractive in the way that Andre was, or some of the other men she'd dated. But he was kind of cute, in his own way, thin and pleasant, though a bit serious. Mostly, she just needed someone different from Andre, someone she could trust. She could never be sure of Andre and somehow, she knew Andrew wouldn't cause her harm.

Now that she thought of them in this context, the similarity in their names wasn't lost on Tina. But she didn't think about it much. There could hardly be two different men than Andrew Grey and Andre James. Where Andre was boisterous and outgoing, Andrew was quiet and introspective. Where Andre was passionate, Andrew was thoughtful. Both men worked hard, but Andre's job at the gym was physical, Andrew's work was mental. Andrew didn't seem exactly ambitious, but his job was in an office and it paid better. Certainly, Andrew's job was better, right? Except that he himself had tried to disabuse her of the notion that one job was better than another just because it paid better or was located in an air conditioned office.

Today, Tina chuckled to herself as she recalled her confusion that day. The choice between Andre and Andrew had never really been a choice. One had led her back to the other, and for that, she would always be grateful.

**

Confusion was something that rarely afflicted Zeke Grey. He was certain of most things in life and those he wasn't, he didn't like to think about. As an example, he was certain that the road he was driving on was old Highway 40. Some of the younger people didn't even know what he meant when he called it that, but old habits die hard, especially if there was nothing wrong with them in the first place. And there was nothing wrong with Highway 40 that necessitated a name change.

He didn't have long to think about it though. Soon, he was on Water Well Road and turning into the church parking lot. Aside from home and work, he spent more time at Salina Free Pentecostal Church than anywhere. Once a month, on Monday afternoons, his boss let him off early so that he could meet with the church council. Zeke took his work as a church deacon seriously. He thought of his church position as similar to his welding job. Just as he welded two pieces of metal together, the church helped put lost souls back together.

"Deke Zeke! Deke Zeke!" The Selmy kids were calling to him from the church door before he was even out of the car. Those kids were incorrigible and Zeke couldn't see why Roger Selmy let them hang out in the parking lot all the time. He grunted a greeting as he walked in. He didn't want to encourage the Deke Zeke nonsense. It was the first nickname he'd ever really been given and in a way he supposed it was a sign of respect. He'd been a deacon for almost twenty years now, so some recognition of the position was understandable. Still, Deke Zeke seemed almost sacrilegious. The Selmy kids should have some respect, though they wouldn't likely learn it from their father.

"Looks like it's just you and me today." Roger said as he shook Deke's hand. There were five of them on council, but Jason Parnell often had trouble getting off work and Bob Searcy was on vacation. Roger was unemployed again, which ironically made him more reliable for council than he'd been when he was working.

"Pastor already here?"

"Of course. Pastor Cartwright never misses a day. He'll be here tomorrow too, even though Tuesdays and Wednesdays are supposed to be his days off."

"It's the Lord's work and I'm sure God provides him the energy to carry on."

"Indeed" Roger agreed as he opened the door and they made their way to the small church office. Walking together, Roger and Zeke provided quite a contrast, both in appearance and temperament. Roger stood six foot one, lanky and gregarious. To his left, Zeke Grey was just five foot six, though seemingly shorter with his hunched shoulders. His face grim and purposeful, he took three strides to Roger's every two, but they arrived together where Pastor Isaiah Cartwright was already at his desk.

"Afternoon gentlemen" the pastor spoke as he shook each man's hand.

"Afternoon Pastor" Zeke replied as he sat down.

"Afternoon, what's on the agenda for today?" Roger Selmy was awfully interested in getting to business for someone with no job.

"Not too many things to discuss today" the pastor replied. "We got through the budget stuff last time. Just a couple of policy change requests from our members to consider."

"Policy changes?" Zeke was skeptical already. God didn't change with the times, so there was no reason his people should.

"Nothing to worry about Zeke. Just because someone requests we change a policy doesn't mean we will approve it."

"Hmph" Zeke mumbled quietly. He'd never disrespect a minister out loud, but he was still concerned.

"Lighten up Zeke" Roger chimed in, slapping his fellow deacon on the back. "We're just talkin'. Who knows, maybe someone will have a good idea. Shake things up, ya know."

"I don't need any shaking up, thank you. But, of course I'll listen. As James said, we should be quick to hear and slow to speak."

"First up" Pastor Cartwright interrupted, "is Nathan Whitman. He'd like to ask that he be allowed to play his electric guitar during services. He just moved to town when he married the Beckmans' daughter and he was mightily disappointed when I explained our prohibition. It seems the Assembly church he attended in Georgia allowed electric. The boy says he learned on electric and doesn't own an acoustic guitar."

"I don't see how that changes anything." This policy had been resolved long ago as far as Deacon Grey was concerned.

"Well, Mr. Beckman is taking up his son-in-law's case. He'd like to remind us that we didn't used to allow instruments at all. Says this isn't really much different." Pastor Cartwright knew where this conversation was headed, but he liked to make sure every proposal got a fair hearing and sometimes that meant giving a bad idea a full explanation before gently squashing it.

"I can see what he means. . . . ." Deacon Selmy started.

Zeke broke in "I can too, and Arthur Beckman has been around long enough to know better. As I recall, he was a deacon himself when we made that decision. Frankly, I still wonder if we did the right thing because it leads to questions like this. But here's the difference: an acoustic guitar makes *a joyful noise*. So does that piano out there, the banjo, and maybe that tambourine we let his daughter play. I'm still not sure about that sometimes either, but if we bring in electrics, what do we end up with? The noise those things make isn't joyful; it's *worldly.* It doesn't matter what they allowed in Georgia. We have standards here and Nathan Whitman will have to live with them if he wants to be a member of this church."

"That's how I thought we'd all feel," the pastor spoke up before Roger could object and before Zeke worked himself up. There was no need in Zeke getting red in the face over something that was never going to happen. "I'll explain it to the Whitman boy. I'm sure he'll understand. He was very respectful when he made his request."

Zeke sat back and slumped in his chair, relaxing just a little. It didn't take much to get a church to lower its standards. You had to be vigilant.

"Moving on," the pastor spoke, as he'd finished making his notes about what to say to the Whitman boy, "Roger, I believe you mentioned you had a request from a parishioner?"

Roger Selmy sat up. "Yes, it was from Miss Nancy Brables. She's finished school now and has moved out of her folks' home. She's teaching down at the elementary on Crawford."

"And what right does that give her to take up the council's time?" Zeke queried. "Shouldn't she be speaking with her father?"

"Well, that's kind of the point. Nancy's out on her own now and John Brables doesn't even attend more than once a month. Less than that during football season." Regular church attendance was a long standing concern of the council and had been the topic of many a sermon. Even Deacon Selmy was on that bandwagon. "Nancy respectfully requests that she be allowed to vote in the congregation meetings next month."

KNOW MY NAME

"You did explain the policy to her, didn't you?" Pastor Cartwright had to wonder how a church deacon could let such a misunderstanding get this far. "Men speak on behalf of their families."

"Paul said women are to be silent in the church," Zeke added, though he wasn't worried this time. He too was surprised that the proposal had even made it to this point.

"It isn't just that Brables is rarely here. Nancy feels he doesn't represent her opinions when he votes."

"Good Lord, what are they teaching at that college these days?" Zeke was about to get on a roll, but Roger interrupted.

"I believe you daughter graduated from that same college. And your boy. Didn't he go out to . . . "

"I know perfectly well where Andrew went to school. That's irrelevant. Nancy should know better. She grew up in this church. These colleges put fool ideas into the kids' heads and then we have to deal with them when they come back to town, if they do come back. It would be better for all of us if our young people took up a good vocation and never let their shadow darken a college door."

"Nancy's point is, John Brables doesn't represent her, even when he does bother to show up to church. Now that she's out on her own, she thinks her own household should have a vote. She's not living at home anymore and she says her old man doesn't listen to her when she shares her opinion on church questions. He just laughs at her."

"I suspect," the pastor broke in, "that Miss Brables is mistaking listening with agreeing. John Brables is a good man even if he doesn't attend as often as he should. I'm sure he listens to his daughter's thoughts and considers them thoroughly. That doesn't mean he has to vote the way she wants. He's the father. He represents the will of the family in all religious matters. Of course, if Miss Brables has more specific concerns, she is welcome to make an appointment and speak with me personally."

"And with that," Cartwright said with some authority. "I think our business for the day is concluded. You'll both be home in time for supper this time. I'm sure your wives will appreciate that."

Both deacons thanked the pastor and they walked out together. Although they often disagreed on the specifics of policy, they shared a certain pride in the service of the church. Good honest debate could only benefit the congregation, Roger thought.

Zeke would disagree on that point and he was fuming as he made his way down Water Well road and back toward the highway. Roger had some nerve, he thought, bringing his kids into a council discussion. Janice wasn't perfect, but she was raised right and would never pull a stunt like this Brables girl. Roger must have encouraged her too.

And Andrew, well he was a sore spot for Zeke all the way around. They hadn't spoken for months; it seemed whenever they did, Andrew managed to pick a fight. Olivia said they were too much alike, but Zeke didn't see it. That young man had no respect for his elders or for God's law. Increasingly, he regretted sending either of his children off to college and especially letting Andrew pick one across the country. Let your kids leave the house and you lose all control of them.

He would be home early, he realized. For all the drama, this had been one of their shorter council meetings. Zeke thought about going back to work, get in a little more time. He never felt guilty taking off for council meetings, it was God's work, but his sense of duty suggested that if the meeting ended early, he should go back and finish his time. But, Gregorson had laughed the last time he'd showed up with just an hour left in his shift. "Go home Zeke," he'd said. "Enjoy your afternoon. Surprise that pretty little wife of yours."

Sayings like that annoyed Zeke. He wasn't even sure whether Olivia would be considered pretty by most men. It wasn't something he considered. The very saying "pretty little wife" emphasized the wrong thing. He wanted a wife who was right with God, one who'd follow his direction and live her life in accordance with scripture. Olivia had a past, one he preferred not to think about, but for more than twenty-five years, she'd been a good wife and servant of the Lord. That was what mattered.

**

A servant is exactly what Olivia Grey felt like today. She was busy making her olive loaf for the Tuesday night Bible study. It had become something of a church legend (or joke) Olivia and the olive loaf. The rumor, which she'd started, was that her mother had been making this loaf on the day she was born. When her mother went into labor and they rushed to the hospital, the Olive loaf burned, thus giving rise to her name, Olivia Bernice Holcomb, now Olivia Grey for more than a quarter of a century. It was, the story held, the first and last time an olive loaf had burned in the Holcomb family. The story was an invention. She'd gotten the recipe from a Betty Crocker cookbook. But as lies went, this was one of the whitest. She thought it best to let them have their simple pleasures, and if they liked calling her "Burnt Olives," so be it. It wasn't the biggest secret she held. Plus, as long as the loaf was good, and it always was, she'd always be in their good graces.

She was finally looking forward to Bible study again. They'd spent the past eight weeks going over the book of Revelations and that text scared her. All the talk of lakes of fire and the liars burning in it, the vivid descriptions of Greek myth-like beasts and all of that apocalyptic imagery gave her nightmares. The way people talked about it made it worse. Half the group seemed intent on using the book to interpret modern events and predict the end of the world. Didn't Jesus say somewhere that you wouldn't know the where and when? If that's true, what's the point in trying to guess?

But, this week would be better. They were focusing on Paul's letter to the Romans. They'd studied it before, but at least it wouldn't keep her up at night.

She was startled to hear the crush of Zeke's truck tires on the gravel driveway. Olivia looked up at the clock, only 3:45, she hoped nothing was wrong. She hadn't even started dinner yet and she had hoped to get a little rest time once the loaf was in. She opened the oven, pushed the bread pans in, and called out to her husband. "Zeke honey, everything OK?"

"Yes, Mother. Council didn't take too long this week. Not much on the agenda except some foolishness from Roger Selmy."

"What kind of foolishness this time?"

"Oh, nothing you need to worry about. Pastor and I put an end to it. He gives Roger a little too much rope sometimes, but Pastor Cartwright knows nonsense when he hears it."

"I'm sure he does. Are you ready for dinner? It's a bit early you know."

"We can wait until the bread's done. Why don't you take a rest?"

"Thank you. I think I will. Did you get the mail? I was hoping for a letter from one of the kids."

"I got the mail and it was nothing but junk, like usual. Neither of those kids is going to send you a letter. They use email and the Internet these days and there's no getting around it. Janice is probably too busy with that new job of hers anyway."

"But, Andrew. He could at least call. I sent him a birthday card not three weeks ago."

"Andrew hasn't called you in what, three months? He's not going to call and he's not going to write. If you want to talk to him, you'll have to call him yourself."

"It's so expensive. He could call me. With that cell phone, he doesn't have to pay long distance like we do."

Zeke Grey wasn't an unfeeling man, but he also didn't believe in giving credence to fantasies. He grasped his wife gently, but firmly by the shoulders. Olivia shivered in his hands. Though she was nearly the same height as Zeke, she looked and felt small, as she often did around him. "Mother, I want you to listen to me carefully. Your son, that boy is gone. We tried. The good Lord knows we tried, but we lost him. He's never coming back to Salina and he's never coming back to church. You're not likely to hear from him more than a couple of times a year, so you'd best put him out of your mind as best you can."

"He's my son. How can I put my own flesh and blood out of my mind?"

"Pray Mother. Pray that the good Lord brings him back to the righteous path. That's the best we can do."

With that, Zeke gave her shoulders a final squeeze, it might have been one of affection, and went into the living room. He had some praying to do himself.

**

If there had been a letter from Andrew, it would have been in Lucinda's hand. She was preparing to leave the Bay Bridge apartment complex once again. As she locked up the last set of mailboxes, she was mentally preparing her list for Lunardi's, where she was headed as soon as she could get the truck turned in. A police officer was removing yellow caution tape from Myrtle Street near Asbury and some kids had grabbed some of the tape and were wrapping their smallest playmate in it. The officer stood to the side, laughing along with the older kids. Lucinda steered around the children and their adult conspirator and made her way toward the Alameda. The faster she could get to the store, the sooner this night would be over.

Lucinda would pay for her decision to take the whole weekend to herself. Since she'd skipped making tortillas on Friday, she was stuck working on tamales this evening. Her mother already had the masa and most of the other ingredients, but Lucinda had to pick up *carnitas* and a couple of other items before heading over. From the amount her mother had requested, Lucinda knew she was in for a long night.

Less than an hour later, she walked into Lunardi's, a paper list in her hand. The *carnitas* she could remember, but she could never keep the spices straight. Her mother seemed to use some that no one else included; despite how much she clung to tradition, Ramira Fuentes was an experimenter in the kitchen, for better or worse.

As she stepped through the door, Alex greeted her, on his way to retrieve shopping carts before the evening rush got under way. "Hey, raindrops girl. Good to see you."

"Hi" Lucinda said, focused, but not entirely unfriendly.

Alex took this as an invitation. "Hey, did you pick up that album I mentioned."

"Not yet. I haven't had a chance." Lucinda already had her eye on the plums. The ones she'd bought on Friday were already gone.

"That's too bad. I think you'll like it. Your name is Lucinda, right?"

"How did you know that?"

"Saw it on your credit card receipt. I looked it up. It means 'light.'"

"I know." Lucinda decided against telling him the story. She'd been nameless for a week after she was born, eventually named after the family noticed that a ray of light from a gap in the curtains woke her up from her nap every day at the same time.

"It suits you" Alex told her as he smiled and headed out to his task, whistling a now familiar tune.

Lucinda made her way through her mother's list, grabbing the *carnitas* last and then changing her mind and heading back for the plums.

Alex was uncharacteristically quiet as he bagged her groceries. "Need help out?"

"No thanks."

"OK. See you soon, I hope."

One reason she shopped at Lundardi's was its proximity to her mother's house. Five minutes down Curtner to St. Lawrence and she was there. As soon as she walked through the door, she was surrounded by her nephews. Lucy's brother seemed to be incapable of producing an X chromosome. Two wanted help with their homework and the third reached his arms out in silent, but obvious request. As she expected though, her mother's voice carried over the din "Did you remember the *cebollas*?" Ramira Fuentes generally spoke English except when it came to food.

Lucinda handed the two bags to the older nephews. "I'll read to you while the *carnitas* are cooling if you'll take these to your *abuelita*." Her hands freed, she picked up little Carlos and carried him into the kitchen where her mother was already at work. "You gave me the list and I followed it. When is the last time I forgot anything?"

"You're right of course, sweetie" her mother replied, giving her a kiss on the cheek and a bigger one to Carlos. "You never forget anything. I just get frantic because we're starting so late. It's going to be a long night I'm afraid. Are you sure you don't want to stay over?"

"I expected a late night, but I'll help as much as I can. I'd rather sleep in my own bed, but if we get the *carnitas* on quick, I should be able to help with everything but the assembling."

"What's this *mija*?" Her mother had reached the bottom of the bag and was holding what appeared to be a compact disc. "James McMurtry? Who's he?"

"What?" Lucinda was startled out of her task of unloading groceries and grabbed the CD from her mother's hand. "That bagboy!"

"A bagboy gave this to you? Who is he?"

"His name is Alex. He's been trying to get me to buy this album since the other day when it was playing over the store speakers. I guess he thought I couldn't be trusted to make my own music choices."

"Your own music choices? You spend all of your money on books. When is the last time you actually bought one of these on your own? Anyway, who is this Alex?"

Lucinda was saved from answering for the moment by the arrival of her sister. She walked through the kitchen door with her daughter in one arm and more groceries in the other. "I brought dinner!" she called. "I knew no one would want to cook anything but tamales tonight, so I brought some Thai food from New Krungthai."

A couple of hours later, the album was playing for its third time and Lucinda's mother and sister were singing along, seeming to have already memorized the lyrics to half the songs. Ramira and Alma Fuentes used corn husks as microphones as they performed the chorus, "Walk between the raindrops, dry as a bone!"

Lucinda was not amused. "Let's just get these tamales done. I'm getting tired."

"Not until you tell us about this Alex," Alma teased. "How long have you two been a couple?"

"We're not a couple. He's just trying to be friendly. You shouldn't encourage him by playing his music over and over."

"I don't think he's outside the house listening," Lucinda's mother said, as she skipped ahead to the songs she'd already picked as her favorites. "Besides, he must be sweet on you. A bagboy doesn't make a lot of money and he spent part of his on a gift for you."

"I didn't ask him to."

"Well, you must have encouraged him, or at least he thinks you did. The real question is, what are you going to do about it?" With this, Ramira grasped her daughter's hands and looked straight into her eyes. "What are you going to do?"

"Probably nothing," she deflected, looking away quietly. "I don't even know this guy."

"There are ways to correct that," Alma said, suggestively.

"I'm sure you know a few, but I don't need to hear them."

"You're right. You don't need to hear from me. You need to hear Alex," Alma replied as the penultimate song came near its conclusion. "He just wants to talk to you." And with that, both Alma and her mother were singing along once again, moving from the stereo to Lucinda's face in the final three lines.

"I only want to talk to you."

"I only want to talk to you."

"I only want to talk to you."

With the final line, Lucinda had had enough. "Thanks for your advice in planning my life, but I need to get home now." She put the paprika on the table and handed her niece to Alma and picked up her keys.

"Hey, you said you'd stay to the end," her mother complained.

"No, I said I'd help get things prepared so that you and Alma could do the assembling. I've done that and I need to get home. I have to work tomorrow."

"We're sorry Lucy. We'll leave you alone."

"It's OK mami." Lucinda gave her mother a quick peck on the cheek. "I'm not mad, I'm just tired. I'll come back tomorrow if there's more work to do."

"Hey, your CD. . . . " Alma called, but Lucinda was out the door and halfway to her car, not interested in the least in raindrops or anyone who only wanted to talk to her.

She was home in ten minutes, not really remembering the drive. She had just started a highly reviewed Joyce Carol Oates book. It was supposed to be about some kind of shapeshifting creature and promised a good scare. She'd only read the prologue at lunch, but for tonight, she put the book down and picked up Pullman's *The Subtle Knife*, dropping it on the bed on her way to the closet. Sometimes, jumping into the middle book of a series was a real comfort.

Lucinda changed into her flannel pajamas and brushed her teeth while Lyra, Will and their cohorts called to her from the bed. She turned out the lights, picked up her book light from the nightstand and crawled under the covers. She held the paperback deftly in her left hand with the right between her knees, and as she curled up and entered the world of cats and hornbeam trees she exhaled more completely than she had for hours. In eight minutes, she was sound asleep.

**

Books were on Molly's mind as well, but not for any enjoyable, much less comforting, reason. She had homework, two chapters to read in history and three in *Huckleberry Finn,* yet she was walking down the outdoor corridor of the Bay Bridge apartment complex trying to keep up with Bridget.

Molly thought she was too old, almost 16,to be traipsing around selling Girl Scout cookies, but her mother had insisted she stay in one more year. "Bridget looks up to you. She wants to do the things you do and she wants to be with you. Stay in at least for her first year." Molly saw little evidence of this. If Bridget looked up to her so much, why wouldn't she listen?

"Bridge slow down," she shouted, worried as the seven-year-old ran down the hallway. "You just missed two doors."

"We already did those two."

"Bridget stop! We haven't done any apartments in this complex." Molly pulled out the list. "We cross off the people who say 'no,'" she reminded her sister, "and come back again to the ones who aren't home."

"I just want to stop at every other door, no, every third door" and once again Bridget was off and running down the hall.

"Bridget the Midget!" This was the name Molly had invented for her sister when she was younger. Bridget hated it and even Molly had grown past using it, mostly. Now, it seemed necessary to get her sister's attention.

"Molleeee, I'm just trying to have fun."

"This may be fun for you, but it's work for me and I have more important work to do. It's called homework. We need to get through this whole complex and we need to do it quickly."

"You should have done your homework right after school. I did."

" You have maybe 20 minutes of homework a night. Mine will take hours. So, we need to get done and get back home. Now, knock on this door and turn on the charm," she said, pointing at 2F. Compliments usually worked, especially after an insult.

Bridget trudged back and pulled out a box of peanut butter patties to serve as temptation. Turning on her sweet smile, she gave the door a knock.

There was no answer at 2F. "Knock again, louder."

Their mother had told them to go at dinner time. It annoyed some folks, but you were more likely to find people at home. Plus, they'd be hungry.

This time, Bridget pounded on the door, loud enough to wake the dead, Molly thought.

"No one's at home" she said and skipped down the hall, pigtails swinging. She skipped 2G and moved to knock on 2H.

"Every door, Bridge. Knock on every door." Molly sighed, quite certain she was never having children.

**

There was, of course, a good reason Andrew was not in his apartment when Molly and Bridget knocked. For if you wanted someone reliable who'd always be in his apartment at dinner time, he'd have certainly been at the top of the list. And, though Andrew wasn't one to give to every charitable organization, the Girl Scouts would have been one of which he approved. They were a civic organization after all and presumably, though he had little direct knowledge of such things, they taught young women important life lessons. So, had he been home, Andrew likely would have ordered a box of cookies, maybe even two.

But tonight, he was lying in a hospital room at the Regional Medical Center with tubes in his nose and monitors attached to his chest. The Center wasn't the nearest facility to his apartment complex, but a traffic problem on the 280 had diverted the ambulance north. But, by this point, the crisis seemed to have been averted.

"He's stable now, just sedated," Jackie was telling her replacement nurse having just gone over Andrew's list of injuries. It had been a long day and Andrew Grey had taken up a substantial portion of it.

"Has his family been contacted?"

"None listed in his wallet. The address is the Bay Bridge apartments across town. There's an insurance card from his employer though. We can call them in the morning if he's still out of it. . I suspect he'll want to call himself though by that point."

"OK, thanks. Get yourself some sleep. You look exhausted."

"You have no idea." Jackie replied. "Sleep tight little Andy," she whispered as she kissed him lightly on the forehead.

**

No one actually called him Andy. Not even his mother. Olivia Grey had always liked the name Andrew, and like many mothers, she preferred the full name to any diminutive. But, for the most part, to his teachers, his classmates, and even fellow employees, Andrew had just seemed more appropriate. Andrew Grey wasn't a nickname kind of guy. Formality suited him.

G-dub was the only one to even try. At the first team meeting after he'd been hired, he'd made a valiant effort. Only Ballard and Davenport had preceded him on the team, and both of them had been reduced to nicknames not of their own choosing. Gilbert Ballard was now Blue-Gil, so named both for the fish and his propensity to wear blue at least three days a week. He'd managed to get most of the team to just call him Gil. Ellie Davenport had long since become Elsie in G-dub's world for no apparent reason. But the attempt to rename Andrew had failed.

Even with just the four of them at the table, Andrew had already been at the far end, a few feet to the right of Ellie. "Everyone, I'd like to introduce you to Andrew Grey, Andy isn't it?" both Gil and Ellie had already introduced themselves, but this ritual was more for G-dub's purposes than Andrew's.

"Just Andrew."

"Alright, Andy. Hmm . . . Andy, the Candy Man. Have some candy, Candy Man." With that, G-dub pushed the bowl of M&Ms down the table, where it landed untouched.

"No thanks."

"Not the Candy Man, heh? Just Andy."

"Just Andrew," Andrew repeated, not insistently, just as patient clarification, as though he assumed G-dub hadn't heard him.

"OK Andy."

At this, Andrew didn't continue to protest. He just raised his left eyebrow questioningly and waited for his assignment. Both Ballard and Davenport were stifling giggles as G-dub finished putting their packets together. The boss looked up and saw Andrew's expression.

"Um . . . Andrew it is, I guess. Moving on . . . "

Even his last name suits him, G-dub often thought. This guy is boring as hell. But, it might not hurt to have one boring guy on the team. Andrew had proven his worth several times since that day.

**

The day had started out well enough. For Andrew, Mondays were generally pleasant. The beginning of the week's work routine gave his existence structure and purpose. He pulled on his khaki pants and ironed his matching cotton button-down shirt. The business casual atmosphere at Silicon Valley firms would not have been what he would have chosen, but it did make his mornings easier. After his oatmeal, he brushed and flossed his teeth, shaved and walked over to his bicycle supplies.

The weather report promised a sunny day and in this area, unlike Kansas where he'd grown up, there was little likelihood of surprise weather. So, Andrew pulled his elastic straps over his ankles and secured his pants to his leg so that there would be no grease marks from the chain. This Civia Derailleur had been one of his favorite purchases. It was perfect for city driving, reliable and maneuverable enough to allow him to react to drivers who never seemed to see, or want, cyclists on the road. Andrew strapped on his helmet, pulled his small knapsack over it, carried the bicycle down the steps, and carefully pedaled out onto Emory toward Myrtle. Although it was legal to ride his bike on the Alameda, Andrew had finally given it up. Initially, he'd thought that by pressing his right to ride, he would eventually convince motorists to respect it. That battle had been lost, so now he mostly took side streets.

Andrew put his left hand down at his side, the signaled for his turn onto Myrtle. He was used to drivers not understanding the signals, but today, he was able proceed without mishap. As was often the case though, it was the mundane moment that produced the unexpected.

**

Ashlynn Parker was busy wiping down her perfectly clean dashboard. She knew it was vain, but this Stingray was so beautiful it almost hurt. Hers was a privileged life, of that she was well aware, but she had made a conscious decision to focus her vanity on one thing, this absolutely gorgeous vehicle.

She knew as she'd been driving down the Alameda that was the classic stereotype rich girl, blond hair blowing in the wind on a bright California day as she drove the convertible sports car. She hadn't been born rich, but the tech boom had been very good to her family, her parents having one of the more successful startups in recent years. They'd worked hard for their money, seventy to eighty hour weeks in the early years and they made no apologies for providing their daughter with a luxury or three.

It was early morning and still cool. Ashlynn wouldn't normally have been in this neighborhood, but she'd been so caught up in her car that she missed her turn a few blocks back. She pulled off to the side road and looked at the sign, Myrtle Street. Traffic was light, so she made a U-Turn, knowing that wherever her GPS took her, it would involve getting back on the Alameda. Having only had the car for two weeks, she wasn't going to risk consulting navigation while going down a major road.

But now, she knew where she was going. The GPS told her how far off her route she'd drifted. She hadn't just missed one or two turns; the Vedanta Society was at least a mile back. Ashlynn's philosophy professor had assigned her to interview someone from a religious tradition outside her own experience and the Vedanta group certainly qualified, if she could find them. And it helped that they were local.

But, while she was stopped, she'd noticed a smidge of dust on the dashboard on the passenger side. She wanted the car to be perfect when she visited her friends later. They'd already been jealous when she'd described it over the phone. She liked using the manufacturer's terms. The car wasn't grey, which sounded boring, but Cyber Metallic Grey. She liked that she hadn't gone with one of the flashier colors. She knew just having this car would make some people think her shallow and somehow the understated grey mitigated that, while *cyber metallic* prevented it from seeming mundane, and just, well grey. She had put a lot of thought into her choice.

She was wiping down the interior, a nice contrasting brown, though GM referred to it as Kalhari. She'd tried looking up that term, but as far as she could tell, it was just a distortion of Kalahari, perhaps referencing the desert. Not a bad description for the color, and went with her desire to tone down the inherent Corvette owner flash.

Ashlynn had dampened the cheesecloth she kept in the glovebox with a bit of water from her square Fiji bottle. The dashboard was clean to begin with, but now, it was spotless. After putting the cheesecloth away, she grabbed her keys, ready to restart the car, but decided to take one more sip. That philosophy professor had chastised her for drinking Fiji water. "You know that comes from a military dictatorship, don't you?"

She knew now, but she didn't care. Perhaps that sounded callous. Of course she cared in the abstract, but she cared most about individual people in her life, not random strangers living under a military junta. The professor had given her an exposé from *Mother Jones* that he said would cause her to never drink that water again. For that very reason, she'd tossed the article. She wasn't heartless; she just figured that any brand of water would present some problem and she didn't have the time for it. These big geopolitical issues have ways of working themselves out over time and she'd rather spend her energy focusing on her family and friends. The local, she could impact. Let world leaders deal with the rest.

But now, as she brought the bottle to her lips, she noticed something floating in the water. She eyed the surface; it was dust from the cloth. Ashlynn chuckled as she opened the door to pour it out on the curb. *If Dr. Burke doesn't want me drinking this water, what would he think of it being wasted in the street?*

KNOW MY NAME

**

Andrew now performed the most spectacular physical feat of his remarkably unspectacular life. As his front tire hit the door of the Stingray, he flew into the air, spinning two full revolutions. At first, the bicycle stayed with him as he clutched the frame tightly with his knees. But when the blond in the sports car let out a gasp, he glanced down briefly and let go. A diver would have called his maneuver a double forward somersault with a half twist. His body was halfway between the pike and tuck positions, but his back was straight and his stomach clenched when he landed. His right shoulder blade and elbow took the bulk of the initial impact, the pain from the former dull, but spreading downward, while the latter shot splinters of pain up and down his arm. Andrew opened his eyes in surprise and the last thing he saw was the word Civia on the frame of his very practical bicycle as it landed across his chest.

MISSING

Pete Massey was worried.

This district's software system was using was incomprehensible. He knew it probably wasn't the fault of the software, but his own limitations. He had learned accounting principles in college and was comfortable with computers in general. But when it came to new software, Massey tended to freeze. They'd gone through three different operating systems since he'd been with Maitland & Mason and they'd encountered at least a dozen accounting and enterprise support systems at the various organizations they worked with. He'd always managed to get by and each time it was for one reason: Andrew Grey.

Grey wasn't judgmental, nor did he complain when Pete asked him the same questions multiple times. He would just patiently show him how to navigate the software, where to find the information needed and on at least two occasions, had created step-by-step tutorials. These made Pete feel a bit like a child, but they also saved his butt on the projects and he knew it.

But today, gratitude was the last thing he was feeling toward Andrew, nor was it worry about his coworker's well-being. Pete was pissed. He'd expected Andrew would have joined them that Monday morning after he'd met with his old pal Danny, who hadn't yet returned his calls, but now it was the third day on the project and still no Andrew.

He'd gotten the fiscal reports and access to their system. But either this district was completely corrupt or incompetent, or Pete was simply looking at the wrong set of figures. He'd find that the top-level figures would match just perfectly, but the detail columns would be off by huge amounts. In some cases, the receivables were half what he expected.

Two hours into the morning, Pete sighed and shoved the spreadsheets aside. He'd have to do what he really had been trying to avoid. "Ellie?" he called to her cubicle.

"No, Pete."

"I really need your help. I'm lost with this and if Grey doesn't show up, I'll never be able to make sense of it."

"You went to the same college I did. You'll just have to muddle through."

"You're not still holding a grudge, are you? It's been months."

"I have a good memory."

At the office party eight months ago, Pete had pinched Ellie's butt. She wasn't so sensitive as to make a big deal about that, especially since Pete had had a few drinks beforehand. But her boyfriend at the time had witnessed it and the incident had caused a fight, leading to their breakup a couple of weeks later. The guy had been a douche and she'd have broken up with him eventually anyway, something Ellie probably knew, but she didn't appreciate Pete pointing it out.

Whining hadn't worked and he knew better than to try groveling with Ellie, but bribery was another story. "Look, I'll buy you coffee for a week. Even that fancy Ethiopian blueberry shit from Peet's no one else likes."

"Nope. I'm busy. It took me a while to understand this thing myself."

"Coffee for two weeks? Plus, I'll wash your car."

"Now you're kissing my ass instead of pinching it."

"Is it working?"

"I've talked to your girlfriends. You're not that good a kisser."

"Look, I'm desperate. I'll review those vendor invoices they dumped on you. Wait, which girlfriends did you talk to?"

"Don't you worry about it. Sold with the invoices, and I'll expect the coffee starting tomorrow. The Sumatra blend this time."

"The invoices and the coffee?"

"That's the price. Take it or leave it."

"I'll take it."

"You're a sucker." Ellie said as she rolled her chair over to Pete's cube. "But a deal's a deal. Look, this software isn't that bad. The problem is, they have to report some things on the California fiscal year and some on the federal. You're pulling the main stuff with the California fiscal year, but you have to select it in both sections, so your details are all using the federal fiscal year because that's the software default."

"Wait, it was that simple? You could have helped me yesterday."

"Yes, but you were still being punished." Ellie said, kissing Pete on the top of the head as she would a child. "Punishment over. Plus, I like my coffee. Make sure it's extra hot. By the time you get here from Peet's, it will be just perfect." With that, Ellie rolled her chair back to her own cubicle and turned on her second monitor so she could compare sheets faster. *Not that speed is that big an issue*, she thought, now that I don't have to worry about the vendor invoices.

**

Lillian's chuckle at the interaction went largely unnoticed. She usually managed to be invisible in the office when she needed to. She hadn't been worried much at all at Andrew's absence on Monday. She'd just assumed he'd join the team whenever he could. She doubted he was hungover as G-dub had speculated; he just wasn't the type. But, a flat tire could happen to anyone, so that had been her guess.

It wasn't until Tuesday that her worry began to percolate. The entire team had arrived, except G-dub, who had meetings with the district brass, and Andrew still wasn't there. She questioned the group one by one, Ballard, Sykes, Davenport, and Massey last, and none had heard from Andrew. Pete Massey was already complaining as he'd expected Andrew's help with the software. The team had just assumed that Andrew had work at the office and would join the project late. But not only had he not shown up at the site, no one had heard from him. Lillian had called him four times during the day, leaving messages each time, but still nothing.

When 9:00 rolled around Wednesday morning, it was time to pull out the personnel file. Andrew's file was thin, reflecting G-dub's minimalist management style and his lack of desire to spend time with Andrew. There were four annual evaluations, all excellent, but with few comments. In the last one, G-dub, feeling the need to provide some direction for improvement, added the line "Andrew should work on his interpersonal and networking skills in preparation for the day when he will be expected to bring in new accounts." Andrew hadn't reacted much to the line. He'd raised his eyebrow in that familiar way, but only briefly, and signed the form.

Lillian only needed one page from the file anyway, the emergency contact page. Andrew rarely talked about his family, but she recalled that his parents lived in the Midwest somewhere. She'd found his mother's name on the emergency contact form and called, but got one of those old fashioned answering machines. She left a message, trying not to sound worried, but just asked for a call back.

But now, the quest was for something deeper. With still no call back from Andrew's mother, and lunchtime approaching, Lillian sat at Andrew's desk. The passwords had to be changed every ninety days, but she knew all four of those Andrew used on a rotating basis. His had been the hardest to memorize because he took security criteria seriously. The others had all been easy. Massey just used the names of his girlfriend of the moment, and whenever there wasn't one of the moment, it always went back to his favorite ex, Naomi, whom Lillian knew was the one that got away. Gil Ballard rotated his passwords back and forth between the names of his two sons. Sykes used characters from Star Trek and Ellie Davenport, who had joined the alumni association just days after her graduation and before even starting at Maitland & Mason, rotated between SpartanPride43 and Spartans4ever34. None of them were especially creative and she'd had their passwords down within days of their being hired.

But Andrew had taken a bit longer and even after watching him enter his password a few times, she had to test it to be sure she had it right. His current one was q9g3&vTT@4. That was the second one he'd chosen and the shortest of the four in his rotation.

Once in, it wasn't hard for Lillian to find Andrew's contact list. His filing system was predictably straightforward, with everything documented and placed in folders for each of the 37 projects he'd worked on since arriving at the firm. Andrew's contact list was longer than she expected. Apparently, he kept a record of each of his coworkers as well as all contact information for every client. But, it didn't take long to scroll down to the G section and find Tina Gamble's phone number. Pulling the post-it from its pad, she logged out and headed back to her own desk. G-dub's team was wrapped up its work and they were used to Lillian nosing around their space, so no one noticed her clandestine activity. This was as she preferred. She was more worried than they were, and it was better not to alarm the team unless there was good reason.

**

Tina was on her route when her cell phone rang. She didn't recognize the number, but answered anyway, unfortunately, just as the Caltrain rolled by. "Hold on a sec'" she called into her phone. Then, in a moment, "Tina Gamble."

"Tina, hi, it's Lillian....Lillian Jacobs from Maitland & Mason".

"Oh, hi Lillian. What's up? I don't think I have you scheduled today."

"No, that's not it. I was just wondering, um, have you seen Andrew lately?"

"Andrew? No. Lillian, you know we broke up, right? It was months ago. Of course you know, I showed you my engagement ring. Andre and I are getting married next month.

"Oh, I know all that. Congratulations again, by the way. It's just that Andrew hasn't been in for three days in a row. It's so unlike him and you were the only one I could think to call."

"I haven't seen him, except when I stopped by the office, and that was usually just the back of his head from his cubicle. Most of the times I've been in, he didn't even say hello."

"I'm sure he didn't mean anything."

"Oh, I'm sure of that too. I don't take offense. That's just how Andrew is. He's so focused on those spreadsheets most of the time, he probably didn't even know I was there. And with Andrew, well, even if he did know, he'd assume I was there for work and wouldn't want to bother me. Even when we were together, he didn't leave that cubicle unless you called him over. Lillian, he does have some family, in Kansas I think. He didn't talk about them much."

"Yes, I have his mother's name from his emergency contact form. I left her a message earlier. If she's heard from Andrew, I'm sure she'll call back. I'm just trying everything I can think of and since Andrew didn't talk about a lot of friends, that led me to you."

"Sorry I couldn't be much help. I'm sure there's a reasonable explanation."

"Probably there is. If it were any of the others, I wouldn't worry. But with Andrew. . ."

"Yeah, I know what you mean. Give me a call when you find him."

"Will do. And congratulations again Tina."

"Thanks."

**

Tina put her phone back in her pocket and began her waddle back to the truck. She still had several weeks to go, somewhere between seven and nine, according to the doctor, but it felt like this baby was going to jump out right here on the sidewalk. She and Andre hadn't planned on starting a family quite this soon, but she couldn't say she was especially upset about the situation. She knew she was doing the right thing, both with Andre and with little BU, baby unknown, as she had begun calling it in her head. They hadn't settled on a name and were still discussing whether to find out the baby's sex now or wait for the birth.

In a strange way, she felt she owed a piece of her happiness to Andrew. She was sure he was fine. It wasn't like Andrew Grey to get into trouble and Lillian had always seemed a bit dramatic. Tina would always have fond memories of Andrew. If it hadn't been for his eccentricities, she'd never have made it back to Andre and now, she patted her belly, to BU.

That last date they'd had had been disturbing. They'd been at an outdoor cafe having just finished lunch and somehow the subject of Andre came up and Andrew began asking questions. "Once someone has cheated on you, it's best to cut things off. I'm proud of you for doing that. Too many people put up with bad behavior in relationships."

"I'm sure they do, but I never actually said he cheated."

"Oh, I thought . . ."

"Andrew, you're not usually one to assume." Tina took the rare opportunity to tease him. You're always so literal and here you are jumping to conclusions."

"Didn't you say you could never trust him?"

"I probably did say something like that, but that doesn't mean he actually cheated."

"So you didn't actually catch him? Or find evidence?"

"I never caught him. And, I don't know about the evidence. I'm not sure if he was cheating or not, yet. I just didn't think I could trust him not to."

Here came the eyebrow. "Why was that?"

"It's complicated. You know he's a trainer at the health club over on Third Street, right? That's where I met him. You probably don't want to hear this, but I slept with him on our second date."

"So, you don't trust him because you feel guilty yourself. I didn't think you were that prudish."

"I'm not. It's just, well, most of his clients are women. Probably 80%." Now, it was Tina's turn to raise her eyebrow expectantly.

"Of course they are," Andrew replied matter-of-factly. "Women always use the trainers more. Men usually assume they know how to use the machines. And they don't like to admit they need the help."

"But, Andre admitted to me that he'd slept with one of his clients before." Tina's tone was almost protesting now.

"Weren't you his client?"

"Are you judging me?"

"Not in the slightest. But it sounds like you're judging Andre for doing the same thing with you, and maybe one or more other women, that you did yourself with him. I'm just confused."

"Wait a minute, you are my boyfriend now, right?"

"As far as I know."

"So why do you seem to be trying to talk me back into a relationship with my ex?"

"I'm not. I'm just confused. You say you couldn't trust him, but you haven't actually said anything he did to cause that distrust."

"I've seen the way those women look at him."

"Presumably the same way you looked at him. You've told me Andre was a good looking guy." Tina noted that there wasn't even a little hint of jealousy in Andrew's voice. "It would seem to me that, to the extent that such a thing matters, his good looks would be a source of pride, not envy. After all, you had him, these other women didn't. Unless they did?"

"I don't know that they didn't have him."

"So, you broke up with him because he had opportunities to cheat?"

"Daily opportunities."

"I'm sure there were." Here, Andrew paused, his expression nothing but analytical. "OK, we've established that Andre is a good looking guy. And, of course, you are an attractive woman." Again, Tina detected neither jealousy in his description of her ex and neither pride nor flattery in his description of her. It was just that, description. "He probably had opportunities to cheat and some minority of those women might have been as attractive as you, or more so."

"Gee, thanks. You're very reassuring."

"Am I?" She should have known by now that Andrew Grey was immune to sarcasm. "What exactly led to the breakup?"

Tina sighed. "The last straw was when I found condoms in his suitcase. He said they were left over from the trip we took to Portland, but I didn't buy it."

"Hmm, well you call that the last straw, but it sounds to me like the first straw because there's no other evidence that he cheated other than his job where women looked to him for fitness advice, and presumably some of them were attracted to him. But, how did you know that the condoms weren't from your trip to Portland?"

"That trip had been a month before I found the condoms."

"Had he made any other trips since then? Ones without you?"

"Not that I know of. But that's not the point."

"What exactly is the point?"

"How could I stay with someone I couldn't trust?"

"You haven't established that you really had a reason to distrust him. He didn't cheat that you know of, he just was around women a lot and had condoms in his suitcase, for which he had a plausible, maybe even probable explanation. So maybe your lack of trust had more to do with you than it did with Andre."

"Andrew."

"Yes?"

"You and I are dating now, right?"

"Right."

"And you'd like to continue dating?"

"Yes."

"So, I'd suggest we drop this subject right now."

Andrew shrugged and looked down at his phone. "OK. We need to get going anyway if we're going to make the movie."

Tina gave him a withering look, but Andrew didn't seem to notice. She didn't remember much from the movie even though it had been her turn to pick. A part of her was hurt by Andrew's questioning. How could someone who supposedly loved her, well, they hadn't exactly started using that word yet, but at least someone who cared for her say things that seemed designed to get her to leave him and go back to her ex. No one was that objective and no one's motives were that pure. Maybe he was just a coward. Maybe he wanted her to break up with him so he didn't have to.

But a nagging part of her was still thinking of what Andrew had said. What if he's right? Regardless of his motives, what if she had been too hasty with Andre, too quick to judge? He'd gotten so defensive when she accused him; at the time, she took that as additional evidence against him. Could she have been wrong?

She left Andrew that day confused and demoralized. She had begun to care for Andrew, but his actions left her ambivalent. Her frustration was only exacerbated when she got home and found Andre sitting on the stoop outside her apartment.

Andre said he only wanted to talk, a line she'd heard before. But this time, perhaps more out of emotional exhaustion than a conscious change of heart on Tina's part, he got his wish. It wasn't so much that Andre got a chance to explain his side of things; he didn't have any new information to offer. But this time, Tina broke down completely. She shared her fears and frustrations. Andre asked a few questions, but mostly, he just listened. By four in the morning, she was back with Andre. She didn't sleep with him that night, she couldn't do that to Andrew, but she did sleep in his arms, fatigue caught up with her near dawn and she lay sprawled across Andre's chest until nearly noon.

Andrew took the breakup quite well and for a moment she even had the thought that maybe he had planned this. All he'd asked was "Are you happy?" When she'd nodded, a sheepish grin spreading across her face against her will, his reply was a quick kiss on the cheek. "Then I'm happy for you." Andrew then walked away and out of her life. For the most part, she'd only seen the back of his head since. as she delivered to his office. Lillian had seemed more disappointed than Andrew, but she held her tongue when she realized how happy Tina was.

As she stepped into her truck, Tina pulled her cell phone back out and found Andrew's number, but all she got was voice mail. Still, she couldn't help but feel this was more a case of Lillian being dramatic. Andrew Grey wasn't the sort of person bad things happened to.

**

Another young woman was worried about Andrew that morning. Ashlynn Parker was at O'Connor Hospital for the third day in a row, frantic and disheveled. She'd heard every excuse in the book from the clerks and nurses at O'Connor, most of them having to do with privacy laws. They wouldn't release information about the man she'd hit or even confirm he was here. Unless she was family, she was out of luck.

At the time of the accident, she was ashamed to think, her first thought had been her car. Her beloved Stingray now had a black tire mark on the inside of the driver's door and the window of that door was cracked vertically. After that moment of vanity, the car had been forgotten. Ashlynn hadn't even wiped down the door, she was so concerned with finding the anonymous cyclist.

The crowd prevented her from reaching Andrew. One man physically detained her, grabbing the keys out of her ignition to prevent her from fleeing the scene. The thought hadn't even occurred to her. A police officer questioned her for a few minutes, but didn't cite her. "Those bicyclists need to be more aware of where they're going," he told her, his eyes alternatively admiring her cleavage and her Corvette. When she asked if the cyclist was OK, the officer's face turned grim, then consciously relaxed. "I wouldn't worry."

Ashlynn had wanted to get to the hospital to check on Andrew, but the ambulance was long gone by the time the officer had taken her information and the crowd dispersed. "We'll have a report ready in about three days if you need it for insurance or anything."

"Insurance?"

"It has to be reported because there's an injury," the officer seemed to be apologizing. "Otherwise, you probably wouldn't even need to bother with the insurance. The damage to your car is pretty minor. A couple hundred bucks should fix that window."

Ashlynn glanced down at the now-forgotten car. "What about the bicycle rider? Where is he? *How* is he?"

"They'll take him to the nearest hospital, the officer looked up at the street sign as a reminder of where he was, "probably O'Connor. I wouldn't worry." he repeated.

Ashlynn took the officer's card and put the address of O'Connor hospital in her car's GPS. Her hands were trembling as she pulled out onto Myrtle. With newfound caution, it took nearly half an hour to reach O'Connor, where she was sure the cyclist would still be in the ER. But no one seemed to have heard of a bicycle accident. It was a Monday morning and the ER was full, but mostly of people with weekend fevers and hangovers. If an accident had occurred, and they wouldn't confirm that one had, the ambulance would have brought the patient directly in from the side doors.

At that point, all she got were HIPAA rules and other stonewalling. "I just want to find out if he's OK," became her mantra, but no one listened.

She finally found a young EMT on his way to a call. He hadn't brought in anyone on a bike, he assured her, but he gave her some advice before his supervisor called him away. "If his injuries are serious, you'll hear about it from your insurance company, especially if it was your fault."

Ashlynn had no doubt that it was her fault. "How can I find him?"

"Sometimes these things look worse than they are." *Why was everyone trying to reassure her instead of giving her the information she needed?* "He's probably already been treated by the trauma team and released. If it's bad, he'll be here overnight. If it's real bad, he'll be in the ICU. Third floor."

She ran into the same barriers in the ICU. Either people hadn't heard of an accident victim or they recited privacy laws. Finally frustrated, she left for home, driving with the same nervous caution, her appointment with the Vedanta Society long since forgotten. Ashlynn tried calling friends, but most of them were in class. Jacie was the only one to answer, and she was adamant. "It wasn't your fault Ashlynn! From what you describe, the guy just ran right into your door."

"But I should have looked before I opened it."

"How many of us have done that? You can't be expected to account for every bike rider. You can't even see them most of the time. It's his fault for not watching where he was going. They really should have to ride on the sidewalk. Besides, the cops would have cited you if it was your fault. Stop beating yourself up about it and get to class. Let's go get a beer afterwards; take your mind off things."

"No, I can't think about class and I certainly can't sit in one. I'll see you later."

Ashlynn paced her apartment, then she paced the streets. Missing class just added to her guilt, but she knew she couldn't sit still and concentrate on schoolwork. She couldn't drive either, touching the keys seemed akin to grasping a smoking gun.

After very little sleep, she was back at the hospital the next morning, but with little impact. Ashlynn used the best of her considerable diplomatic skills, but could find no information on an accident victim. Any accident victim. She started walking the halls, from the ICU down, but it took a bit of time to surreptitiously check charts and eavesdrop conversations to find out about every patient. After the second "Can I help you honey?" from an orderly, she went home, frustrated again, but knowing she couldn't and wouldn't let it go.

Wednesday morning, she was back again, this time with a more systematic plan. She had a notebook in hand and a list of rooms in the ICU. Since she had to dodge nurses, orderlies and custodial staff, not to mention patient families, she'd use her list to narrow things down. There were quite a few rooms, she started by crossing off the cancer patients and other non-candidates and figured she'd be able to find him by the end of the day. All she knew about him was that he was a white guy, thin, and youngish, probably still in his twenties. That didn't narrow it down much, but she could still cross a lot of people off the list just by using those criteria.

Her system was working, or at least it seemed to be. By mid-morning, she had been through most of the ICU and had crossed off half the rooms. There were several she still had to get back to because there had been medical testing going on when she stopped by, family visiting, or someone watching as she was about to enter.

Now, she looked both ways, as had become her custom, stepped in the door of room 341. The patient was a thin white guy, around 22, she guessed. She looked at his face and couldn't tell much. He had the same light brown hair as the guy she'd hit. She couldn't be sure because most of the hair was covered by a head bandage and only a few tufts stuck out. Ashlynn reached for the chart.

Just then, she heard voices outside the door. She snuck around the corner unseen. The voices became clearer; apparently, one of the nurses was showing a new CNA around, making sure she was able to check vitals and knew each patient. Ashlynn listened in as they stepped into room 341. The voices were muffled, but a few words slipped through.

"MVA . . . Mr. Jamison is heavily sedated . . . swelling in the brain . . . those bikes are deathtraps; I saw enough when I worked in the ER that I'll never let my son have one and he's been begging for two years. . . . Not sure whether he'll make it. . . how much damage there is. . . the family comes in the evenings, father works in the day. . . here at 5:30 like clockwork. . . keep a record of his vitals and make sure he's clean. Don't answer any questions from family, direct them to the charge nurse."

Ashlynn's heart was beating so fast her hand went

absentmindedly to her chest. She took several deep breaths to calm down. She knew from old reruns of ER that "MVA" stood for "motor vehicle accident," but it was the bikes comment that confirmed it. This had to be the guy she hit. As the two employees exited 341 and walked around the corner, she gave them her best "I belong here" smile and walked right by, stepping into the room. She pulled down the chart and looked over what little information was there.

Kevin Jamison Junior was her victim. There wasn't much on the chart that she could make sense of but his vitals and medications. His blood pressure had apparently been up and down quite a bit over the past day, which was the only time period listed on the chart. The bandage on his head was the most visible sign of injury, but his left arm was also in a cast from mid-bicep to below his elbow. There was also a slightly faded scrape that ran from his lower jaw down his neck to below the edge of his hospital gown. That must have been from the asphalt, she thought.

As she approached his bed, emotions overwhelmed her. She hadn't really considered her next steps, other than an apology. With the focus on her task behind her, guilt returned full force, now accompanied by helplessness. What was she to do for this man now that she'd found him? She turned a half-step toward the door, then stopped. Clenching her jaw, she took a breath, then another. *The one thing I'm not going to do is walk away*, she thought. Ashlynn moved deliberately to the chair at the other side of his bed, sat down and grasped Kevin Jamison's hand in both of hers. Leaning forward so that her neat blond ponytail was draped over the patient's arm, she exhaled and whispered, "Tell me. Tell me what to do."

**

At another hospital, eighteen hundred miles to the east, another young nurse was in training. It had been an overwhelming day for Janice Grey, but a good one. Wesley Medical Center might not be big by the standards of New York or Los Angeles, but it was among the best in the Wichita area and it was close to the university, so she didn't even have to change apartments. Janice accepted change when she had to, but didn't relish the prospect. She was glad to have been offered a job there, though daunted by the challenge of the ER.

Although it was a Wednesday, the emergency room still seemed busy to Janice. Things would slow down after a few weeks, her charge nurse had told her. She'd also been assured that she'd done very well for her first few days. Still, it seemed like a whirlwind and two thirds of the way through her shift, this was the first chance she'd had to take a breath.

Stepping outside to a veranda, Janice pulled out her cell phone and pulled up the number for her parents' home, sighing slowly as she recalled their reliance on outdated technology. "Hello?" came the nervous and timid voice at the other end.

"Hi Mom, it's Janice. I saw you called me earlier."

"Oh I'm so glad to hear from you. Why did it take so long to call me back?"

Janice sighed again, impatient and relieved that she now lived two hours from her parents. "I'm at work, Mom. And you didn't leave a message, so I figured it wasn't important."

"You know I don't like to leave messages on those machines. I hung up when I realized you weren't going to pick up. That saves me a long distance call on my bill."

Janice's sigh was mixed with a bemused chuckle this time. Her mother was actually proud of her Luddite-ness. "What's going on, Mom?"

"Honey, well, I don't want to alarm you, but . . ."

"Mom?"

"Have you heard from Andrew lately?"

So that's all it was. Janice's jaw tensed at the memory of her last conversation with her brother. "No, but Mom, you know, we don't really talk all that often." Janice now realized that her mother was still talking.

"I got a call from his job, that accounting place in San Jose. The woman there, I think she was the office manager or something, she said Andrew hadn't been in for three days and they hadn't heard from him."

"Did you try to call him?"

"Of course I did, twice, but his phone goes right into that voice mail thing. I think I'll probably get charged for both of those calls."

KNOW MY NAME

"Did you leave him a message?"

"No, I hung up right away. But, I think I'll still be charged."

It was time to get harsh. "Mom, if you really thought this was an emergency, the money wouldn't matter, would it? You'd just leave a message. Andrew probably isn't going to call you back until he realizes how panicked you are. And, he's not going to know that if you keep hanging up on his voice mail."

Olivia Grey was silent. She hated being chastised and Janice knew it. But her mother had a tendency to avoid harsh realities and lose focus. Still, Janice felt the need to temper her criticism. "Look Mom, I'm sure Andrew is OK. He knows how to take care of himself."

"But in that big city, anything could happen."

"It could happen in this medium-sized city or in a small town like Salina too. But it probably won't." Janice knew the truth was almost always more boring than what went on in most people's heads. "I'm sure Andrew is fine," she repeated. "It always takes him a long time to return your calls, doesn't it? I wouldn't worry mom. He'll call you back in a day or two, if you leave a message."

More silence. "Look Mom, I gotta go. My break is over and this is a new job. Let me know when you hear from Andrew."

When she again heard nothing, Janice looked down at her phone to see if she'd lost her connection. She hadn't. "Mom, you still there?"

"OK hon', I'll try not to worry. Janice?"

"Yes Mom? I really gotta go."

"You coming home for Christmas?"

"I don't know. I'll try, but I'm the newest nurse here and everyone will want it off. It's not likely I'll get it."

"I understand. I love you sweetie."

"Right back 'atcha Mom. See you soon."

Janice wasn't ready to head back to her station just yet. She pulled out her pack of cigarettes and lit one. Health care workers' high smoking rates were a poorly kept secret, and she was trying to quit, but just now, she needed one.

Not that she was really worried about her brother. Andrew was likely being stubborn, a trait that often had been a source of tension between them. Most recently, it came up in that ill-fated phone call.

That had been two months ago and it still rankled. Her mother's pressure about Christmas had been one more reminder. Because, that was exactly why she'd called Andrew.

He hadn't even been decent enough to make up an excuse for not coming to Kansas for the holidays. He had no other plans, didn't complain about the expense, or the chaos of travel in December. He didn't even mention the Kansas weather. No, he was old reliable Andrew, direct and inappropriately forthright.

"Janice, I just don't see the point in coming. It's always a fight every time I visit."

"Andrew, don't leave me alone with them. It's not fair. And, you share some of the blame for those fights."

"Oh really?" She could see his eyebrow raised over the phone.

"Yes, do you really think it was a good idea to bring a Christopher Hitchens book into their house?"

"It's what I was reading at the time. Where was I supposed to leave it?"

"You couldn't read something else during that three day visit? Something less incendiary?"

"I don't find it incendiary. I thought it was enlightening."

"You would. That's not the point and you know it. You can read anything you want; you're an adult. But bringing an atheist book into Dad's house was unnecessarily provocative."

"I didn't provoke him. I didn't even bring up the book."

"Other than sitting on his couch reading it in front of him?"

"Like you said, I'm an adult. I wasn't bothering anyone. I was sitting and reading. He saw the author's name and went on a two-hour rant."

"It seems to me that you had some part in that rant. You know how he is. Why bring that book? Why debate Zeke Grey on religion. You're going to lose every time."

"I didn't lose."

"I don't mean lose the debate, numbnuts. A family isn't a forensics team. Sometimes you avoid a topic if you know it's a sensitive issue. Dad gets worked up over this stuff and he can't believe his own son could be an atheist. Of course he was going to go

KNOW MY NAME

off about it. You provoked him and then you argued with him for two hours. The reasonable thing would have been to just let it go."

"I'm not the one who got unreasonable. I simply defended my position calmly and logically."

"For God's sake Andrew, religion isn't logical. Faith isn't logical. And most importantly, Zeke Grey isn't logical!"

"Exactly my point."

"And like usual, you exactly miss the point. Keep your logic and leave him his faith."

"Are you really equating the two? One is based on facts, research, and sound analysis. The other, superstition."

"Call it what you want in San Jose. But you were in his house. Calling someone's beliefs superstition in his own house is insulting. How can you not see that?"

"He taught me to think for myself didn't he? Wouldn't he want me to . . ."

"He taught you no such thing and you know it. He taught blind faith and obedience to authority and nothing more. Anything else you picked up on your own and he certainly does not approve."

She had finally gotten a chuckle from Andrew. A miracle. "I guess that's true. But you'd think he'd be proud."

"You know him better than that. He'd be proud of you if you worked hard, lived in Salina for the rest of your life, and married a nice girl from the church. Education and independent thinking aren't high on the old man's list of values."

"Well, I guess you have his approval then. Stayed right there in Kansas."

"Hey, don't make this personal. I got out just like you did. Got a degree just like you. And in case you didn't know, Wichita isn't Salina."

"It's not that far away. And neither was your degree. You went to nursing school."

"What the hell is wrong with nursing? I'm going to be keeping people alive. Better than pushing papers around."

"I'm just saying, you know Dad didn't want either of us going away to college, especially you because you're a girl."

"I think I qualified as woman a few years ago, big brother."

"I know. But not in Dad's mind. If you were really going to rebel, why'd you stay in Kansas? Why'd you pick a safe, female career like nursing?"

"Look, this isn't a competition as to who's more rebellious. Nor was rebellion really on my mind when I picked a major. I happen to like nursing. And, I'm good at it."

"I'm just saying it would have been a different story if you'd picked another major, say engineering, or science. He'd have said you're wasting your time. He probably still expects you to get married and quit work before you're thirty."

"Not likely. I don't make my decisions based on what he likes or doesn't like. I went to WSU because it's a good school. I'm a nurse because I like taking care of people."

"So when are you moving back to Salina?"

Janice drew a quick intake of breath at the thought. "Not anytime soon. But I'll visit them at Christmas and I won't pick any fights. Can I say the same about you?"

"I'm afraid not. I can't go back to a house where I can't think for myself."

The problem isn't with what you think; it's with your need to shove it in Dad's face, she thought. But there was no point in arguing any further. Her brother wasn't going to change any more than her father was. Better that they stay apart. Though the two of them deserve each other; they're so much alike.

"Where have you been; cases are getting backed up." Janice's unsettling reminiscence was cut short by her training nurse. As she turned back toward the ER, she blew out another lungful of breath, half smoke, half frustration.

"I'm coming" she called. No need to get in trouble her first week on the job. Her big brother could take care of himself. That's the way he liked it anyway.

**

The one thing Andrew wanted most right now was to be allowed to take care of himself. His roommate at Regional Medical Center was a snorer and he wasn't getting much sleep. He'd asked to go

KNOW MY NAME

home since yesterday, but he barely saw the doctors. His nurse had laughed at him the day before, but today, she just seemed reluctant. The doctor, she explained, thought he'd be best off staying one more day. "You can rest here one more night and then he'll feel more confident about sending you home."

"I'll get more rest if I can sleep in my own bed. I'll be fine."

"We'll let Dr. Nguyen decide that. He'll be here in a few min . . . oh, here he is now."

Dr. Nguyen strolled into the room, all confidence. He pulled down Andrew's chart from the wall. "So, I hear you're not a big fan of our company, Mr. Grey."

"Your company is fine; I'd just be more comfortable at home."

"Well, I was thinking of keeping you here one more day, just in case. I understand you live alone."

"Yes," Andrew replied simply, not sure why it mattered.

"So who would take care of you if we send you home? Do you even have a ride?"

"I'll take care of myself. I have for years now. And I can take the bus home. There's a stop right around the corner from my house."

"That's out of the question, I'm afraid. If you do go home today, and that's still a big if at this point, we'll get you a cab. It would take at least two bus changes to get near your apartment. You'd be half passed out by the time you arrived. Tell me, what kind of support do you have at home?"

Andrew now realized he faced a difficult choice. He lived his life by a certain code and honesty was at its core. But he needed to be away from this hospital, its smells and noises; the snoring wasn't the half of it. "I've already spoken with my landlady," he lied. "She's going to check in on me and get me everything I need. She even said she'd go to the grocery store if I didn't feel up to it."

"Well, I guess you have some support then. Still, I'm not sure you shouldn't stay one more night. Let's go over your injuries a bit."

"I'm really going to be OK. I just need a few days to rest."

Doctor Nguyen wasn't listening; he was glancing through several pages on a clipboard. "I'm not really worried about your concussion at this point; it was pretty minor. If you hadn't been wearing a helmet, we wouldn't be having this conversation, by the way. Your ribs were pretty badly bruised though. How's your breathing? Can you take a deep breath for me?"

Andrew breathed in heavily making sure not to show the pain he still felt. He was glad the nurse had brought his morphine pill just a half hour ago. Watching the expression on the doctor's face, Andrew wasn't sure whether his performance was convincing.

"Hmm...." was all the doctor said as he turned to the next page.

"My biggest concerns are your pain level and possibly infection. It's not that any one of your injuries are all that major, but together, they could impair your ability to get around and take care of yourself. How's your pain right at this moment?"

"It varies some" Andrew said, thinking he shouldn't be too definitive, "but right now, it's about a 2 or 3."

Dr. Nguyen chuckled, "you've got our scale down pretty well by now."

"Yes."

"The nurse said you were limping as you took your exercise down the hallway this morning. How's that ankle."

"I'm told it was just a bad strain. It was stiff, but I can get around. Want me to demonstrate?"

"It's not necessary. When your leg got twisted, was it the bicycle chain or the frame?"

"I don't know, I was out cold."

"Well, we thought it was the chain because there was something that looked like grease in your leg wounds. But that could have just been gravel and tar from the road. We made sure to clean it out. Still, there's the risk of infection." The doctor now looked through two pages of readings from Andrew's charts. "It looks like your temperature has been pretty stable though, 98.9 this morning? Hasn't been higher than that since Monday."

It didn't seem to be a question, so Andrew just looked at him expectantly, slowly shifting his weight to ease the pain in his lower ribs.

"So, you were able to get up and down the hall, but with a bit of a limp. Do you usually exercise at home? Gym membership?"

"I do about half an hour of calisthenics each morning and evening."

"Calisthenics?"

"You know, sit-ups, pushups, jumping jacks. Basic exercise." Andrew's voice was patient, as though he were used to explaining his exercise habits to strangers.

"Oh, you're a bit old school. Well, you'll need to take it easy for another day or two. Walk around your apartment, maybe to the mailbox, stretching would probably be painful. When you feel up to it, try to get back into your exercise routine, but do so gradually. Understand?"

"Got it."

"Now, back to the risk of infection. Do you have a thermometer at home?"

This time, Andrew didn't have to lie. A first aid kit had been one of the first things he'd purchased after renting the apartment, even before he had most of his furniture. "Yes, digital."

"I'd like you to check your temperature at least four times a day. If it goes above 99.6, get your butt to your doctor immediately or to the ER if it's after hours."

"Not a problem."

"All right, I guess we can let you go. It will take an hour or two to draw up the paperwork. Have you spoken with your employer?"

"No, my cell phone was smashed in the accident. But I understand the nurse called HR the day I arrived."

"So, no problems with them? They won't give you any hassle for missing time."

"I think I have a good excuse."

"OK, I'll write you a note just in case. How long would you like to be away from work?"

"I'm not sure I understand."

"Well, we can be pretty flexible. I know some employers are understanding, and some less so. And sometimes, you just need a little extra rest after a trauma like this. So, what do you think you'd like?"

"I'd like the amount of time off you think is medically necessary. No more." Andrew's voice probably sounded colder than he realized, but his moral judgment at the doctor's "flexibility" was reflexive.

Dr. Nguyen didn't react. "I'll just put down that you need to be off for the rest of this week and all of next. I'd like you to make an appointment with your doctor for next week. He may extend it if he thinks it necessary. Any other questions?"

"Not at this time. Thank you doctor."

At that, Andrew took another breath, a bit more shallowly this time. By this time, Dr. Nguyen was halfway down the hall.

**

The office doors banged open as G-dub made his afternoon entrance. He did a quick head count, Massey, Sykes, Davenport, Ballard; Grey wasn't here. "Where's Andrew?" he called.

"Bathroom" Lillian replied casually.

G-dub seemed to always miss Andrew this week. He would have been anxious to hear Andrew's weekend story, whatever had kept him from making the project launch meeting on Monday, but he wasn't that hopeful. Andrew had always been tight-lipped about his personal life. If he'd finally gone on a bender, or better yet, gotten laid, G-dub would probably never hear about it. "The daily reports ready?" he asked Lillian.

"Be in with them in a moment."

Lillian, in fact, had four of the daily reports. G-dub didn't expect much from these, just half a page or so on what each person had found for the day. Four were ready, but she was still finishing up with Andrew's. His tended to be more detailed than the others, so it was taking her a couple of minutes to finish it.

On Monday, she'd taken an old daily from the Dubner project; Tuesday, it had been the Phillips Petroleum audit. If she was going to cover for him, she thought it best to choose different projects so that G-dub wouldn't suspect anything. The man was clueless sometimes, but he wasn't a complete idiot.

The problem now was that the daily she'd copied over to her flash drive an hour ago was from the audit of Patterson-Crews, a biotech startup they'd worked on four years ago. Although G-dub insisted that the dailies be no more than one page, and he preferred shorter, this one was two and a half pages. That biotech firm had been a mess and it had shut down less than a year later. It was too late to go back to Andrew's computer and pull another file, she'd just have to use this one. But after getting rid of most of the content specific to the Patterson-Crews findings, the size of the file was no longer the problem. It was now less than a page, but there wasn't much substantive. *No worries*, she thought. Lillian channeled her inner Andrew Grey and inserted some blather, specific accounting-sounding blather, about the receivables at San Jose Unified. She hoped this was the last time she'd have to do this. The content of these reports had to get more specific as the audit progressed and the detail Andrew typically included would get harder to fake. Lillian finished up her three paragraph summary of Andrew's findings at SJU and sent it to the pool printer. She pulled the still warm page out and placed it in the middle of the five.

"Here you go." Lillian dropped the dailies on G-dub's desk without fanfare.

"All of them in on time?" her boss asked.

"Every one."

At that, Ellie Davenport looked up at Lillian, but said nothing. It was a dangerous game Lillian was playing. Not because G-dub was going to find out, Ellie was sure Lillian could fake reports from any of them to the boss's satisfaction, but Lillian hadn't considered what was going to happen when Andrew returned. He was so obsessively honest he'd never let something like this slip by. Andrew would rat her out in an instant.

"Good work team!" G-dub called out from his office. His job was easier when all the dailies were in on time. He had a four o'clock deadline for them. That allowed him to read the reports, to the extent that he thought necessary, and finish up by five. It also allowed the members of his team a little time after their work for the day was over to take care of personal items. He knew that in most modern offices, employees did this kind of stuff on work time. They'd spend part of their day browsing the Internet no matter what he did. By requiring the dailies be done early, he managed to have them get the work done and they pushed their personal business to the last hour of the day. That way, he lost less productive time than most of his fellow supervisors and kept his team happy.

Happy team, happy boss, he reflected as he set the reports aside and opened a browser. He needed a birthday present for the wife.

MICHAEL CARLEY

**

Just over two hours after leaving the hospital, Andrew concluded the doctor had been right. He should have taken a cab. Instead, he'd walked around the corner to the nearest bus stop. It turned out not to be the one he needed, but there were several nearby. Finding the right route was made more complicated since he didn't have his phone but he wasn't willing to go back and risk their insistence on the taxi. He knew the transit system well enough, and once he got a schedule, decided it wouldn't be too difficult, just a two-step process, first on the 70, then a short walk to a stop for the 62.

While on the 70 bus, he was sure he'd made the right choice, though the bus' bouncing wreaked havoc on his legs and ribs. The alternative route was the 22 bus. He and Tina had taken that when she'd wanted to attend a Hitchcock festival in Palo Alto. That had been a ride of more than two hours. It was early in their relationship and Tina had said the ride would give them time to talk and get to know each other.

He'd thought it a good relationship and had been disappointed when she broke up with him. But, there had been no point in arguing. He didn't understand those who made a scene and beg to stay with a person who didn't want to be with them, plus Tina had seemingly good reasons. She'd misjudged Andre and was correcting her mistake. Andrew took some pride in having played a part in her newfound happiness. He tried to keep his distance when she came to the office, to avoid awkwardness.

Still, it would have been nice to have been in a relationship just now. Andrew didn't mind being alone, but some things, logistically at least, were easier with a partner. If the accident had happened while he was with Tina, she'd have visited him in the hospital, but more importantly, she'd have given him a ride home.

Andrew wasn't insulted that no one had visited him in the hospital. He didn't have many friends in the area. He knew the day he'd arrived, the nurse on duty had called the office. He'd expected G-dub to show up, but he hadn't, and thankfully so. G-dub's gregarious style grated on Andrew. But that was just who G-dub was, and he mostly left Andrew alone.

None of the other team members came either, but that didn't concern him. People visited friends and family in the hospital, not coworkers. He mostly liked his coworkers, though not their antics, but he didn't consider them close friends.

Their nonappearance did spark a spiral of speculation in his mind though. It would seem his absence had hardly been noticed. Andrew was not a proud man; he knew he was a good accountant, better probably than most, but he also knew that his skills weren't exactly unique. He was a bit surprised that none had even called to ask questions, but then he remembered that Monday had been the start of the San Jose Unified audit. There were no projects outstanding to ask questions about. G-dub had probably been pissed he missed the project launch meeting, that is, if he'd noticed. Andrew hoped for Pete Massey's sake that there was no new software involved. But, regardless, they were getting along fine without him.

Andrew did wonder, if he had died, who would have missed him? They'd have found his wallet and cell phone, as they had in this case, and they'd have called his parents, his sister perhaps. Andrew cringed at the thought of Zeke Grey presiding over his funeral preparations. He'd have to prepare a will just to avoid that possibility. He mentally chastised himself for not having done so already.

But what if he'd just disappeared? He hadn't shown up for work in three days and no one seemed concerned. He'd heard from no friends or family and really, his mother was the only one who ever called anymore, and that was usually to guilt him into coming for Christmas.

Andrew wondered what would happen if he went on vacation and didn't come back. G-dub hardly noticed on the rare occasions when he was late. He'd turned in an absence notice once when he'd been sick and the boss expressed surprise that he'd been gone. What if he just stopped showing up? How much dust would his desk collect before they noticed? How much longer before they sent someone to check on him? Would they even do that or would they wait a couple of weeks, fire him and direct deposit his last paycheck to the bank?

He knew there were days, even weeks when he hardly spoke with anyone, just a few pleasantries to coworkers or store clerks. If there were no meetings, he could go an entire day or two without speaking a word. Sometimes, if it had been hours since speaking, he'd have to clear his throat when addressing someone because his larynx wasn't used to the activity.

He had supplies in his apartment to feed himself for a couple of weeks. This was good because the doctor had said he wouldn't want to travel for a while. He could stay at home for some time and not have to deal with others. He'd have to get his cell phone replaced, but that could wait since the office was already aware of his absence. He should probably check in next week though.

But what if he didn't? What if he never showed up again at work or anywhere outside his apartment? How long before they figured it out? He guessed it would take G-dub a week or two at least to even notice his absence, unless there was something wrong with something he'd turned in, and there rarely was. His coworkers would probably take note, but he doubted they'd say anything. They were quite keen about protecting one another when making mistakes or coming in late and though Andrew didn't party like they did, the shield of the team would likely extend to him. Who knows, maybe he could stay home a month or two and still collect a check. And with his family several states away . . . *it would be an interesting little experiment*, he thought. Andrew almost chuckled before the bus hit a small bump and the pain jolted him back to the present.

He hadn't thought of the pain as being this bad at the hospital, but this was more movement than he'd made in three days and the morphine was wearing off. The scrape on the upper part of his left leg made sitting uncomfortable but standing was no better. With every bounce, he adjusted his position, but then the next movement would affect another body part. The largest bruise was on the back of his left thigh, so he'd move to his right. Then, bounce, his ribs would scream out in pain. He thought of taking some of the medication they'd given him, but opening a bottle of pills on a public bus didn't seem like a good idea.

The walk from the 70 to the stop for the 62 should have taken only a couple of minutes, but he took it slow; his body seemed to have stiffened up. Reaching the stop, he realized he'd just missed his bus, so he had a fifteen-minute wait for the next one.

It was on the ride on the 62 though when he really began to have reservations. He was standing at first because the bus was crowded. He didn't mind standing, he told himself, but he had to hold onto the overhead bar and that stretched his rib injury. He tried switching from right hand to left just as the bus lurched and he fell into a man holding a toddler in his lap. Offering his apologies, he finally started looking for a seat.

Other than his facial injuries and stilted movements, the rest of his injuries were internal, so there was no way he was going to ask for a seat from someone else. But, gradually the bus cleared out and Andrew was able to sit down. He passed the time by counting the stops. Twelve had passed so far; eight more to go.

Andrew actually cried out as he reached up to pull the cord for his stop on Taylor Street. Several heads turned as he held onto the cord. He was afraid that if he sat back down he wouldn't be able to get up again. "Excuse me," he said to the young man in the aisle as he cautiously stepped over his feet. The nine feet between his seat and the rear door took him nearly a minute to navigate.

"You all right man?" the father with the toddler asked as Andrew approached the door. The little boy looked up from his *Boom Chicka Boom* book questioningly. He turned to reply, but then realized that the door was closing.

"Wait!" he shouted toward the driver. The last thing he wanted was to miss his stop. Who knows how far he'd end up from home? Slowly, he made his way down each step, falling to one knee on the sidewalk at the last one but getting up quickly, too quickly, lest someone think he needed assistance.

The five minute walk to his apartment took nearly twenty and two different people asked if he needed help. But he knew better than to stop and rest; he might not be able to get back up if he did.

The stairs were the worst. He usually didn't mind stairs, considering it a bit of added exercise that helped make up for his sedentary job, but now, he was thankful there was only one flight. He paused a moment at the top, then walked past five doors to his sanctuary, apartment 2F. His hands shook and sweat dripped down the back of his neck. He fumbled with the keys, but managed to insert the right one and open the door. He made it three steps into the entryway, dropped his bag from the hospital and collapsed to the floor.

**

Lucinda inserted her key into the set of mailboxes for the south side of the Bay Bridge apartment complex. The bundle was fairly small as it often was mid-week. Still, the residents must have been expecting something important, probably paychecks. Two were already watching her, waiting. A middle-aged woman looked out her first floor apartment window and a boy, maybe about four years old, had been sent to wait for Lucinda, key in hand.

It didn't speed things up when people waited like this; it just made her nervous. But, she tried to go as fast as she could. The little boy reminded her of her nephews. "*Como estàs*?" she asked, correctly guessing from his appearance that Spanish was his first language.

"*Bien*," his eyes lit up again just like her *sobrinos*.

"*Dame dos minutos*, OK?"

"OK."

Lucinda continued sorting, dropping groups of flyers, bills, and personal items into the slots for 2A, B, C, D, and E. She'd seen the little boy come out of apartment 1D, but that was on the lower group of boxes. Next was 2F and she looked up toward that apartment, as was her habit. She'd only spotted him once and then just for a moment, but still, she always looked for the mysterious Andrew Grey.

Now, she dropped the packets of mail for apartments 4G through 4K and her heart caught in her throat. There he was!

At least, she assumed it was him. Andrew Grey, her ever unrequited crush, was stepping into apartment 2F. She only saw a bit of him this time, a black, non-descript bag was the last thing through the door, but she was sure it was the same light brown hair that had proceeded it. Lucinda tried to memorize what she'd seen as her heart raced. A green denim shirt black bag, and, was it khaki pants again like last time? She wasn't sure.

The little boy made a questioning noise that brought her out of her daydreams. "*Lo siento*." she mumbled under her breath as she went back to the mail. She dropped Andrew Grey's in his box, noting he hadn't picked up the last couple of days' worth on his way in. That was unusual. As little as she knew about this man, she was aware of his mail habits, and he was very conscientious about his mail. She flirted briefly with the forbidden thought of walking it up to him, blushing at the idea. Lastly, she picked up the mail from the other apartments on the second floor, then, in businesslike fashion, distributed the first floor mail and nodded to the little boy as she went along her way.

Only once before had she caught a glimpse of the elusive Andrew Grey. In certain hyperrealist moments, Lucy was a bit embarrassed by how far her fantasies extended. But luckily, she had few such moments. Besides, no one was really hurt by a few stray thoughts.

She'd seen his name on envelopes for a couple of years without ever seeing the man behind the mail. But that day, it must have been almost a year ago now, he'd been wearing a light blue pea coat with a striped scarf. She watched him, walking across the outdoor balcony toward Apartment 2F, and he appeared every bit her ideal man. Lucinda had a fascination with all things British, born from the pen of C.S. Lewis and nurtured through her teen years on Tolkien. She'd read the American copycats like Brooks and Paolini, and she did occasionally venture into other genres. Her mother introduced her to her favorite Latin American writers. She found Marquez and Allende interesting, but her mother's favorite, Victor Villaseñor, proved too vested in the real world for her taste with no sense of fancy or whimsy at all. Needless to say, Ramira Fuentes was exasperated with her daughter's literary choices.

Whatever the source, Lucy was a full-fledged Anglophile. The British seemed to have cornered the market on imagination, the ability to create new creatures and entire worlds that seemed so real. At times, they were more real than her own. She'd rarely been outside California, just a few trips to Michoacán to visit relatives and one to Portland, Oregon where her uncle lived with his new husband. The Fuentes family was not especially adventurous. But the one place she'd always wanted to visit was Great Britain. After her new bookshelves were installed, that was the next thing she was saving for. She planned to visit every part of the islands: Big Ben, King's Cross, Oxford and the Midlands. She'd see it all if she had to save every penny until she was forty.

Andrew's look that first day, at least from the back, had been decidedly British, or at least she'd thought so. In truth, all she really saw was the jacket, scarf, and his short-cropped light brown hair as he took a few steps down the hall, paused and entered 2F.

Lucinda had never been one to fall head over heels. In fact, she'd never had a serious boyfriend. It wasn't that she didn't want one, it just seemed that the life in her mind, and in her books, was preferable to any actual humans she managed to encounter. And she'd never of course, really encountered Andrew Grey. She just saw him once and let her own fertile imagination take flight. And he probably hadn't seen her at all.

Since the Bay Bridge apartments were near the end of her route, they provided a good breaking point for her day. Before arriving, she'd think about what type of mail Andrew might have, not that it was especially interesting. She was disappointed on those days when nothing at all arrived, but those were rare. He got flyers from the local grocery store, letters from the alumni information at San Jose State, and local bills. The university choice surprised her. Why would someone so obviously British have come to a mid-ranked state school? The thought of an undercover spy alias crossed her mind, but that was trite and overdone. More likely, he'd come to California as many had, for the adventure. He picked up his mail almost every day, but was never at home during the day, so perhaps he taught there. A university professor would be quite a catch in her mother's eyes. She hadn't been to the university herself since the Amy Tan reading last year. Maybe if she stopped by, she'd spot Andrew.

Then he started getting newsletters from something called the IMA. She was sure the "I" stood for International, though upon looking closer, the organization appeared to be called the Association of Accountants and Finance Professionals in Business. Obviously, a bad acronym, maybe International was implied? But high finance? That gave a whole new perspective to her dreams of Andrew. He must be an influential businessman keeping a low profile in town. Thoughts of private jets and vacations on the islands filled her mind for weeks.

Last week, Andrew had gotten his voter registration packet and sample ballot. She wondered, is he a Republican or Democrat? Did she care? Most big business guys were Republicans, weren't they? But she was sure he'd be someone who'd care about the little guy, so maybe a Democrat. Lucinda wasn't political herself. Her brother Jaime usually had to remind her to vote. He was involved in the local chapter of the National Council of La Raza and often had pointed advice for Lucinda, not that she necessarily followed it.

Maybe, she thought, Andrew was a member of one of those small parties, the Greens, the Libertarians or maybe the Peace and Freedom people. One of those fighting the good fight against the system. She couldn't help it, she glanced at the sample ballot. Andrew was listed as *decline to state*, no party affiliation. She should have guessed. A standup guy like Andrew Grey would never tie himself down to a party. Lucinda was proud of him for that.

But now, as she left the Bay Bridge apartments, her face flushed with excitement, there was just one thing on Lucinda's mind. *What is in that little black bag?*

**

"Bridget the Midget!" Molly yelled, as her sister once again got distracted by whatever shiny object was hanging in the window of apartment 2G.

"Stop calling me that!"

"Then pay attention. I have homework due tomorrow and this is the last night for you to sell cookies. You want to win that bike, don't you?"

"Yes."

"Then, you have about . . ." Molly glanced down the row of apartments to her left " . . . six more doors to knock on before we go home. It's almost seven o'clock."

"Couldn't we try the houses down the street too?"

"No. We can try these six doors and then we're going home. Now, break out your big pretty smile and knock."

Bridget knocked. Loud. Then she knocked again.

"There's nobody home, Bridge."

"Wait, I hear something."

"Let's go."

"No, wait!"

Slowly, the doorknob turned and the door opened a crack. Molly had to walk around her sister to see whoever was inside.

As she put her hand on Bridget's shoulder, Molly almost gasped. At the door was a disheveled young man, or maybe he was middle-aged, it was hard to tell. He was holding himself up by the doorknob, apparently unable to stand otherwise. The man had a bandage down his left arm and his legs were trembling. There was another bandage on the right side of his face, but it was small. The thought that he might be on drugs went through the teenager's mind. Molly gripped her sister's shoulder protectively as the younger girl went into her script.

"Would you like to buy some Girl Scout cookies? We're saving money for a camping trip and I'm trying to win a bike."

"It's nice you want a bike; they're good exercise. Will you wear a helmet?"

"Yes."

"And you'll ride safely?"

"Yes." Bridget was fidgeting now.

"That's good. Still, I'm not sure if you're more deserving of a bicycle than another scout. Tell me about this camping trip?"

"We're planning to go to Yo...Yosum..."

"Yosemite." Molly corrected.

"So, is this just for fun or will you learn something?"

"Well, it's mostly for fun, I think, but we'll probably learn stuff."

Molly saw that it was time to intervene. "It's an educational trip for the girls," she began authoritatively. "They're learning survival skills, leadership, and studying the various flora and fauna so that they can be responsible environmental stewards." Molly could never remember the difference between flora and fauna, but she knew the terms from biology class and they sounded impressive. "The camping

KNOW MY NAME

trip will be next month if the girls sell enough cookies. They'll be learning new things every day."

"We will?" Bridget now sounded dubious about the whole project. Molly nudged her and tightened the grip on her shoulder. Bridget squirmed, but smiled at the man. "How many boxes would you like to order?"

"I think I can help you out with one box. Which ones are the best?"

"Peanut Butter Patties!" Bridget exclaimed.

"Actually, the Thin Mints are the most popular," Molly corrected. She was hoping she'd heard the man wrong. All this trouble for one box? "Here's the list of the choices."

The man took his hand off the doorknob and took the list from the teenager. Molly saw him hesitate and widen his stance. She wondered if he was about to fall and hoped she wouldn't need to go into his apartment if she had to call 911. Thankfully, she remembered that she had her own cell phone with her. *See Mom, it really is for emergencies*, she thought.

"I think I'll try the shortbread" he replied, after looking closely at the list.

"How many boxes?" Bridget batted her eyes expectantly.

"One. Like I said. I live alone; one is enough." With that, the man walked several feet and reached down for a small black bag. "Oh" he exclaimed quietly as he pulled his wallet out of the bag.

"Are you OK?" Bridget asked as he slowly stood up. She was fidgeting again, eager to move on to the next door.

"Bridge," Molly whispered. "We are *not* going into that apartment." She was as impatient as her sister to get away from this door, but caution seemed in order.

"I'm fine. Just a little slow today. Or tonight, I suppose it is now." It took him almost half a minute to move the few feet to the door. The man was grasping the doorknob again, and again, his legs were trembling. "Five dollars, is it?"

"Yes sir." Molly replied, answering for her sister, eager to get away.

"Here you go. When will the cookies arrive?"

"Two weeks," Bridget replied, taking the cash and heading down the walkway.

Molly followed up. "They're arriving to us on the 3rd and we'll be delivering them over that following week after school. Bridge, what do you say?"

"Thank you sir!" The youngster called over her shoulder, pigtails swinging as she moved toward 2E and knocked, even louder this time.

"Thank you. Molly smiled at the man apologetically. "I hope you're feeling better soon."

**

Andrew exhaled slowly and moved slowly toward the bedroom, black bag in hand. He was a bit surprised because he'd never passed out before, at least not that he could recall. But now, it was all he could do to keep from collapsing again. He suspected the pain itself was the only thing keeping him awake.

He managed to make his way to the bathroom, put the bottle of Vicodin on the counter and pull out one pill. Best not to overdo it. Just one to take the edge off.

So much for that *interesting little experiment*, he thought, reflecting on his morbid thoughts from earlier. The idea of not going back to work held a strange kind of appeal. He had food in the house to last for weeks and he could stay in the apartment until someone noticed his absence. The landlady might pick up on it eventually, though the rent was paid automatically from his account at the bank, so there would be little reason to expect that quickly. Maybe G-dub or, more likely, Lillian would eventually inquire. But none of them really cared. They probably wouldn't notice.

He was accountable to no one, which was exactly how he liked it. If he wanted, he never would have to leave this apartment. Andrew yawned, the medication beginning to take effect. Crawling under the covers, he thought, I don't even have to leave this bed if I don't want to.

Except, now he was accountable. To two Girl Scouts he didn't even know. He'd have to open the door eventually.

Damn cookies.

BOOKS

It was early yet and she was tired, but Ashlynn was already up, bright eyed and determined. She wanted to get to the hospital early so she could catch Kevin up on the story. She'd decided they should be on a first name basis as perhaps familiarity would cut through any barriers between them. She doubted that Kevin knew she'd caused his accident, but in case he picked up on any vibes from her, it was best to be as positive and casual as possible.

After she'd finally found her victim, and recovered from the shock, Ashlynn resolved to do whatever she could for him, however ineffectual that might be. She arranged the flowers in his room and gave them water. She fluffed his pillows. And to the extent the nurses would allow, she helped with his sponge bath.

All of that, of course, seemed superficial, but she was determined to stick it out. She'd heard stories of people waking from comas when they heard family and friends talking to them. And though he was unlikely to recognize her voice, she talked to him. That Wednesday, she'd talked for hours. The thought of apologizing came to mind of course, but whether it was the weight of her guilt or her determination to keep things positive, she avoided doing so. She didn't talk of the accident at all.

And since she didn't know much about his life, she told him about hers. There wasn't much to tell, she was sure, that wouldn't sound shallow and unimportant, especially given the circumstances, but she talked anyway. She told him about her classes, the math class she'd aced, the history professor who'd dressed up in period costumes in a misguided effort to keep their attention, and of course, Dr. Burke, the philosophy professor, whose assignment had led to her and Kevin's fateful meeting. She skipped over the accident itself, instead veering into a discourse on the Vedanta Society she'd been there to study. She'd missed her appointment of course, but the research had proved fascinating, or at least that's what she told Kevin. In truth, any religious tradition would have been outside her experience; her parents had little time for such things. But, the Vedanta group seemed quite devoted.

She also talked about her family, what they'd done for her, the things she'd enjoyed, and the things she'd missed by not having a different set of parents. She worried that she was stepping again into the shallow end of the pool; everyone had such regrets, didn't they? She told Kevin of her difficulty in choosing a major. She'd never need to work, though her folks had told her that once she found what she was passionate about, the rest would take care of itself. But what was that? It certainly wasn't philosophy, or any of the other subjects she'd taken so far.

At one point, she wondered if Kevin was someone she'd want to date. With a little cleanup, he seemed like a pretty good looking guy. Assuming he recovered, which she hoped with every breath, his injuries wouldn't likely be disfiguring. Even if they were, she could look past them. He wasn't much older than she, maybe in his early twenties.

"You should wake up soon. We could go out for coffee maybe. I know you haven't seen me yet, but I'm told I'm kind of pretty." Ashlynn quickly regretted that last statement, not only for the false humility, but because she could tell that Kevin wasn't the kind of guy to place beauty over more important values. Her charge, she was sure, was a serious, compassionate young man.

Eventually, though, she did run out of things to tell him. Though she'd shared more with Kevin in one afternoon than she had with her friends in her entire teenage-hood, anything more would lead her into the realm of self-importance. His recovery was of greater value than his knowledge of her story and it would best be furthered by focusing on him.

So, she started reading.

At first, she read from a fishing magazine Kevin's father had left in his room, then she moved on to waiting room magazines. She read from *Time* and *Newsweek*, though most of the copies were old, *Scientific American, Popular Mechanics,* and several medical journals. She avoided *People* and the other tabloids. She couldn't imagine Kevin was interested in celebrity gossip.

Ashlynn was a fast reader, always had been. By mid-afternoon Wednesday, she'd burned through all the magazines of interest, and several of no interest. She knew she'd have to leave by 5:30, when Kevin's father would arrive, but for now, occupying her time, and his, was paramount. So she took the elevator down to the hospital gift shop. The book selection there was better than she'd expected. Apparently, those visiting family and friends had many hours of boredom to occupy. Right now though, it wasn't her own boredom she was concerned about; she wanted to occupy Kevin's mind, activate any nerve, emotion, or sense that would lead to recovery. Hell, she'd have slept with him if she thought it would help.

Though the selection was large, most of the choices didn't seem appropriate. Kevin's tastes would be literary she was sure, serious, but not intense. Oh, for Christ's sake, she had no idea.

Then she pulled a title off the shelf she'd never heard of. A host of superlatives swirled across the cover in a vortex. *Everything Matters!* by Ron Currie Jr. She knew nothing about it, but the title was good and maybe Kevin would appreciate that the author, like him, was a Junior. If she could convince Kevin that in fact, everything, or at least something, mattered, she'd be well on her way. Ashlynn pulled out her credit card, handed it to the smiling clerk, and headed back to her charge.

Back in the room, she started the book just before 4:00 in the afternoon. It was engrossing from the first page. It started with the main character's infancy, even prior to his birth, and she found herself laughing for the first time in several days. Kevin didn't react as far as she could tell, but she got into the story within minutes. She almost missed the time to go. Looking up at the clock, it was 5:28, so she scurried out of the room right in the middle of a chapter.

But she didn't cheat, at least not Wednesday night. Though she was as restless as she had been, this book was her shared experience with Kevin Jamison Junior. She waited until the next morning to finish her chapter and move on to the next. But all day Thursday was spent reading to Kevin. She left the room only for restroom breaks and when the nurses needed to do something. She knew all the nurses' names by now; to them, she was Kevin's devoted sister who worked at night and kept vigil at his bedside through the day while their father was at work. By the time for the father's arrival Thursday night, she was already a third of the way through the book.

But that night, she couldn't put it down. She hadn't been able to sleep wondering what was happening in the novel. So, she'd been up half the night reading. The only thing that mattered was everything and everything mattered now.

Now it was Friday morning and though she hadn't slept more than four hours, she was making her way to the hospital. She felt bad about reading without Kevin, but more than that, she wanted to share what she'd read with him. She wanted to talk about the book, what others they'd read together. She wanted to walk him up and down the ICU hallways while he recovered, she reading, he making sure they didn't crash into anyone while she had her face buried in the book, or perhaps it would be the other way around. She wanted to walk with him in the park nearby, read those sections again he might have slept through, let him read some parts to her. Ashlynn was by now convinced that this book was essential to Kevin's recovery, and maybe to her own.

Stepping off the bus, through the glass doors, and onto the elevator, she pulled the book out of her purse and moved back to where she'd left off with Kevin the night before. She wanted to be ready the moment she stepped into the room. Despite her anxiety, she was still watchful as she walked down the hallway of the ICU. Though Kevin Senior's schedule, as she understood it from the nurses, didn't permit him to visit in the mornings, there could be other family members or friends coming to visit. Not only did she not want to explain herself to them, she valued her alone time with Kevin.

But the room was empty, save for a nurse's assistant, who

seemed on her way out. "Your brother seems to be doing a little better this morning. His fever's down."

"Really?" Ashlynn couldn't suppress a surge of hope. "Has he . . . "

"He hasn't woken up. It's still serious. The swelling's not going down enough. But there's always hope." The young woman squeezed Ashlynn's hand for a moment as she stepped out of the room.

Ashlynn took several breaths and remembered her task. She removed the bookmark and placed it next to her water cup from the previous day. Interlacing the fingers of her right hand through Kevin's, she opened the book with her left. "We're on Part II now," she told her charge. "Another chapter about Junior. Here we go. 'Though she's hoping to slip in and out of town without me finding out, of course I know when Amy comes back . . . '"

**

Across town, Lucinda awoke with a tired euphoria. She'd been on something of a high since the Wednesday Andrew Grey sighting. The mystery of the black bag had taken on a life of its own, having undergone several transformations in just under forty hours.

The first iteration had been perhaps the most obvious. Andrew was a doctor. For much of Wednesday evening, she was sure of it. He was an old fashioned doctor who still did house calls, travelling from patient to patient as crises presented themselves. Perhaps he was such a medical throwback or perhaps he was an obstetrician, attending home births for those people who eschewed hospitals.

Another of her longstanding Andrew fantasies had been that he was a pilot. If so, he'd surely travel the world once they were together, or rather, they'd travel together, Andrew with his English scarf and pilot gear. In some of these dreams, Andrew worked for one of the major airlines and she got to travel for free whenever she wanted. She'd make trips to London, Scotland, Ireland, or if she wanted, to Morelia to visit her great aunts. Sometimes, they'd travel together, but just as often, she'd simply make the trip with him, exploring the local atmosphere while he worked. When he returned, she'd take him out to dinner at some quaint little place she'd discovered, show him the sights, and spend the evenings telling him of her adventures.

The black bag could be some of that efficient luggage pilots carried. Airline people always had the best because they used it so much. But the bag would fit just as well with the other version of her dream, that he was an amateur pilot, a rich entrepreneur who used his pilot's license to travel the world without impediment of schedule or flight plan. He might travel for business, or in a private capacity as part of his volunteer work; in many of her daydreams, he was a do-gooder, alternately lending his expertise to impoverished countries in improving their water supplies or simply adding a shovel and a set of hardworking hands to whatever project was already underway.

The bag would coincide quite nicely with one specific fantasy, that of Andrew's work with Doctors Without Borders. She'd become so enamored with this idea that she'd begun donating to DWB. It was the only charitable organization she followed, except for some of the local work in which her brother was involved. In this case, the bag could be either that of a pilot or a doctor, or somehow, he could use it for both. In his DWB work, Andrew might take on assignments for six months to a year, wherever he was needed, but given the singular character he presented, she thought it more likely that the organization flew him from site to site, a surgeon who was brought in to deal with their more complex and difficult cases.

Before work on Thursday, she'd gone so far as to conduct an internet search for "black bag," garnering a new set of ideas for what kind of life her secret love led. One of the leading search results was something called "black bag jobs" an apparently nefarious and illegal practice among law enforcement when they wanted to frame people they didn't like. There was still some appeal to the idea of Andrew as a member of a secret organization, but she still thought it too cliché, too common a fantasy for someone of her imagination. And the more she read about it, the more she disliked the practice that seemed to be associated with the targeting of political groups. Lucy wasn't political, but something about what she read just seemed wrong. She discarded it completely.

Another search result was for a technology company, which made a lot of sense. Of course, he'd be in the tech field; this was Silicon

Valley after all. But the name of the company had little to do with bags themselves; again, she'd ventured into some kind of surveillance industry work. She moved on.

Then there were several results for apparel and fashion companies. She could see Andrew in the industry; he was certainly dapper, what with that scarf and pea coat she'd seen the first time. But aren't most men in the fashion industry gay? Lucinda had gotten over any latent homophobia when Uncle Jimmy came into her life; his humor and warmth had completely set her at ease. But no, more likely Andrew was one of those rare straight men in a field dominated by women and gay men. He could have any woman he wanted, but he was devoted to his dear Lucy, or at least he would be once they met.

Such thoughts had occupied her entire day Thursday, making the workday go by faster than any she could remember. At the Bay Bridge apartments, she'd lingered over his mail. He still hadn't picked up yesterday's, which was unusual. She scanned his apartment door for any sign that Andrew was home. But, though she thought she saw the flicker of a light behind the blinds, her love was not in sight. Maybe Friday.

But now that Friday had come along, she was excited for another reason. The black bag had certainly not exhausted its value as a source of fantasy, but real life had intruded. Today was finally the day! Her new bookshelves were going to be installed.

Her mother had hated the idea from the start. Why pay to have new bookshelves installed in a rented apartment, she'd asked. What happens when you get married and move out? Lucy's reply was that she had no intention of marrying any time soon, though that certainly wasn't the answer that would provide any relief from maternal nagging. She'd quickly followed up that she'd enjoy the bookshelves as long as she lived there, which, since she'd just signed a new lease, would be at least two more years.

Now, it was finally happening. She'd given the apartment keys to the cabinet people, she'd notified the landlord, and the installation was to be done by five o'clock. She wouldn't even have to see the work in progress. Lucinda would just come home from work to her entire south wall redone with bookshelves with that deep-red cherry stain she'd selected. She could spend the evening and most of the weekend filling them.

In preparation, she'd finished the Joyce Carol Oates book at lunch on Thursday. It had been a good one, with intrigue and uncertainty. She'd been surprised when so many of the characters had been real historical figures, presidents, authors, and others. Most of the authors she knew; she'd liked Jack London quite a bit, but couldn't remember much about Upton Sinclair and he took up a good deal of the book.

Lucinda had been so intent on finishing the book, she hadn't noticed how cool the day was, but it wasn't the cold she shivered from at lunchtime; it was the scary story. She was so into the novel that she'd neglected most of her lunch, but that didn't matter. She could eat while driving.

The fun part, upon finishing, had been thinking of where the book would fit on the new shelves. There were certain books that had special places, but the rest would be placed alphabetically, by author. Given the books in her collection, the Oates ones would be more than halfway, but less than three quarters through, alphabetically. She suspected, they'd be in the fourth column of shelves, about half the way down, midway across the third row. She still had the book with her, along with a China Miéville for today's reading as she dropped off her own car and picked up the mail truck, she wondered how close her guess would be. She was going to find out if it took all weekend.

**

Lucinda's unrequited love interest wasn't having such a good day himself. Andrew was determined to begin getting back into his routine. He'd spent most of Thursday in bed, but not sleeping. He'd drift off for an hour, or two at most, then the pain would return. He tried to will it away, avoiding medication as long as he could stand it, but each time, he'd eventually break down and take a Vicodin. His ribs hurt more than anything else, but his left buttock was also sore and his right knee was now a problem. No matter which way he'd shift his weight, he was uncomfortable and each time he tried to settle into a position, one body part or another would scream for his attention. At nearly four AM Thursday night, he finally gave in and took two pills, thus managing his first unbroken sleep of more than three consecutive hours.

The mistake he made Friday morning was to think that he'd turned a corner. Since he'd been without medicine for a few hours, he took one pill and got up. Andrew was glad the nurse had given him forty tablets. She'd told him it was so he didn't have to pick up his prescription until the following week and he now saw the wisdom in that. He certainly wasn't going anywhere today.

But in preparation for getting life back underway, he did need to exercise. The doctor had told him to get back into his calisthenics routine as soon as he could. He knew it would be uncomfortable, but if he kept it light, he could get a start today.

His normal regimen included twenty old fashioned jumping jacks, designed to get his heart rate up for the rest of the session, then twenty sit-ups with his feet lodged under the couch and twenty pushups using a dining room chair. He usually repeated each of these twice each morning before heading off to work. Today, he thought, maybe one set of each would suffice.

He wasn't pain-free, but he wouldn't be for some time, so he might as well get over it. But the first jumping jack displayed his folly. The impact, small though it was, caused his knee to buckle as his legs moved outward and as he brought the legs back together, the knee collapsed altogether. He came down hard, adding a bruise to what was probably a torn meniscus already.

Determination, or one might call it intransigence, is part of the Grey family DNA. Since he was already on the ground, Andrew rested for only a moment, then swiveled around so that his feet were under the couch. He had to rest again, but only for a moment so as to not lose his focus. He gritted his teeth, moved as much of his weight as he could to his right side, sucked in his breath, and thrust himself forward full force into his sit-up.

"Aahh!! . . . ggrr" is the closest thing to the sound he made as his body moved forward, then shot back again. The pain in his ribs caused him to recoil immediately, his instinct to lie back down. But that just made things worse as the same pain shot through his torso as he moved backward as he'd encountered on the upswing. No longer having any conscious control of his body, he rocked from right to left, searching in vain for a way to relieve either the ache in his hips or the sharp throbbing in his midsection. His mind told him relief was just a few minutes away if he could manage to live that long. But each time he attempted to take a deep breath, it would cut short in his throat; very little expansion of the chest cavity was going to be permitted by his injuries.

With his limited breath and uncomfortable position, Andrew would need all of his self-discipline to survive the next hour without passing out. He continued to rock back and forth ever so slightly. He managed to put most of his weight on his left buttock, still rocking his torso slightly to the left and right. After about ten minutes, he began the arduous process of relaxing his upper body. Each attempt to untie the tension in his abdominal muscles would result in a sharp draw of breath starting the process all over again.

This went on for well over an hour until he could relax his muscles enough to move. Slowly, he began to crawl the twenty feet to the bedroom where his savior Vicodin was sitting on his nightstand. He took two pills, swallowed them dry, and began the excruciating process of lifting himself up onto the bed.

Exercise, maybe tomorrow.

**

Zeke Grey, on the other hand, was already finished with his calisthenics. He hadn't missed a day in more than thirty years. He'd exercised on his honeymoon with Olivia at that little motel in Branson. He'd done so five months later the morning Andrew was born, and again two years following that the day Janice had made her way into the world after eighteen hours of labor. To Zeke, a difficult day was just another reason to maintain routine. It helped keep him calm amidst life's many storms.

Not that this was expected to be a difficult day. It was Friday and he just had work and to prepare for the weekend. Pastor Cartwright had selected him to do the reading for his sermon on Sunday. He took this responsibility very seriously. Zeke wasn't a fast reader, but he did his best to imbue his recitations with the reverence that sacred scripture deserved. All scripture was equally sacred of course, but he especially connected with the letters of the apostle Paul. This week's choice was one of the best; Zeke had to admit that Pastor seemed to get what was wrong in the world and what Christians needed to do to address it. He hadn't been sure for some time.

His voice rose as he moved into the latter half of Romans 1. Zeke had himself considered that perhaps he might be called to serve the Lord as a minister, but it wasn't to be. That decision had been made for him, or at least he'd made it indirectly. Zeke wasn't one to look to the past. Quite the opposite in fact. He had his sights set on a glorious future, one after the trials and tribulations of this world were but a memory. A future with streets paved with gold, if only he remained on the righteous path. For that, Paul's letters provided direction. They were, in Zeke's world, the closest he came to ecstasy.

**

Olivia was in the kitchen putting away the breakfast dishes. She nearly jumped out of her skin as her husband's voice rose again without warning. *Good heavens*, she thought, she should be used to it by now.

Nonetheless, Fridays were her least favorite day. It wasn't that she didn't look forward to the weekend, though things were lonelier now that it was just her and Zeke. But the Pastor was depending on him for the readings more often lately, which meant these Friday practice sessions. She knew that Zeke loved his work at the church; it gave him purpose. But, she worried that he'd be late to work and get into trouble. He never really had been in trouble at work, not in more than twenty years. The only time he'd ever been written up was the morning after Janice had been born when he'd been twenty minutes late. But still, she worried.

She was just finished scraping the biscuit pan when Zeke came into the room. Small beads of perspiration stood on his forehead. "You home on time tonight?" she asked.

"Not too late. I just have to drop off some supplies at the food bank on the way home."

"Do they need more food again?"

"No, just some utensils and that new oven we got for them at the Salvation Army. Bob Searcy said he'd pick it up in his truck, but he'll need some help unloading it."

"That's very good of you. You OK with chicken and dumplings for dinner? Maybe we could invite the Selmys?"

"The dumplings sound good, but I'd rather not listen to Roger Selmy's jibber jabber. Maybe I'll just bring Bob home with me. He's been alone since Jeanine died."

"The problem is, without Jeanine, I'll have no one to talk to."

"Maybe he'll bring Darlene along, if she's not too busy with schoolwork. I gotta go; I'm running a bit late this morning."

"OK sweetie, I'll see you tonight."

Olivia abandoned the dishes and headed for the living room. She wasn't looking forward to an evening listening to Zeke and Bob talk or watching Bob's sullen teenage daughter look at her cell phone, but company was company. She'd take time to prepare later.

For now, she reached into her sewing kit, fumbled past the needles and pin cushions for the book at the bottom of the box. She'd picked up the latest Harlequin romance at the library the day before, but had been too busy to start on it. She'd never have pulled it out in front of Zeke. He didn't approve of such books, especially the ones with the racy covers. The one time he saw one of them, she'd expected a lecture, but what she got was worse. "I can't believe you brought such trash into my house." he'd told her quietly before retiring to his room for the night. She'd been so ashamed, she took that one back to the library unfinished.

The closest thing to romance she read with him around was a Janette Oke. Several of the women at church read those, and since they passed them around, it saved everyone money. But as much as she appreciated the sharing, Christian romance just didn't cut it. She needed the real thing and a month after being caught by her husband, she was back at the Salina public library looking through the stacks for her favorites and furtively glancing around to make sure no one she knew was nearby. Whenever she could, she tried to get the four books in one versions, which saved on trips to the library, but they didn't always carry those.

Of her church friends, only Tabitha Selmy would have understood. Tabby had a wild side, though she was careful who she allowed to see it. If rumors were to be believed, she had a wild past as well, but Olivia tried to avoid the rumor mill. That could only lead to trouble.

The Harlequins gave her a link to her own past as well, though she'd never have admitted it. The descriptions of lovemaking brought to her mind a kind of vicarious eroticism that she'd long since abandoned in her real life. Her love life with Zeke was nothing like the characters in these books, but that wasn't the nature of their relationship. He was her husband, and a devoted father, the best she could hope for or deserve.

Olivia sometimes wondered if anyone had relations like the scenes described in these books. It didn't seem possible. But they provided her opportunity to fantasize, to wonder about a different kind of life.

She was careful not to allow these fantasies to venture too far. Olivia knew it was dangerous (not to mention sinful) to think too much about actually being with other men, physically or otherwise. Her own past came to her only in flashes, often during these early morning reading sessions, her mind fleeting between the scenes described in the book and those actually, or not actually experienced by a teenage Olivia.

In either narrative, or perhaps both, there was a handsome rakish rogue, whose silver tongue loosened the will of the naive, inexperienced girl, page-turn, heaving bosom, page-turn, legs splayed in wanton, shameful, guilty passion, page-turn, worry, a missed period, ignorance, passion, confrontation, self-delusion, page-turn, more confrontation, abandonment, page-turn, parental shame, should she run, accept her fate, what kind of girl am I, page-turn, shame, guilt, fear, page-turn, Olivia, running, running, page-turn, characters, these are fiction, you cannot run forever, page-turn, exhaustion, collapsing, literally falling at the feet of a serious young man she hardly knew.

Questions, what's wrong, page-turn, denial, confrontation, exhaustion, proposal. No, this was too real, page-turn, but I can help you, keep your secret, page-turn, Harlequin secrets are delicious, no, your secret, page-turn, marry me, I've always admired, liked you, page-turn, handsome rogue, seduction, page-turn, short, serious young man, young, but older than she, only twenty-five, he said, not too old for you, you need me, I need a wife, page-turn, a life with you, you're all wrong for me, page-turn, a life with you, I hardly know you, page-turn, rogue, kissing down her neck, danger, page-turn, I'll take care of you short serious man says, if you'll commit, commit what, commit your life to Christ, page-turn, will rogue stay with her, is he really reformed this time, page-turn, stay with me, I'll take care of you and your baby, page-turn, rogue won't stay, will never stay, will never change, page-turn, marry me, you don't know me, all I need to know, what, will you devote your life to Christ, raise your child, our child for the Lord, what, will you...for Christ, what, I can't, I can take care of you, I've always thought you were pretty, a good person, page-turn, the rogue leaves, he always leaves, page-turn, ok, I will, what will, where will, let me take care of things, take care of everything, my baby, our baby, it'll be our baby, you'd really, I would, if you'll let me, let me, I need a wife, I'll be a father, your baby's father, page-turn, the rogue is gone, she is alone, page-turn, yes, my baby needs a father, but people, people will know, our secret, it will be our only secret, in everything else, we'll be right, right with God, but this, our secret, I'll take care of everything, the short serious man, what was his name again, it was to be her name, what was she giving up, it didn't matter, he was a good man, he'd said so, she was tired, so tired, yes, this would solve everything. Yes, he'd take care of her.

Olivia closed the book. It appeared, and things might change, but it appeared, that the rogue was going to stay, going to reform this time. She didn't believe it. She knew she'd come back to the book tomorrow, but for now, she didn't buy the story. The rogue didn't reform, he didn't come back. The rogue was gone, the serious man was here, the short, serious man she didn't know then, but now knew quite well.

They hadn't talked about it again after that day. He never wanted to. And he was true to his word, his every word. Zeke Grey had married her, been a father to her son, the only father he ever knew or ever would. And as true as he'd been, as faithful, she'd been as well. She'd committed herself to the Lord, to the righteous path as she understood it, as he'd explained it to her, both patiently and determinedly. He'd been a good father, a good provider, as stable a man as she could ever have wanted. The son, conceived in spontaneous, momentary shameful irresponsibility, was born into stability, structure, legitimacy. Then, there had been the daughter, both of theirs, cementing the marital bond should any doubt have existed.

Gratitude can cover shame, it can smother doubt, fear, and other worries about whether the choices are right. And when gratitude is combined with the business of motherhood, of raising them, raising children to be right with the Lord, a serious little boy, so like his father, though he'd be tall, taller at least. A not-so serious girl, flighty, looking for every chance to escape, climb trees in her dress, fidget in her lap during Bible stories, and wander toward the door. She'd be a tough one to rein in.

Olivia had enjoyed every minute of raising them. She accepted Zeke's corrections when he thought her methods too liberal, deferred to him on matters disciplinary and religious, but the joy of motherhood was hers. Whatever she'd given up, she'd always have her children.

Now, her face a bit flushed, she returned the book to the bottom of the sewing kit. She'd check tomorrow; maybe the story would take a turn; sometimes they did. But this she knew. The rogue was the rogue. The serious man sacrificed, stayed. And so, she stayed.

**

Tina had no need for romance novels; she had the real thing right under her thighs and she was enjoying it. She loved watching Andre's face as he tried to hold out for as long as he could. It appeared that he was alternating between pain and deep concentration. She wasn't sure at times whether he was prolonging his own pleasure or making sure she got hers, but in the end, it didn't matter. As their mutual climaxes ebbed, not exactly simultaneous, but that was overrated, she smiled, waiting for him to open his eyes. "Mmm," was his only expression has his gaze met hers. It was halfway between a chuckle and a moan.

The one thing she was beginning to miss as her pregnancy progressed was that, although being on top was the most comfortable position, she couldn't simply collapse forward onto his chest at the end of their lovemaking and fall asleep in his arms. But now, this little bundle was in the way, and increasingly so. Slowly, she disengaged and lay next to her fiancé, leaning in for their customary concluding kiss. "Is it hard?" she asked.

"Not anymore."

"Ha ha. I meant, is it hard for you now, you know, to make love with me? Does it hurt now that I weigh more or is it harder to get aroused with me so big?"

"You're kidding, right?"

"Not really," Tina leaned on her elbow and looked at him. "I'm curious."

"Babe, it just gets better all the time. More than I ever thought it would." Andre paused for a moment, searching for words. "But if you want specifics, first of all, you're not that heavy. You've gained less than 20 pounds. And in case the past little while wasn't enough evidence of how much you arouse me, I guess I'll have to show you again tomorrow."

She kissed him again and relaxed onto the bed. "I'm glad we took the day off."

"We took it off for your appointment mostly, so don't fall asleep." With that, Andre grabbed his book off the night stand to make sure he didn't make that mistake.

Tina knew he'd not let her miss the doctor's appointment; he hadn't missed one himself so far. So, she nestled against him and considered a catnap.

Andre was right of course. Their lovemaking was better than it ever had been. She was less inhibited this time around and as the pregnancy progressed, she seemed to want him more often rather than less. She wondered if that was typical.

This was her first pregnancy, though they'd already discussed a second child at some point, maybe three years from now if all went well. For now, well, they could keep practicing.

Andre was hers and this was real and forever. She wouldn't ever make love with anyone else, of this she was now sure. Tina took some modest pride in the fact that the number of lovers in her history could be counted on one hand.

First there was Corey, if he should really be counted at all. Their awkward encounters in high school were more about relieving both of them of their respective virginities than either love or sex. And frankly, the whole affair, while precious in her memory, had taken less than half an hour. She hadn't even missed curfew.

She and Corey had tried again on prom night, but between the triteness of the occasion and embarrassment over the first experience, they'd both broken down in giggles and decided to remain friends.

Next, during her time at San Jose City College, came Joseph, the one who really had cheated. That example of male infidelity hadn't been her imagination; the evidence was everywhere, from the text messages she'd found on his phone to the panties in his car. She'd stayed with him far too long for her own self esteem. The insult to her intelligence, she now reflected, was probably worse than the cheating.

Then, after her first insecure few months with Andre, came Andrew. Despite the strange way their relationship had ended, Tina felt nothing but warmth for Andrew Grey. The first time they'd made love had reminded her of some of the same teenage awkwardness she'd experienced with Corey. It was their fifth date and at first, he seemed content with a parting kiss. It was she who'd initiated the next step by inviting him in.

When she moved from the couch toward the bedroom, he hesitated. She thought for a moment that maybe she'd overplayed, maybe he wasn't ready, but with a nod of understanding, he'd followed. She still had to take the lead, to such an extent that she began to wonder if perhaps he was a virgin, or even gay, but a check with her left hand put such fears to rest. She'd chuckled slightly and he'd flushed and stopped short. "Protection?" he'd asked.

"I have some. In the drawer." After a bit of hesitation, he stepped over to the night stand and pulled out the small box of condoms. After pulling one out, he looked at it with trepidation and moved to remove his clothes.

"Here. Let me," she said and took the prophylactic from his hand

and placed it onto his erect penis. Andrew was shivering and again, she wondered if she'd moved too fast, but after a few moments of foreplay, he seemed to relax.

Over the next several minutes, they explored one another, he hesitantly, but with growing arousal. As consummation began, at first, her own libido took over. It had been more than three months since she'd last been with Andre. She reacted almost frantically, kissing him on the chest and face alternately. Her approaching climax stalled though as he seemed to pull back, withdrawing, not physically, but somehow, moving away. He seemed to be staring at a spot on her forehead or just above. She pulled him closer, first with her legs, then with both her legs and a flurry of kisses, redirecting his gaze toward her. He shivered again, his face an expression of mild panic. Then, his eyes moving upward once again, he increased the pace. Tina moved with him, but as he concluded, she felt disappointment rise within her, not having reached her own orgasm. That was common enough for new couples, she thought, as she reached up for another kiss. As his eyes met hers, he shuddered once again, this time for several seconds and with a final, unexpected thrust of his narrow hips, he took her by surprise and she found it to be her turn to tremble, her orgasm mild, but pleasantly rewarding. Tina looked down Andrew's body, contrasting his thin, pale legs with her the dark tone of hers surrounding his waist. She used her ankles to pull him into her once more before sliding to the side. Andrew still had his eyes closed.

They were together again another handful of occasions before that fateful day at the movies led her to return to her happy life with Andre, and each time, his pattern seemed similar. He was attentive, but in the midst of the action, he seemed to retreat and withdraw into himself. Her efforts to improve their intimacy were met with fear and withdrawal, his eyes widening as long as they were in contact with hers. But he was a devoted boyfriend, right up to the day she broke it off, just what she needed to restore her faith in men.

"What are you reading?" she asked Andre, pulling out of her reverie and back to the present.

"A book."

"Let me see," she snatched the book from his hand. "This book is little. I know you can read something more sophisticated than 'See Spot Run'. She turned over the cover and read, *Crawling: a Father's First Year* by Elisha Cooper. She was touched. "Is it good?"

"So far it is. I just started."

"You know, I had no idea how into this you were going to be."

He shrugged. "It's what I've always wanted, to have a family, to be a dad."

"You never talked about it, you know, before."

"We didn't get that far. You broke it off before I could."

"I'm sor . . ."

"Don't," Andre interrupted. "We've been through it. That's in the past and we're looking at the future." A pat to her growing belly showed what he meant by future. "Everything is about little Andra there."

"Andra? What kind of name is that?"

"Boy or girl, a combination of your name and mine." He looked at the clock and reached for his pants on the floor. "You know we have a decision to make. In the next half hour to be precise."

"I know. I just can't decide. I keep going back and forth. I want to know, but I don't. What do you think?"

"I've been thinking about it. I know my mother wants to paint the room blue or pink and buy all the right clothes, but, well, how many real surprises are there in life these days?"

Tina smiled, "Not many."

"So, we don't find out? Let the mystery be?"

"Let it be," she sighed. But what about names? I don't know about Andra."

"That's just a placeholder. We don't know if it's going to be a girl or a boy."

"We could pick one of each so we'll be prepared."

"Why don't we see what she—or he—looks like, then decide?"

"You hoping for a girl?"

"I am hoping for a beautiful, healthy baby, a happy, tired mother, and a lifetime with both of them."

Another contented sigh. "Good answer. Let's go."

MICHAEL CARLEY

**

Lucinda forgot to eat her yogurt again.

She'd been doing that more and more lately, but in her defense, she was nowhere near the yogurt. She was in London, or rather under London, in Un Lun Dun.

Newhall Park probably isn't the best in the city, but it works well for a quiet place for lunch. Lucy just sets up her blanket a little ways from the playground and hardly anyone ever bothers her. The parents are usually pretty good at keeping their kids on the swings and the book in her hand lets them know she doesn't want to be bothered. In her mind at least, it is an effective shield.

It was a bit cold, but she didn't really notice until it was time to leave. Now, she found herself shivering. She was really not really supposed to have food in the truck, but she'd have to make an exception again today and eat bites of the yogurt as she made her stops. Maybe it wasn't ideal, but worth it.

It wasn't her fault really. She blamed Miéville. He's the one who created Un Lun Dun. Every time she delved into one of amazing worlds he created, this one right under the city of London, she felt the need to travel and whenever she finished one of his books, she felt like she had been on a long adventurous trip. Sated and without ever having left the safety of San Jose.

And what a world this one was! Giraffes walking the streets, and not just ordinary giraffes. These were carnivores. Some of it was pretty scary, but kids read this book, so there was nothing really bad. She'd read most of what Miéville had written, yet she still felt as though she never knew what's going to happen next. The more she read, the fewer surprises there were to be found, so when an author pulls off a really good one, it's a special feeling.

A while back, she bought a timer to track her lunches. Sometimes, she was so lost in the story that she'd completely lose track. It wasn't just the time that disappeared, it seemed the whole world was swallowed with it. The kids, the park, everything. Once, a teenager threw a Frisbee and it landed on her leg. She didn't realize it was there until he walked all the way over and picked it up, startling her in the process. The kid looked at her with a strange face and asked if she was deaf. Apparently, he'd been calling to her for a couple of minutes.

It was Terry Pratchett who really caused the problem. She'd always been a fast reader and would sometimes get through two Discworld books in a day. Old standby characters like Sam Vines were a comfort. But, once he introduced Tiffany Aching, she was entranced. So much so that she took a nearly two-hour lunch one day and had to rush through the rest of her route to avoid getting in trouble.

The timer helped though and she had it down to a science. Since Newhall was the closest park to her route, she didn't have very far to go. She just parked on the street, walked over to the grass and laid her blanket out. Each day, she set her timer to fifty-one minutes and made the fullest use of her lunch period. Sometimes, she could get through a hundred, maybe a hundred-fifty pages in that time.

But Miéville got her today. She'd been waiting to read this one for a while because she'd already read everything else of his and didn't know what to make of it since it was really written for children. Now, she was sorry she had waited. The book had captured her from the first page and before she knew it, thirty-six chapters were gone and her timer was going off with the yogurt not even opened.

She'd heard some people say they felt naked if they didn't have a book with them. It's not a bad metaphor, but it really doesn't cover it. It had happened to Lucy a few times when she used to bring only one book with her. If she finished it too early, she'd have nothing left to read. This uncomfortable feeling would come over her as though she were more than naked, but exposed in a visceral way. The last time it happened, she felt as though other park patrons were starting at her. She looked down as though her breasts were exposed, but nothing was amiss. She crossed her arms and left the park early, wanting to stop at the bookstore before resuming her route, but knowing there wasn't time. The nervous feeling stayed with her through the whole afternoon until arrived could get to Hicklebee's. They mostly carried children's books, and it was where she'd picked up Un Lun Dun, though she hadn't started reading it until today. But somehow, having it on her lap for the drive home had been calming.

Now, she couldn't wait to get home and finish it. She had to find out what's happened to Zanna and Deeba and she had to know today. Plus, she knew exactly where it was going in the bookcases. Miéville had his own section.

For now though, the conclusion was clear. The timer wasn't enough. All it accomplished was to get her to keep her from taking too long a lunch. It couldn't get her to actually eat that lunch.

Darn yogurt.

**

Driving back to the office, Pete was again worried. He'd finally managed to get a lunch meeting with his old college acquaintance Danny, and the tale he had been told was disturbing indeed. According to Danny, two district assistant superintendents had been siphoning off bond money and lining their own pockets. They even had a little dummy corporation set up to receive the funds. Danny's story was filled with lurid details of parties these guys were holding with district funds. The dummy corporation even had a web site, which Danny described as a sham. It was a bare bones site that described little about what the corporation did.

He knew this news wouldn't be welcomed by G-dub. Danny had insisted that he not be quoted; everything he said had to be anonymous. Pete had to find some way to document all of this for their report. Something this serious would likely end with a criminal investigation.

He had to talk to someone. Andrew could have pointed him to how to document the abuses. He could imagine the conversation he'd have had with Grey. Andrew wouldn't have expressed any shock or dismay at the allegations; his entire demeanor was always so matter-of-fact. He'd have put together a checklist of things to look into, ways to verify Danny's allegations without involving him. He'd have described step-by-step how to document every violation in explicit detail and he wouldn't have even asked for credit.

But Andrew hadn't been in all week. Lillian was covering for him with G-dub, a practice Ellie suspected was going to blow up when Andrew returned. Ellie would be next on his list, but though their relationship had thawed somewhat, she was busy in her own work and could be so mercenary, Pete didn't want to bother. He thought of going to Lillian, who could sometimes provide advice on her boss's thoughts, but if she got fired for protecting Grey, Pete didn't want to be caught in the fallout. That left G-dub himself. Pete had called Lillian right after his meeting and got an appointment with the boss.

He took a deep breath as he walked into the building, going directly to G-dub's office, and knocked on the open glass door. "Pete, come in. So, you finally got your lunch with the old college buddy. Took long enough."

"Yeah, sorry, he put me off until today." Pete hesitated, surprised at himself. He wasn't usually nervous around the boss.

"Well, spit it out Pete. What'd you find out? Must have been juicy if you asked for a special meeting with me. I don't think you've done that since the Christmas party when you were worried Elsie was going to file sexual harassment charges." Pete saw Ellie look up from her cubicle. Her eyes were shooting him daggers. He was no longer forgiven.

But he had to focus on the task at hand, so he spilled it all. The corruption, the embezzling, the wild parties, the web site. He told the boss everything Danny had revealed. Throughout, the boss looked skeptical and by the end, even seemed to be smirking a bit. Pete was wondering what he missed.

But now G-dub's face turned stern. "Well, these are serious allegations indeed. What was the web site your friend mentioned again?"

"Keep-pucks dot com. Apparently, they're Sharks fans and they're worried about rumors the team will be moving.

"OK, let's see." G-dub pulled up the web site on his laptop. "Yes, just as I expected. This is indeed serious."

"What is it?" Pete thought he must have missed something. The web site itself had seemed rather innocuous when Danny had described it, just a front for the dummy corp's business operations.

"Pete, let me ask you a question. Did you do any investigation at all before you came in here?"

"Well, I . . ."

"Yes, that's what I thought. And this 'friend' of yours from college. Is this the one you wouldn't let into the fraternity?"

"Yeah, he pledged the year after I did. But he was kind of a dork, so he didn't get in. What does that have to do with . . ."

"Well, I'm guessing the Sigma Alphas have taken a few steps backward since my time. It looks like they chose the wrong guy. Maybe I did too. Maybe I should have hired this Danny McDowell instead of young Massey out of college. He's not so great with the word scrambles though."

"What are you talking about?" Pete began just as his boss was turning the laptop around.

Keep-Pucks dot com was indeed a scramble, and yes, a bad one. But it had been enough to fool Pete Massey and have him worried for an hour and a half. The banner across the top of the web page read

Keep Pucks=Pete Sucks
Revenge is Sweet

(By the way, if you think I'd rat on my bosses even if they were doing something wrong, you really didn't know me. I like my job)

Pete turned red, then ashen, then red again with anger. Danny McDowell had made him a fool in front of his boss and knowing G-dub, he'd never live this down. Even now, his laughter was carrying across the floor. "Look guys. Check your email in a minute. I'm going to send you a message direct from Pete's friend Danny."

"He's not my friend," Pete interjected lamely.

"I'd guess not." G-dub clicked send on the email and turned the laptop back around so that it was facing Pete again. "Massey, I really thought you were smarter than this. I expect your revenge on your 'friend' Danny will be both more embarrassing and more creative than this little web site. And I expect you won't wait half a decade to exact it."

"Will do," Pete was short on creativity, but he knew Sykes could help him with that. Duane Sykes was forever playing practical jokes and would have a host of ideas. But G-dub wasn't finished with him yet. He was still half laughing, but Pete knew that on issues like this,

KNOW MY NAME

he meant business.

"You expect to sit in this chair one day, don't you?"

"I don't want to be presumptuous."

"Bullshit. You said as much in your interview. It's why I hired you. I respect ambition. But ambition has to come with some smarts and common sense."

Pete was abashed again and said nothing.

"Speaking of bullshit," G-dub now reached onto the shelf behind his desk. "You need a better BS detector. Yours seems to be defective." With that, he tossed a small book over to Pete. It was a tiny book, almost a pamphlet. *On Bullshit* the cover read, by Harry G. Frankfurt. The laughs began again. "Now get out of my office. You're wasting my time."

The laughter had spread to the rest of the office, which by now had received the email. Sykes and Ballard were both laughing out loud. But Duane gave him a reassuring look as he passed his desk, so he knew he'd have the help he needed. Ellie was smirking, but she wouldn't look at him, her eyes were glued to her screen.

When Pete arrived at his desk, she rolled over quietly. "Told the boss about the party, huh. You just added two weeks to your sentence. And today's doesn't count; it wasn't hot enough."

Pete nodded, assenting as Ellie rolled herself back to her own cubicle. He'd gotten off easy and he knew it.

**

Bullshit was exactly what Janice was dealing with, and it was getting on her nerves. Drunk Jerry, otherwise known as "patient grab-ass" had already been in three times during her short stint in the ER. This time at least, he had a semi-legitimate reason; he had fallen, outside the liquor store, of course, and had a nasty gash on his forehead. She knew the blood made the injury appear worse than it was, and it didn't seem to stop Jerry from feeling her up. As she tried to find a vein to put in an IV, his left hand wandered to her behind. She moved it twice, more patiently than she felt, the second time warning him "I'm going to have to put you in restraints if you keep it up."

"Ooh, tie me up baby."

Janice sighed. For the third time, she looked for a vein and again, fingers moved from the bed to her clothes, crawling toward her like the itsy bitsy spider. *He thinks it's a game*, she thought. This time, he didn't just grab her ass; he managed to slip his hand under her scrubs. That was it. Janice pulled his hand out, and shooting a glance toward the door, quickly bent the middle two fingers back nearly to his wrist. That got his attention, but his scream was loud enough to alert nearby patients as well. He'd have her colleagues running their way if she didn't quiet him down.

"You can't keep your hands to yourself, I'll make sure you do," she told him. Before releasing his hand, she grabbed a roll of tape and lashed his wrist to the gurney. Within a minute she had his IV inserted. By the time she was finished cleaning and bandaging his head wound, which, as she suspected, was superficial, Jamie was crying and apologizing. "Tell it to someone else," she warned, "I've had enough."

Just then, the charge nurse looked in, and as she always seemed to, took in the scene in about half a second. "Why don't you take your break Janice? I'll finish up with patient grab-ass."

Janice nodded and stepped out of the room, walking down the hall, and to the balcony where she could grab a smoke. *Shit,* she thought to herself, *what have I done now*?

She probably should have found a better way to handle Jerry. From what she'd heard, she'd have to deal with him a couple of times a week as long as she was in the ER. That is, if she still had a job. She hadn't run into any trouble with the charge nurse yet, but the woman had a no-nonsense reputation.

Janice knew she had a problem with authority figures, especially when it came to her sexuality. She'd had a feminist college professor whom she mostly found annoying, but on this issue, she agreed. Women had the right to control who touched them and when.

She'd gotten her first lesson in this from her father. She was studying in her room with a classmate when discussion of honors chemistry led to flirting, which led to kissing. Unfortunately, Zeke walked in just as the boy's hand began moving from her waist to her breast outside her shirt. The brief jolt of forbidden pleasure led to a scream as her father's voice caused her suitor to jump. The teens bumped heads before the boy ran from the room terrified of the short man with the beet red face.

Janice was pulled from the honors class and forbidden to date her entire junior year, which wouldn't start for several months. At the start, her brother had been her advocate, or so she'd thought. He'd called Zeke a bigot, a sexist, and a prude. And, though he hardly dated at all, he insisted she had every right to. For a brief time, she was honored to be his sister, bonded by shared parental persecution and perceived systemic injustice.

But just two months later, Andrew had abandoned her, and left the state entirely. He wanted to get as far as he could from Zeke, and from Kansas. He'd been in such a rush, he'd somehow found a work study job before his freshman year and left Salina less than a week after high school graduation. Her feelings of sibling love turned to those of abandonment as she was left to deal with her last two years of high school alone. Through college and thereafter, Andrew visited a total of three times, all for holidays, and all ending in heated, and to her mind, unnecessary, arguments.

And though she'd thought Andrew had stood up for her out of shared loyalty and brotherly love, it was he who disabused her of that notion. In one of their increasingly strained phone conversations, he'd explained, no, this was about principle. He'd have told his father off regardless of whether the victim was his sister or a stranger. Well, she'd thought, it was nice to know where she stood. And, Andrew had taken every opportunity since then to reinforce that point. He picked fights with his father whenever he could. Janice wondered why she wanted him around. Because, *misery loves company*, she thought, hating herself for not thinking of a better cliché.

Taking a final drag of her cigarette, she turned to head back into the building. Time to take her punishment. But, the reprimand seemed to be finding her; as Debbie, the charge nurse stepped out onto the balcony.

"Have one?" she asked.

Janice shrugged and handed her boss a smoke.

"Health care workers and smoking. Another of life's great ironies." Debbie mused. She was expecting Janice to stay and wait for the hammer to fall.

Janice didn't believe in small talk. "So, does this health care worker still have a job?"

Debbie chuckled. "You're going to have to do a lot worse than pick a fight with a drunk who'll never remember it to get out of this department. You're going to pay your dues here whether you like it or not."

Janice sighed, something that seemed to be becoming something of a habit lately. She wasn't sure if she should relax or not. Clearly, Debbie wasn't finished.

"A piece of advice, just to cover your ass. If you have to restrain a patient, call for help. Not that you couldn't handle Jerry alone; you seemed to do just fine (*was that admiration in her voice?*), but you never know when someone will make false accusations. Always have two in the room if you have to restrain someone and use something better than tape."

"Will do," was all Janice could think to say.

Before she could head back in, Debbie crushed out her half-finished cigarette and turned to walk away. "I've got to quit these things" she said. Then, turning around, she added, "Oh, and by the way, bending the fingers back will work on drunks, but if you try that on a meth-head, he won't even notice. Those guys are scary. Be ready for anything."

Again, Janice nodded, glad she was a worker bee. Bosses, you could never figure them out.

**

Authority figures weren't a problem for Andrew. Of course, he'd fought with Zeke. The man's narrow-mindedness never ceased to amaze Andrew. He believed things simply because he believed them, and drew conclusions based on no evidence. He built his whole life around these beliefs, and worse, he judged his children on whether they adhered to these ridiculous standards. Andrew was standing up for what was right. Increasingly, he saw no reason to engage with Zeke and so travelling to Kansas held little appeal, despite his sister's pleas for solidarity.

But now, he was restless. With the help of a substantial dose of Vicodin, he was ambulatory, though his back muscles remained tight. But he was bored. Afternoon television was a disappointment. Talk shows that celebrated scandal, soap operas with implausible storylines, and twenty-four hour news channels with pundits talking past each other, each making their own bad arguments.

Seeing those arguments led him to his lone bookshelf. The volume he went back to most was a college text *The Power of Logic*. He had taken Dr. Burke's Philosophy class to meet a general education requirement, but for him, logic and reasoning held enormous power. He'd devoured the text of reasoning and argumentation. He had ammunition, not only against Zeke, but all the bad arguments he heard on a daily basis, whether from fellow students, on television, or especially from religious sources.

He had even briefly considered switching his major to philosophy. He met with Professor Burke, explaining his passion for logic and reasoning, and his desire to study it further. But as he had no desire to teach, he wondered what career options would be available. Unfortunately, the meeting had not gone as expected. Dr. Burke had more questions than answers and finally, he'd walked away disappointed.

"I usually don't recommend changing your major based on one class. What appeals to you about philosophy beyond what you've seen so far?"

"I love studying the logic and argumentation. It makes so much sense and explains so many of the problems in the world. If we only followed these rules, it would solve so much."

"Where do you find it most useful?"

"In class discussions for a start."

Professor Burke chuckled. "Yes, I've noticed that in my class. Do you use it in other classes?"

"Of course. Though it isn't always appreciated."

"How do you use it?"

"Mainly, I point out logical fallacies and bad reasoning. Unfortunately, that includes most of the arguments people make, so it doesn't make me very popular."

"I suspect you don't care much for popularity anyway."

"Exactly right."

"How about in your personal life. Do you use the devices we discussed?"

"Yes, mostly with my father."

"And how does that go?"

"He has no patience for it. He places mythology above sound logic. Every point he makes is based on biblical text and faulty reasoning."

"Your father is a religious man."

"Very much so."

"So how has this affected your relationship with him? With the rest of your family?"

Andrew hadn't really thought about it. "We haven't gotten along for a while. Now, I understand why."

"You see his bad reasoning as the source of your relationship problems?"

"Yes. He doesn't care for it when I point out the flaws in his reasoning. Everything he says is based on 'the Bible says' or 'God tells us'; it's all fallacy."

"Most people don't appreciate having their every flaw pointed out. Have you found a common ground?"

"I don't think there is any. I prefer logic; he always goes back to his religious mythology."

"And that religion has no appeal to you?"

"Of course not. There's nothing to it. Too many contradictions. Yet my father denies those contradictions even exist. Or he says it's not for us to understand."

"Sometimes those contradictions are what make it worth study."

"You aren't suggesting I take it seriously?"

"I am."

"I don't understand. I thought that logic and reasoning was what drives philosophy."

"That's a part of it, but again, you've only taken one class. There's much more to what we study than logic and reasoning. Have your considered taking my comparative religion class?"

"I saw it in the catalog. But what's the point? It's all mythology. I

KNOW MY NAME

could get as much reading from a book of fairy tales."

"Don't underestimate the power of fairy tales."

"I don't understand."

"Fairy tales, mythology, and religion provide a framework on which people base their lives."

"But they're not true. Logic . . . ."

"There is more truth in them than you may realize. Faith has its place."

"Faith is blind. It's not based on evidence. My father even used to quote it. It was his favorite verse. Hebrews 11: 1, 'Now faith is the substance of things hoped for, the evidence of things not seen.' It is, as your class made clear, tautological. It makes no sense whatsoever."

"But to the faithful, it carries much value, provides them structure and comfort in their lives. It's a foundation . . ."

"A foundation built on sand. They'd be better off if they knew it was all fiction. Then, they could base their decisions on facts."

"Do we always have all of the facts?"

"Of course not."

"Are we always right about the 'facts' we do have?"

"No."

"Then facts won't necessarily provide the comfort you think. And there's a larger problem. Facts are certainly important, as are the logic and good argumentation we've been discussing all semester. But no society anywhere on Earth has ever based their culture primarily on these things."

"Why couldn't we?"

"It's not how we're wired. Humans need so much more than that. We're not inherently, or even primarily, rational creatures. The human brain is more complex than that, as you'll understand if you take a course or two in anthropology or psychology. Those aren't my areas of expertise of course, but culture plays a big role in my comparative religion course."

But Andrew had little interest in comparative religion and he quickly cut off the conversation and went back to his dorm, frustrated, yet determined. Soon after, he found accounting, a field which carried fewer contradictions. It provided him not only an income, but rules on which to base a career and a life. The rules of accounting confused others, but they had a clear internal logic, and as he later told Tina, if followed, prevented problems. In any of the recent corporate scandals, had accounting standards been adhered to, there would have been no scandal, no problem, no issue. Accounting was logical and legal. Plain and simple.

The problem today, in picking up *The Power of Logic*, was that he had the book virtually memorized. He could, when any argument arose, quote his opponent's logical fallacy. He'd stopped doing that with most people, save for Zeke, of course, long ago, finding that it generally wasn't appreciated. Though in reality, those arguments still ran through his mind each time he found himself in those discussions, and though he rarely chose to point out his acquaintances' bad arguments, the mental train of thought would often derail his ability to maintain a conversation. Losing himself in the unvoiced arguments, he'd lose track of the actual discussion and his silence would soon betray him.

But logic was a habit Andrew could not turn off, and happily so.

Still, he was bored and restless, and needed reading material. Other than the logic book, he had several accounting texts leftover from college, but they too, or at least their important principles, were long committed to memory. There were no novels on the shelf. He did find an old copy of Steinbeck's *The Pearl* in a drawer, but though he recalled finding it mildly instructive, he saw little reason to reread it.

Andrew hadn't read a novel since college; he found fiction superficial. In a theoretical sense, he could see the value of literature. But as a practical matter, he had little use for it. As he looked around his living room, he saw a few textbooks, three dictionaries, an atlas, and a public transit map for the Bay Area. But there were no other novels.

He'd done little moving about the apartment and had only this afternoon changed clothes since the hospital, so there was no laundry to be done. He'd cleaned over the previous weekend and he didn't believe in dusting surfaces that hadn't yet had a chance to collect dust. He'd taken his temperature three times and, it hadn't gone higher than 99.3. He needed a new cell phone, but he knew better than to try making his way to the store.

Finally, he spotted the sample ballot and voter pamphlet on the counter. He'd already gone over the candidates last weekend and made a few notes, but there was no reason he couldn't do a bit more research. He picked up the pamphlet and fired up his computer.

Andrew was neither a Republican nor a Democrat. He distrusted the parties and most politicians and he was especially distrustful of ideology. His perspective was that when most people aligned themselves with a party or ideology, they generally turned off their brains and stopped listening to contrary evidence.

For Andrew, policy choices were all about what was practical. When he heard a political argument, he tried to evaluate the facts and determine whether the policy being advocated would improve on what was, or make things worse. There were certain things he supported generally, good infrastructure, education, and sound fiscal policies. He was glad that this was a local municipal election. There were no parties involved; the candidates on the ballot weren't even identified with a party, though a few (and Andrew was suspicious of those) tried to make their party obvious when they thought it would help them.

For those attached to a political party, the lack of party identifiers probably made things more difficult. But Andrew thought this was preferable, and he enjoyed taking the time to research and evaluate the candidates.

The first thing he looked at was the person's occupation. A member of any profession could make a good candidate as far as Andrew was concerned. But too many members of a particular occupation in a group might pose a problem. Andrew despised groupthink and his vote was cast in ways he thought would limit it.

Two candidates for city council identified themselves only as "businessman." Andrew found this somewhat suspicious, so he sat down at his computer to begin his research. He'd just taken two pills, so his pain was at a minimum. Still, he groaned as he sat in the desk chair. There was no comfortable way to sit for any period of time without his ribs or hip throbbing. As before, he simply alternated positions and gutted through it.

The name of the first businessman sounded familiar; Andrew was sure he'd read about him in the Mercury News. He looked him up and found the same articles. The erstwhile candidate had petitioned for an expansion of his business and been denied by the planning commission. He'd taken his fight all the way to the city council and been denied again. Andrew recalled that he thought the guy never had much of a case and it looked like he was running for council to line his own pockets. He crossed him off the list.

The second businessman owned a couple of sandwich shop franchises. As far as Andrew could tell, he'd never had business before the council. He'd served on a couple of city committees, for arts and for parks and recreation. He was involved with the local boys and girls club. The guy appeared to have a history of civic service, which Andrew respected.

Some of the other candidates were obvious no votes, so Andrew ended up putting the "maybe" into the "yes" category. He turned next to the school board race. There was a retired teacher running, of her, Andrew was unsure. He was often ambivalent about teachers running for public office. If they're good teachers, they're probably better off staying in the classroom. If they're bad teachers, why should they get to make policy? Teaching should also give someone experience that might be valuable on the school board, but she might have too many friends in the classroom to be objective. Andrew put her in the "maybe" pile.

The next candidate was an accountant. She wasn't someone Andrew knew, just a CPA with her own shop who did mostly tax work for individuals and small businesses. Generally, he liked the idea of an accountant on the school board; she might keep them focused and make sure the budget was well spent. And, she could help the fellow board members' understand the state's byzantine accounting and budget rules. Andrew checked whether there were any accountants already on the board. There weren't, so she went on the strong "maybe" list.

It had only been twenty minutes, but he was already feeling low arrows of pain shooting through his left side. Shifting from side to side was no longer effective and he had to get up. The spasm that clenched his lower back caught him completely by surprise as it was on his right side, rather than the left which had been giving him the most problems. He grabbed the desk and tried to sit back down. The desk chair began rolling away and he gripped it with his buttocks while holding closely to the desk with both hands. The spasm began to subside, but his desperate attempt to keep from falling put a strain on his entire torso and the rib pain made his breath shallow.

Once stabilized, he slowly, ever so slowly, began to ease himself to the floor, first to his knees, grateful to be free of the chair, which he now viewed as a danger. He made a mental vow not to sit in it for at least a week. His injuries would need to substantially heal before a rolling chair would be a smart choice again. From his knees, he began to regain his breath. He pushed the chair away. He moved first his right leg, then his left from underneath him to in front, then began the slow process of sliding down to a supine position. His back spasmed again, not quite as badly this time, and he held his breath and waited for it to pass. Resting his head on the carpet, he slid his feet under the desk until they hit something. He lifted his head to see, it was just the power strip. He lifted his feet gingerly and rested them on top of the surge protector and tried to relax. As it had before, this took several minutes of patient practice, but eventually, he was lying on the floor, legs under his desk and staring at the apartment ceiling.

Now what?

**

While Andrew examined the ceiling, Lillian stared at her monitor, worried. She'd completed four daily reports on behalf of young Mr. Grey, who had better appreciate her covering for him. He'd never quite thanked her for introducing him to Tina, and though the relationship hadn't worked out as she'd hoped, she still considered it a success, at least on her part.

But it wasn't just daily reports now; it was the weekly summary, a longer report which G-dub took home for the weekend. Each team member had to complete one of these, outlining a list of their findings on the project for the week and tasks to be addressed the next week. The boss told them that since half of them came in hungover every Monday, having a plan would help things go more smoothly.

It wasn't so much that the weekly had to be well written. Lillian had written the four dailies of which it was largely comprised, mimicking Andrew's style to the best of her ability. She was rather impressed with herself if she did say so, though only silently. Plus, Lillian knew what the accountants didn't—that G-dub didn't really read the weekly reports at all. He wanted them to think he took work home for the weekend, but it was mostly an exercise for them, not for him. Only Ballard had ever figured it out. He'd noticed the boss would get details wrong, so he put a few X-rated tidbits into one of his weeklies last year and G-dub had never noticed. Lillian had caught it though and had sworn Gil to secrecy, figuring this was one of the boss's tricks that might actually have some value. So far, Ballard hadn't told the others.

No, Lillian's worry wasn't about the weekly she was writing; she could fool G-dub in her sleep. She was worried about Andrew. She never thought he'd be gone a week without a peep. She'd gone so far as to drive by his apartment the night before. His Civic was still in the carport and concerned as she was, she couldn't bring herself to get out and knock on the door. But he still hadn't returned her call.

She was just about finished with the weekly report when her desk phone rang. It was Nikki from HR.

"Hi Nikki!"

"Hi Lillian, how are things?"

"Fine here. What can I do for you?" It was better to get to the point with Nikki. That girl was way too chatty, especially for someone working in HR. They were supposed to have discretion.

"Lily honey, you have an accountant over there by the name of Andrew Grey, right?"

"Of course we do." *For crying out loud, this company isn't that big.*

"Well, did Jodie call you about him the other day?"

"No, what was she supposed to call about?"

"Oh dear. I thought I left her a note. You see, I took the last couple of days off. My daughter is on the dance team at her school and they've been invited to regionals. You should have seen my Arial . . . ."

"Nikki, what about Andrew?"

"Oh yeah. We got a call about him the other day. Wednesday, or was it Tuesday? I don't recall."

"Nikki, get to the point."

Nikki didn't notice the indignation in her voice. "Anyway, a nurse called from Regional Medical Center. Apparently, your Andrew was in an accident on Monday."

Lillian felt her throat tighten. She lowered her voice; if this was bad news, it was better if she got the details first, then relay them to the others. "How is he?" she was almost whispering.

"Oh, he's fine it seems. They sent him home. They said he'd need at least two weeks off though for his recovery, possibly longer."

"Longer?"

"I'm sure he's fine. They sent him home. Sorry about the message. I thought I left a note for Jodie. Oh, here it is right here. I guess Jodie never would have found it in my purse, would she?"

Lillian gritted her teeth. "Nikki, are you sure there's nothing more?"

"Nope, that's all I have written down."

This girl would lose her address if she didn't have it written down. "OK then," Lillian replied in her best 'pat a child on the head' voice. You have a good weekend Nic. Wish that Arial of yours luck for me."

"Thanks Lil. She'll really appreciate it. My daughter is the best on the team, I'm sure of it . . ."

Lillian had already hung up. Now, she was really in a quandary. She'd been covering for Andrew all week and she was sure she could convince him to go along once she heard his explanation for where he'd been. She had hoped it would be juicy, even if Tina wasn't an option. The possibility Andrew had finally found someone had been in her thoughts since Monday.

But the real excuse was mundane. He'd been well enough to send home, so she didn't need to worry about him anymore. But the bigger problem was what to tell G-dub. With all the daily reports she'd been turning in, she could hardly tell him that Andrew had been out all week.

And he wasn't coming back next week either. Next week! That was the solution. Nikki had said Andrew would be gone for at least two weeks, maybe longer. She had her solution.

Lillian sent his weekly to print. Andrew would have his accident on Monday just like Nikki had said.

Next Monday.

**

As he pushed through the doors of O'Connor Hospital, Kevin Jamison Senior. walked slowly down the corridor toward his son's room. He'd made this same trek every day for the past two weeks, and the staff had begun to recognize him. Kevin was so regular with his visits; they could set their clocks by him. Each day after work, he picked up Harry, his second son, and together they went to visit Kevin Junior.

Now, Harry was beside him as usual, somehow matching his father's slow pace. Harry was a sensitive kid, as though he was aware that his father's knees, now seemingly devoid of ligaments after a lifetime of construction work, prevented him from walking as fast as he'd like. Normally, Harry would have run down the hallway to check on his brother, but he stayed without complaint as though this was the pace he'd have chosen for himself. Kevin Senior knew his son was doing it to prevent him embarrassment and though he didn't embarrass so easily, he happily noticed his son's caretaking nature. He'd done well as a parent.

As well as he'd done with his boys, there were a few regrets, primary among them being getting Kevin Junior that motorcycle. His eldest had always been a responsible kid; the bike was the closest he'd come to rebellion. But though the accident wasn't his fault, he'd likely never have been hit if he'd been driving a car.

Kevin steeled himself for the worst before entering the room. Every night, he worried he'd find the bed empty. He knew that was unlikely; the hospital had his cell number and would call if there had been a significant change in Kevin Junior's status. Still, that image came into his mind each time he entered the third floor ICU and didn't leave him until he saw his son's face and felt his breath.

Only as they approached the room did Harry begin to outpace his father. But then, he stopped suddenly and looked back, a quizzical

KNOW MY NAME

expression on his twelve-year-old face. Kevin picked up the pace as much as his weary knees would allow and looked in.

His son was still in bed, in exactly the same position as he'd been each of the previous nights. But sitting next to the bed was a young woman. She was wearing jeans and a simple green cotton shirt, her hair in a ponytail that was draped over the bed. Her left hand was holding Kevin Junior's right, their fingers intertwined. A book lay closed in her other hand, about two thirds completed, at least if her finger was acting as a bookmark as he suspected. She was fast asleep, her head laying across Kevin Junor's chest.

Harry was bewildered, but respectful. "Who's she?" he mouthed silently to his father.

"No idea," he replied, but he was about to find out. If Kevin Junior had a girlfriend, he hadn't mentioned her. And this girl certainly seemed devoted. He tapped her gently on the elbow. "Excuse me?"

Ashlynn looked up, first groggy, then startled. The book fell to the floor and she bent over to pick it up, grasping several times before she managed to get the book without disengaging her hand from Kevin Junior's. Before looking up at the baffled father and son, she found her place in *Everything Matters*.

"I'm Kevin Jamison" the older man said, then seeing his need to clarify, he added "Senior."

Ashlynn still hadn't spoken, still was trying to find her voice. "I . . . I'm sorry."

"How do you know my son? Are you friends at school?"

"Sorry, I'm so sorry," was all Ashlynn could manage. Then, she ran from the room, dropping the book at Harry's feet along the way. She was halfway down the hall before her the youngster could pick it up and read the title.

**

Pulling up to her own apartment complex, Lucinda's heart was racing. She pulled her car into the carport and raced up the steps. The doorknob was locked along with the deadbolt, so she knew they'd been there. The keys fell from her hand to the floor next to the shelf as she stepped through the door and looked to her left. There they were! Along the entire long south wall, at a cost of over

$1,800, were thirty feet of bookshelves, just waiting for her to fill them.

Lucy ran her hands down the third, then the second of the six shelves. There would be dust eventually, but none yet. They were pristine and in a cherry red so deep it was almost crimson. She wondered for a moment if the stain she'd chosen was so red as to be unrealistic, perhaps not even recognizable as cherry, but ultimately she didn't care; she loved it. The shelving was broken up into five six-foot sections. She'd given a lot of thought to what would go on each shelf. She was happy that she'd chosen the adjustable shelves. She could move things around, shortening the space needed for paperbacks and she'd need at least one shelf for oversized books.

It would take all weekend to get the shelves stocked, but it was a task she was looking forward to. Most of the books were in boxes in the complex storage facility downstairs. She'd brought three up the previous night and was both winded and exhilarated by the time she finished. The oversized books were the ones she wanted to start with tonight, so she adjusted the shelf at the top so that the space was long enough to accommodate *Tolkien's World: Paintings of Middle Earth*. She quickly found that the allotted space wasn't nearly enough. Several of the dragons and mythical creatures encyclopedias and art books were a good 14 inches tall. Lucy had never tried drawing, but the art books held appeal anyway. She enjoyed seeing what the artists were able to accomplish and contrasting how their visions differed from the images in her mind.

Shortly, she had two nearly full oversized shelves and extra slats. She was beginning to wonder if she might have more shelves than she needed, but there were a lot of paperbacks downstairs. Those boxes were the heaviest, so she was saving most of them for the morning when she was fresh. For tonight, she just had the box of those with authors A through D. She'd have to leave space on each of the shelves for some to be added later. That would be another of the fun parts.

But first, was the book of honor. The first book to go on the shelves was something she'd planned carefully, though once she thought of it, it had been an easy choice. No, it wasn't Tolkien. And, it wasn't even one book; there were several. Carefully, she pulled out of the tissue paper wrapping her precious three three-volume sets of the *Wheels of Time*. No other book, or at least no other single copy of one, held as much value.

This was the last gift she'd received, would ever receive, from her father. He'd driven more than 300 miles to a book signing in Santa Barbara to get it for her birthday. He didn't even know who Robert Jordan was, but he knew his daughter talked about his work incessantly and eagerly awaited each new volume. Three boxes, each with three books and her father had pestered Jordan until he signed all nine copies. Arturo Fuentes had been a reserved man and incessantly polite, so the image of him waiting for a famous author to sign each and every copy with other readers waiting in line was forever implanted in her mind.

These copies were paperback and other than to read the inscriptions, which by the eighth and ninth books were nearly illegible, she'd hardly opened them. She had other copies when she wanted to read the books, and she couldn't bear touching these. Both Jordan and her father had passed away just months later, so this was one of the last and her most precious memory of each of them. Even when the hardcover fourteen-volume box set came out three years later and her mother hinted that she might be willing to buy it for her, Lucy had declined.

The Jordan volumes went on the top shelf, far right, in their own section. Everything else would be alphabetized. A calm settled over Lucinda as she pulled out the books that would go in the A section. *Watership Down* went on the first shelf, but before long, she was already correcting herself. Silly girl Lucy, she thought. Ábalos comes before Adams. She moved the Adams volume to the right and placed the copy of *Grimpow* in the first spot, reaching for the next handful of books.

What a great night this was going to be; what a great weekend!

**

Ashlynn was shaking and out of breath by the time she reached the elevator. She couldn't believe she had fallen asleep and missed the time to leave. She'd been reading almost the entire day, mesmerized by the book and, in a strange way, feeling that Kevin Junior was as well. She'd been holding his hand and reading and a couple of times, it had seemed—though it might well have been her imagination—that he'd squeezed her hand a little. But each time, when she looked up, there was no movement in his face.

Just as the elevator bell rang, she heard the voice behind her. "Hey! Wait up!"

Ashlynn didn't want to turn around, but she couldn't add discourtesy to her list of offenses against this family. She looked at the young boy approaching; he couldn't be more than ten or twelve. "I'm sorry. I have to go. I'm late."

"Wait a minute," he said, holding his hand out. "I'm Harold Jamison."

"Ashlynn," she replied timidly, not sure she should give her full name. Then she remembered. I'm the one who committed a crime against his family, not the other way around. "Ashlynn Parker."

"How do you know my brother?"

"I really do have to go. I'm sorry I can't help you."

"Not until you tell me what's going on. The nurse said you've been here every day. She thought you were my sister. KJ's sister."

It was time to escape. The elevator doors started closing and Ashlynn stepped in. "I'm sorry," she repeated, wondering how many times she had said it and whether it sounded as pathetic to him as it did to her.

As she was about to exhale, a foot wedged between the elevator doors. "Hello again," young Harold said. How could he be intrusive and polite at the same time? "If you won't come back with us, I'm going down with you."

Ashlynn nodded. She had no idea what to say. It was only two floors down to the lobby, yet it seemed to take several minutes and she just stood there fidgeting. Harold stared at her, his face full of patient expectation. She had no answers for him.

As the bell rang and the doors opened again, he stepped in front of her, his eyes insistent, but not threatening. "My brother is going to die, you know."

She knew, but didn't want to know. She willed herself not to nod again, but she was shaking so much, he probably perceived one. Finally, she steeled herself, "I'm sorry. I just don't know what I can do for you."

"Why are you here? Why did you run? What are you so afraid of?"

Just the act of speaking had given her some resolve. She swallowed. "I didn't want to intrude on your family time." This sounded plausible, didn't it? "I'm not . . . family."

The boy just stood there, waiting patiently for further explanation. "I talked to the nurse. You've been here every day for at least three days. You've been here all day. You fell asleep reading to my brother. You may not be family, but he obviously meant—means something to you and probably you to him. Come back with me."

If only you knew, she thought. *He never knew who I was, will never know. He knew me for about three seconds, probably never caught a glimpse of anything but my door. That damn car.* A tear streamed down each of her cheeks and again, she was unable to speak.

They were standing only a few feet from the elevator and he had to move closer to her as the door opened and more visitors stepped out. "Come on," Harold spoke quietly, taking her limp hand in his. It was neither a command nor a request. It was closer to encouragement.

As the elevator emptied, he stepped inside, still holding her hand. He said nothing, just watched her patiently. Ashlynn was frozen to the spot, but as the elevator began closing, Harold put his foot in the door, holding it open for her to come to her own conclusion. She stepped through with him, lacing her fingers through his as they'd held his brother's for most of the day. The boy smiled reassuringly and patted her hand. *Wasn't he the one with the dying brother two flights up?*

Ashlynn breathed slowly and deliberately on their flight up and studied her young caretaker. The resemblance was obvious. Harold was thinner, but that could just be his youth. The same slightly oversized ears, maybe even the same tiny mole on his chin, just to the right of center. Harold's hair was slightly lighter; it might even be called blond. What had her mother called hers when she was a kid? "Dirty blond" or something. At the time, she'd thought it meant something naughty.

The bell rang again and her chest tightened. "Harold?"

"Harry. I go by Harry." With that, he squeezed her hand and led her out, returning to the familiar third floor ICU.

**

Kevin Senior had by now reached the elevator doors. He was reaching to push the button when his son came through, holding the hand of the distraught young woman. He looked at her, then looked at his son. As was becoming their custom, Harry took the lead.

"Dad, this is Ashlynn Parker. KJ's friend." Harry looked his father in the eye expectantly. Clearly, this girl needed some help and he was expected to provide it. He extended his right hand. She took it in her left, the right still clenching Harry's.

"Nice to meet you, Ashlynn."

"You too," she replied, meekly, but as one who seemed to be regaining her confidence. She looked at Harry, then stepped forward.

Again though, it was Harry who took the lead. "Let's go see how Kevin is doing. Then maybe we can get something to eat. I'm starved." He moved forward, Ashlynn in tow, then, remembering, slowed his pace so that his father could keep up.

As the trio reached room 341, they looked toward Kevin Junior, his status unchanged. As long as it had felt, fewer than ten minutes had passed.

There were only two chairs in the room. By now, Kevin Senior had collected his thoughts and remembered his manners. "Ashlynn, why don't you sit where you were; I'll grab one of the spare chairs at the nurse's station."

"Oh, I couldn't," she began, but Harry cut her off.

"I'll get it."

This left her with little choice and in case she was still wondering, Kevin Senior pointed toward the chair next to the bed and nodded. Ashlynn sat down, but paused first to pick up the book.

She clearly wanted to take the patient's hand again, but didn't want to be presumptuous. It was Kevin's turn to try putting her at ease. "Looks like a good book."

"It is. It's very good."

"What's it about?"

"Well, it's hard to describe. There are aliens, or maybe they're not aliens; it's not really clear. And they, well, it's hard to explain without it sounding ridiculous."

Kevin chuckled. "Sounds complicated. Having something to read is important though if you're going to spend a lot of time here."

Ashlynn just nodded, blushing slightly. Clearly, he too had spoken with the nurse, or been present when Harry did. They both knew of her lie.

Kevin continued. "Well, I just like to keep 'em simple. Give me a straight mystery or detective story. Nothing I have to spend too many brain cells on. I just finished my last Spenser novel. Damn Parker had to go and die on me. They're not the same without him."

Ashlynn smiled meekly. At this point, Harry returned with the extra chair and straddled the chair backwards, resting his chin on its back. Then, as if remembering his manners, he turned the chair around and sat properly. "How's KJ?"

"Nurse says no change," his father replied.

"No news is good news?"

Kevin shrugged. At this point, stability might seem like good news, but they needed something to happen soon. The doctor had said that if the swelling didn't go down in the next day or so, brain damage would be permanent, even if he somehow came to.

Ashlynn spoke up. "His fever was down a little this morning. I thought that was a good sign, but the nurse said we shouldn't get our hopes up."

She was reddening again and Kevin knew why. It was quite presumptuous to use the word "we" in referencing their family. And she still hadn't explained who she was or why she was there.

"You've been reading to him all day?"

"Yes," she replied. "It's a really good book." As though quality literature explained not only her presence, but how she knew Kevin Junior at all. Perhaps it could. His son had always liked English, had considered majoring in it, but then he did well in all of his subjects. Maybe she was a classmate, though she looked a bit younger than Junior. She couldn't be more than twenty.

Minutes passed in silence. Ashlynn reached her hand up, tentatively. She wanted desperately to hold Junior's hand. She seemed to need it like breath.

Again, Harry took matters into his own hands, and with his typical tact. He took the book from Ashlynn's hand. "Can I see this?" he asked as he pulled the book away and placed her hand on top of his brother's.

Ashlynn smiled sheepishly, but clutched Kevin Junior's hand tightly, then interlaced her fingers with his as they'd been most of the day. Harry pretended not to notice as he paged through *Everything Matters*. "This does look like a good book," he confirmed, both absentmindedly and irrelevantly.

Silence returned, but somewhat less awkward. Finally, Kevin had to ask. "So, do you take classes with Junior, I mean Kevin?"

The girl shook her head slowly and didn't look at him. For a moment, she stared straight forward, then to the left at Junior. Finally, her eyes settled on the book again, longingly as though it were a life preserver.

Kevin was almost whispering now, realization upon him. "You were at the accident?"

Ashlynn simply nodded, clutching his son's hand in hers more tightly.

"You saw it."

She paused, and then nodded again, her eyes brimming.

Kevin reached forward and touched her elbow. "Thank you for being here." He paused, unsure of how to proceed. He didn't want to upset the girl again, but the details of the accident itself were still largely a mystery to him. "How? What did you?. . . the accident?"

Hot tears were now streaming down the girl's face. She took in a shallow breath, then looked him in the eye. "I caused it." She looked at Harry as well and repeated, in case he hadn't heard. "I caused it."

Kevin Senior glanced over at Harry who was already moving his chair toward her. Together, they grasped her arms, Kevin at her right, and Harry at her left, just next to the bed. She let go of Junior's hand and leaned forward into them, her arms folded, swaying forward and back. The tears flowed freely and silently now.

But, this time, she didn't run away.

**

For two and a half hours, Andrew lay on his back, half under the desk, legs propped on the power strip. He thought he'd be able to relax that way, but it didn't seem to be in the cards. He started shifting from side to side started less than an hour in, and it was soon clear that this wasn't going to provide any relief. Yet stubbornness prevailed and he waited as long as he could. He needed to find his way to both a better position and some medication.

Bending his knees, he pulled himself away from the surge protector, then he scooted himself backwards away from the desk. He moved over to his left side before trying to sit up. He managed to make his way to a kneeling position. Next, he took several breaths because he knew there was no way to make it to his feet without risking both additional rib pain and more back spasms. First, he lifted up to his right leg, protecting the ribs on his left side. Then, using that leg, he pulled himself to his feet in one long, deliberate motion.

He was pleased. He hurt all over, ribs, back, buttocks, and hamstring, but all were a rather low, anticipatory pain, and perhaps its diffusion would allow him to move around a bit. He would have been tempted to head out to the mailbox, test his limits, but he knew that was premature. What he needed right now was medication so that he could get more rest.

Walking disjointedly, yet deliberately, he made his way toward the bedroom. Finding the door, he held onto the wall as he sidestepped toward the nightstand next to the bed. It wasn't until he reached the nightstand that the spasm hit. It was almost as though it was in his ribs and back at the same time—or was it alternating? Either way, Andrew collapsed, fell backwards, his shin hitting the bed railing just before his butt hit the floor.

He had managed to keep the bottle of pills clutched in his left hand. He moved it to the right before reaching down to feel his lower leg. Great, another body part injured; what next? In the grand scheme of things, the shin injury would never rise above a minor nuisance, but at the moment, he could afford a bit of self-pity.

He considered the pills. The nurse had said to take one or two at a time, as needed. At the moment, he felt like he needed five. But Andrew was smarter than that. Still, he was sure that two weren't going to provide any relief. Three were too many, but maybe with two and a half, he could get some rest. He broke his first pill in half, got two more from the bottle then swallowed all three dry. He looked over at the stale water next to the bed, and ignored it. Until medication kicked in, he wasn't going to be doing any reaching, even if it was only two feet.

But it was best not to wait to get into the bed. Pain or not, he wanted that over and done with. As the worst of the pain subsided, he pulled himself to his knees, then launched into the bed full force. He cried out uncharacteristically, bunching his legs up toward his chest. For what seemed like the twentieth time just that day, he began the slow process of relaxing his muscles, one at a time.

There was no way he could relax completely; it would take close to an hour before enough medication circulated through his system to permit that. As he waited, Andrew considered his situation and how it could have been different.

What if he'd hit his head instead of his shin? What if one of his injuries had prevented him from moving altogether? He had no home phone; a landline seemed redundant in the 21st century. His cell phone had been destroyed in the accident and he wasn't ready to go pick up another. No one at work was expecting him for a couple of weeks. The rent was paid and the landlady, contrary to what he'd told the doctor, rarely stopped by, and never without written notification. With his family out of state, and mostly out of mind, there were few people in his life who would notice his absence.

Andrew returned to thoughts of his experiment. What would happen if he just stayed in the apartment, stayed in bed? Who would be the first to come looking for him? Tina was no longer in the picture. There were no other girlfriends, nor the prospects of any. In fact, the only women Andrew could recall spending any time with lately were Lillian and Ellie, neither of whom were dating material, especially as coworkers. He'd hardly even seen any others, except his landlady a time or two, and that pretty Latina who delivered the mail, whom he'd only seen once from the window. Since his rent payment was automatically made from his checking account and the landlady didn't have an inspection scheduled for another five months, he had no expectation of seeing her. Lillian would eventually notice he was missing at work and might start asking questions; she was that nosy. But for the most part, he lived his life independently and anonymously, which is how he liked it.

He didn't like the feeling that the need for medical attention might whittle away his autonomy. Yet, he still believed that his physical needs wouldn't. But intellectually, he was intrigued by how long he could avoid interactions with other humans if he so chose. Maybe he'd just stay home until it was time to head back to work. There was enough food; the bills were paid. He needed no one.

Yes, maybe he would just stay home. Maybe, he'd stay right here in this bed.

PRAYERS

Zeke began his day as he began most, in prayer. The good thing about Sundays was that there was extra time. Church service didn't start until 9:45, nearly two hours later than he reported to work most weekdays. This made for a relaxing morning and extra time for devotion to the Lord.

On weekdays, he would say a quick prayer just after getting up, typically kneeling at the side of the bed for a few minutes. But on a Sunday, he took his time, spending half an hour or more in devotion, using the coffee table in the living room as a makeshift altar.

His prayer followed a common pattern, thanks before requests. The reverse would seem presumptuous to say the least; asking something of God before acknowledging all He had already provided was tantamount to sacrilege. Zeke thanked the Lord for his health, his family, his faith, honorable employment, and the community of His servants he'd been allowed to share his life with. He was often irritated by his fellow congregants at Salina Free Pentecostal and he questioned the devotion of several, but it wasn't for him to judge. Sundays were the day he reminded himself of this fact and focused himself toward the path to humble service.

His requests followed a pattern as well. He asked God to keep him on the righteous path and to protect him from the temptations of the world. He acknowledged to his God that all of the worldly things that could be offered were nothing compared to the promise of eternal life that was available if he were to remain true to his Lord.

Though he wondered if it was presumptuous to quote sacred scripture to God, he often recited one of his favorites from the seventh chapter of Matthew, "For strait is the gate, and narrow is the way, which leadeth unto life, and few there be that find it." He knew this to be true and beseeched, "Lord, if it be Your will, let me be one of the few who is able to keep to the narrow way. Keep me on the path toward You and all that You have promised for us, should we heed Your teachings."

Though it seemed to his wife that Andrew and Janice rarely crossed Zeke's mind, he was always careful to include them in his supplications. His family was important to him, second only to his devotion to God, and he had long hoped that the two could be reconciled. He prayed not only for his own moral strength, but for Olivia's as well. And he asked that God bring his children back to the righteous path, toward His way and back into His holy fold. In his mind, he hoped that this would mean they'd come back to Salina as well, but that seemed a bit much to ask.

In Zeke's world, God was at the center, then family, community, nation, and world. And that was the order his prayer followed. After asking for God's good graces to be bestowed upon his family, he added similar intonations for the town of Salina as well, for Kansas, the United States and the other diverse nations as well. There was less certainty about this as he knew that it was a small minority in this world that would come to the true faith and find salvation, but the Lord's mercy was infinite if only we asked, so indeed, he asked.

Coming full circle, he closed his prayer with a return to the humility he knew was central to his dealings with the Almighty. "If these things be thy will, thy will" he repeated several times, "I ask you these things in Jesus' holy name, if they be thy will. But not my will, but thine be done. Your will be done O God. Let your will be mine and let your will be done on earth as in heaven."

**

In the next room, Olivia began her own prayers. Hers lacked the structure of her husband's, but there was power in them nonetheless, or at least so she hoped. There were certainly themes in her entreaties, and though they lacked Zeke's orderliness, the sincerity was ever present. Today, she began, as she so often did, with those things she wanted from God. Her needs were simple; she had no desire for earthly riches, she reminded herself; on some occasions, she reminded God of this as well. She wished only for her family's safety and happiness and most of all, their presence. She wanted her Andrew and Janice, together in her home, for the holidays and as often as was possible after that. Tears streaming down her face, she pleaded, "Bring them home O Lord, please bring them home." She lacked the words, so she repeated, with only minor variations, "Bring them home, keep them safe and bring them home. Bring them to Salina, bring them to family where we'll keep them safe and loved. Bring them home."

Today, she asked for something she didn't always dare bring up, grandchildren. She asked the Lord to bring her children home so that they could meet good mates, "a husband for dear Janice and a good and faithful wife for my Andrew." She promised, and, at the risk of bartering with the Almighty, vowed, to be the best grandmother she could be. She knew she would spoil them; there was no avoiding it. But she gave her word that she would care for her grandchildren as she had her own, teaching them, and helping their parents keep them true to His teachings. She'd use the same book of Bible stories she'd read to her children. Zeke didn't like that one because it showed Jesus with long hair, but he'd let her keep it.

Olivia worried that her prayers would not be answered due to her own sins, so she confessed them regularly. She avoided mention of her teenage past, allowing herself the subtle fiction that, though the Lord knows all, he need not be reminded of all. But she admitted to many sins, both real and imagined, stray thoughts, impatience and mistakes as a mother, and ignorance. It was ignorance that most concerned her, ignorance of the will of God and why He would punish her as He had. She was sure she had committed many sins of which she was unaware and pleaded with the Lord to share His will. Unlike her husband, who asked to be kept on the narrow path to heaven, she was sure she'd strayed off of it, but in ways she was too simple and limited to understand. She asked that God lead her back, allow her to make recompense and to do whatever it is he required to atone for her many and myriad errors. She too knew of His limitless mercy and wished only that she be allowed to return to the fold, to do His will. If she, or any member of her family had erred, let her pay the price, for the fault most certainly lay with her. Her ignorance of His will was at the heart of any mistakes that had been made. Let her take the blame, let her right the wrongs, so that they could all be reunited in love, home, and hearth.

Her eyes were still red as she was preparing breakfast. She knew how to time things well after decades of marriage, and Zeke joined her as she was pulling the biscuits out of the oven. The sausage gravy was his favorite and she liked to make it for him on Sundays, especially when he was reading scripture. Comfort food helped calm him. Plus, she had a request of her own to make.

She waited until his mouth was full and started by reminding him. "I'm still hoping the kids both make it home for the holidays, or at least Christmas."

He looked wary already. "Well, I hope you're right. But don't get your hopes up, especially about Andrew. I think he's made it clear that Kansas life is too slow for his fast living ways."

"I know. I just hope anyway. And if he doesn't make it, we'll still have Janice. She may not make it for Christmas day. She might have to work. But she'll be here some time, maybe Christmas Eve."

Zeke waited, so she continued. "But anyway, I was wondering, if they don't make it, I was thinking maybe we could go out to California to visit Andrew. Maybe Janice would come with us."

"I'm not sure how welcome we'd be there."

"We're family. I know he might not have room for us in his apartment. We'd probably have to stay in a hotel. But of course we'd be welcome. Andrew could show us the sights. Yosemite, the Golden Gate Bridge."

"I have no interest in San Francisco. Those hippies have ruined . . . ."

"Andrew lives in San Jose, dear."

"It's just down the road as I understand it. And that bridge you want to see is in San Francisco. No thanks to that."

"Oh, well we don't have to see the Golden Gate. That was just one possibility. We could go to Yosemite, see the redwoods, the ocean. I've never been to the ocean."

"Be awful expensive."

"I know. But, I can budget. We have months to plan, dear. I can cut down on household expenses. I think I can save enough. Plus, we have a little savings already. We haven't taken a vacation in five years. More than that if you don't count camp meetings."

"Why wouldn't you count camp meetings?"

She didn't want to give up any ground, but it was time for a momentary retreat. "Oh, they count. I misspoke. And, I do so enjoy the fellowship we find there. I just mean we haven't gone anywhere else. We haven't seen much of the world."

"Much of the world is just worldly."

"Andrew is not worldly. He's our son."

"I'm afraid those two things aren't necessarily mutually exclusive. The boy . . . " Zeke trailed off, not wanting his morning to devolve.

His wife was not to be deterred this time. She grasped both of his hands and uncharacteristically looked him right in the eye. "Zeke," she paused, not for effect, but it had one. "Zeke, please?"

"Well, maybe we should pray about it. I have always wanted to see those big trees. We'll see if the good Lord's willing."

"Oh, He is. I know He is." Olivia couldn't hide her elation as she headed off to get ready for church. It would be quite an adventure. And, if she could get Janice to join them, they'd all be together again.

**

Andrew Grey had no prayers.

If he was capable of faith in the first place, it had been driven out of him. He could never see past the logical inconsistencies seemingly inherent in the religious doctrine he'd been presented. Science provided better explanations for the phenomena he saw around him. Logic and reasoning provided better methods to understanding. He wouldn't have prayed for healing because he didn't believe in miracle healing. He wouldn't have prayed for wisdom and knowledge for his doctors because medical school existed to provide that. Humans created these things. Religion, it seemed to Andrew, had been created to allow humans to avoid responsibility, both credit

KNOW MY NAME

and blame, for their actions.

At the moment though, his actions were inaction. He spent most of his time in bed. The Vicodin made his brain fuzzy, but without it, every movement hurt. He'd taken two and a half pills three times on Saturday, then four to get to sleep that night. After waking at 4:00 Sunday morning, he took just two, hoping to conserve enough to last through the upcoming week or longer. He'd decided to stay in this apartment until he had recovered enough to go back to work, or at least to the drug store.

He wasn't sure yet how long that would be. But, he'd last as long as it took.

**

The story had come out gradually, at least theirs had. After her tearful confession, Ashlynn hadn't been up to talking more about herself, much less the incident that put Kevin Junior in the hospital. The three of them bonded over their hopes for his recovery. After leaving exhausted Friday night, she'd come back early on Saturday and met them in the lobby. Through the whole weekend, she'd done more listening than talking.

She had learned quite a bit about Kevin Jamison Junior. He was in his last year of college, planning to be a middle school teacher and maybe a soccer coach. He'd coached Harry's team last year already and they'd placed second in their age group. Just months earlier, he'd started his student teaching assignment. He loved it, though he was exhausted in recent weeks with the work and school schedule.

The family had never been wealthy, but after the boys' mother died, things had taken a turn for the worse, just as Kevin Junior was starting college. The construction industry had taken a big hit and work had been scarce. Though he was skilled, heading into his fifties, Kevin Senior had found it more difficult to get consistent jobs. He'd lost at least one job because he couldn't keep up. The supervisor had been sympathetic, advising him to apply for disability. But he hadn't wanted that, both because of pride and the fact that disability wouldn't provide the income to cover his mortgage.

Kevin Junior had helped out enormously. He seemed to have an endless reserve of energy, taking care of Harry, serving as a mentor to his younger brother, who clearly worshipped him. He'd taken a job at a motorcycle shop when he turned sixteen, working as many hours as they'd give him, and he used most of the money to help the family, even against his father's protests.

He'd kept the shop job through college, working thirty hours a week and taking fifteen to seventeen units through four years, finishing on time when it was taking most of his peers five or six years. He was still spending fifteen to twenty hours at the shop while doing his student teaching. The exhaustion had finally caught up to him and this, his father had gently suggested, may well have contributed to the accident.

Ashlynn just looked away when he said that; she knew better.

Kevin Junior had been hoping to get a teaching job as soon as his credential was issued. He already had some leads. The principal at his student teaching site was impressed with him and said she'd hire him herself if an opening came up. If not, she'd give her highest recommendation to colleagues around the district. She was sure he'd get a job right away.

Kevin Junior had promised that if he did get a job, he'd pay for Harry's college tuition. This contribution his father hadn't objected to; he knew how important the money was and that he could never afford it. Harry, for his part, thought he was ready now. Though he hadn't quite hit his teens, he was already a year ahead and was set to start high school in the fall. Starting in his sophomore year, he'd take at least one, maybe two night classes each semester at San Jose City College, getting a jump start. Combining this with AP classes, by the time he finished high school, he'd be a college sophomore at least. He hoped to finish college in two and a half years and have his own credential shortly thereafter.

Yes, he was following in his brother's footsteps, though not exactly. He hoped to teach high school math or biology. "The market is better for that," he'd told Ashlynn. She was impressed by the research he'd done already. With a degree in math or one of the natural sciences, he'd never be without a job. And, he'd be able to take care of his father. Once both boys were finished with school, they were determined to give their father a chance to retire, age

KNOW MY NAME

qualified or not.

When Harry told her that, Kevin Senior's eyes moved from one son to the other, then met hers with a sheepish pride. His boys had taken over leadership of the family, yes, but it seemed the family was in good hands.

For the first time, Ashlynn was embarrassed by her advantages. She evaded their questions about her college work. She hadn't been to class all week, and she hadn't notified any of her professors. She'd even stopped responding to messages from her friends.

Her parents had planned her entire college budget. They'd looked at the estimated costs the college provided, padded them by twenty percent, and then added $5,000 per year "for personal stuff" she was sure to need. They put all these in her account, and Ashlynn made the payments. Her parents thought this would teach her independence.

She didn't mention the car, for more reasons than one.

When the nurse entered the room, she was startled to see Ashlynn still there. She stepped to the side and looked directly at Kevin Senior and his son. "The doctor will be here in a few minutes. He's concerned that Kevin's temperature hasn't come down enough and there's still too much pressure on his brain. He has some options for you to consider."

Ashlynn broke in "What does that mean?"

"I'm sorry, but this conversation is just for family."

Harry stepped in quickly, "She's my sister."

"I thought . . ." The nurse was flabbergasted. The expression on Ashlynn's face was equally confused, so the surprised nurse turned to the father. "I'm sorry, but I had been told . . ."

"It's complicated," Kevin Senior replied patiently. "But she's family. Anything you need to say can be said in front of her."

The nurse turned again toward Ashlynn, but there was no triumph on her face, only surprise and gratitude. "Well," the nurse began, "the doctor will explain fully. But the procedure he's suggesting is called a decompressive craniectomy. Basically, the surgeon removes a small piece of bone from Kevin's skull to relieve the pressure."

"That sounds pretty risky." Kevin Senior's voice was shaking and both Harry and Ashlynn took his hands. The nurse relaxed her attitude toward Ashlynn. She must really be family after all.

"It is risky. But as the doctor will explain, we may have come to the point where the risk of the surgery is outweighed by the risk of doing nothing."

"He mentioned it the other day," Harry said. "It is risky, but they do it quite often. They know what they're doing Dad."

"Of course they do." Kevin Senior turned to the nurse. "When do they want to do this?"

"Well, they need your permission of course, but the doctor has already notified the surgical team." Then, she quickly added, "Just in case. They'd like to start this afternoon. The procedure takes several hours."

"If he thinks it is necessary, we'll do it."

"Actually, the doctor will explain further. And there will be some forms for you to sign."

"Just ask the doctor one question. If this were his son, is this what he'd want done? If this surgery is the answer, just bring me the papers and I'll sign them."

**

When she entered the small room at the police station on Mission Street, Ellie saw her coworkers with their heads on the metal desk. She took her car keys and banged them as loud as she could on the desk. Clang! Clang! Clang! The keys rattled against the desk as loud as the bells rang for Ebeneezer Scrooge in the Dickens story, which was actually as she intended. Pete and Duane both groaned and Pete reached for the keys. "Uh uh. These are mine and the two of you don't need to be near keys or cars any time soon," Ellie dictated. Clang! Clang! Clang! "It's time you two woke up."

"OK already," moaned Sykes. "I thought you were coming to help."

"Oh I am, but that doesn't mean you get off easy. You're both idiots and if the SJPD isn't going to make you pay, I certainly will."

"What do you mean the cops aren't making us pay? What did you do?"

"We'll get to that in a minute. Now let's hear the story."

"It was his fault," Pete began. "He planned too big of a . . . "

"Get real. If it wasn't for this dumbass . . . "

Clang! Clang! Clang! "One of you better start talking," she pointed to Sykes. "You, go first."

"Well, you know we had to get back at Pete's friend, Danny."

"Of course. Because you're both twelve years old. Go on."

"Not that. Well, not just that. But what he did cannot go unpunished. Plus, G-dub practically ordered it."

"Get on with the story."

"Well, I wanted to do something creative. But our friend here has very little imagination."

"Hey!"

"It's true," Ellie reminded him. "Plus, you'll get your turn." Turning back to Sykes, she nudged, "Go on."

"We decided to do something to his car. But all Pete wanted to do was the old magnet and beer can trick."

"What?"

"You put a beer can on top of his car, connected with a magnet. It's supposed to stay there when he drives, gets him in trouble."

"Sounds pathetic."

"No kidding. Like I said, he has no imagination." This time, after a quick look from Ellie, Pete kept his mouth shut. "Anyway, we didn't have time for something truly original, but I managed to talk dumbshit here into one just a little better. We hooked up a reverse beeper to his headlights."

"And what's the point of that?"

Sykes laughed out loud and Pete joined him. Clearly, they were impressed with themselves. "Every time he turns the lights on, his car will beep like a garbage truck in reverse. It will be weeks before he can figure it out and in the meantime, he won't be able to drive at night."

"Well, pathetic sounds about right. You two are both imbeciles."

"Hey, it would have worked if it wasn't for Pete. He couldn't get his first idiot idea out of his head."

She turned to Pete. "OK, your turn."

"Well, Elsie . . . " he began, still slurring a bit. Her heel got him in the testicles before he could get started.

"Now I know you're not going to start acting like the boss in here."

If there was anything she knew about Pete Massey, it was that he was easily chastised. Abandoning his futile attempt at folksiness, he took over the story.

"I still think that the can on the hood thing was the better prank. It would have really gotten him in trouble."

"If it had worked," Sykes broke in.

"It would have worked if that damn alarm hadn't gone off."

"Wait a minute," Ellie interrupted. "You mean to tell me that this guy managed to rewire his headlights without a peep, but you can't put a beer can on the hood without tripping his car alarm?"

Sykes leaned back, beaming with pride. Ellie was disgusted; she hadn't meant it as a compliment.

"It would have been fine, but there was wind and the can kept falling off."

Duane couldn't keep to himself. "That's because that prank is older than dirt. There's a reason no one uses it any more. Most of the beer cans are made of aluminum now. Magnets won't work."

"So instead of getting your friend . . . "

"He's not my friend!" Pete interjected.

She kicked him, this time in the knee. "Don't interrupt me. Instead of getting your *friend* in trouble with the cops, you get yourselves arrested for public drunkenness, and I had to come and get you."

"That's all they've got. They really wanted us for drunk driving, but they couldn't find our car."

"Duane, public drunkenness is enough. But it's your lucky day. You're home free."

"What do you mean?"

"I told you before, my cousin is the sergeant here. I managed to convince him you had taken the bus to your friend's neighborhood, so they stopped looking for your car. They're not going to press charges. I hope I was telling the truth."

"My car was around the corner. But we really hadn't been drinking that much."

She shook her head. "Yeah?" Clang! Clang! Clang! "Maybe that's

KNOW MY NAME

why you were both passed out when I got here? Dumbasses!"

Pete was finally wising up. "You mean we can go? And you knew all of this before you came in?"

"Yes, but for some masochistic reason, I wanted to hear the story from you. I now regret that decision. Let's go."

Both men stood up and Pete moved to embrace her. She put both hands out. "Keep your distance. You smell like piss and beer."

Meanwhile, Sykes gloated. "You know, at least we got Danny. My prank worked even if yours landed us here."

"Well . . . ."

"Spill it Pete. What else is there?"

Pete turned to Sykes, but didn't lift his eyes. "You know that wire you had hanging from the headlight switch? I kinda tripped over it when the cops got there."

"Tripped over it how? Did it?"

"Yes, it came loose. Your beeper isn't going to work."

"You idiot. Now we're going to have to . . . ."

Now it was Sykes Ellie was striking. "No, you don't 'have to.' And if you do, you'd better pray I never hear about it. This is the last time I'm coming down here for either of you. That clear?" She grabbed both of them by the elbow and steered them toward the door, pressing on their respective ulnar nerves for full effect.

Sykes shook his head in disbelief. Pete turned quietly and whispered. "Thanks. You seriously saved our butts." Ellie just nodded.

But Pete Massey never knew when to quit. "How many more weeks?"

"Oh Petey. We're way beyond coffee."

**

Andrew Grey had no prayers.

He'd never have prayed for help or for a friend to come pick him up at jail. He didn't drink and he considered pranks childish beyond comprehension. It was one more thing that put distance between himself and his coworkers.

Not only did he not engage in silly pranks, but Andrew had no real hobbies to speak of. He lived in a small apartment, so he didn't garden. He liked bicycling (other than his last trip) but considered it largely a mode of transportation, not a pleasure activity. He considered it important to be civically engaged, but detested interest groups and partisan politics. His family was several states away, which was the way he liked it.

Even the mundane activities were unavailable to him. He couldn't concentrate to read, everything on television was inane and browsing the internet bored him.

It would be rather inaccurate to describe Andrew as disconnected, for that would imply he'd at some time been connected in the first place. If he had been, it was long ago and long forgotten. For while it is true, as the saying goes, that not all who wander are lost, it seems equally true that some are lost because they have forgotten how to wander, or never learned. No one would later recall a specific moment when things had fallen apart for him, when his bonds with his fellow humans, to whatever extent they existed, had become severed. It might be easy to suggest that it was one of the many arguments with his father, but in truth, these days, Zeke Grey hardly entered his mind.

**

The Hitchens book hadn't been the biggest fight, nor the first. Janice remembered them all because it always seemed as though she were in the middle just by being present.

The biggest one, at least in her memory, came from his days in high school. Andrew had been placed in honors biology, which he took seriously. They had come to the section on evolution and Zeke had gotten hold of Andrew's homework.

"What kind of trash are they teaching you over there?" he'd asked.

"It's just evolution, Dad. You know, DNA, all that stuff."

"But what are those pictures?"

Andrew didn't want to get into it, but he pointed to each in turn from his textbook. "Homo-habilis, Homo-Erectus, Neanderthal, Cro-Magnon, and Homo-Sapien. That's us."

"So, these are supposed to be how humans evolved from monkeys?"

"Humans didn't evolve from monkeys, Dad. But all life on earth has a common ancestry. Humans are related to modern day apes. Closest to chimpanzees."

"So where does God fit into all of this?"

"He doesn't, as far as I know." Andrew's voice was matter of fact as he turned back to his homework.

"That's what I thought. They're teaching this evolution garbage, but they won't let God into the classroom. I'm going to go down to that school."

"There's no need for that, Dad."

"I'm your father. I have a right to know what they're teaching you. My tax dollars are paying for you to be taught that God didn't create the Earth."

"They never said any such thing."

"They can't both be true. Either God created the Earth and man in his likeness or we evolved from monkeys. So, they're teaching you that the Bible is wrong. That you're great grandfather was some chimp named Bobo swinging from trees in the jungle."

"My great grandfather? Dad, this didn't happen in three or four generations. Humans evolved into their present form over hundreds of thousands of years. All life over millions. They didn't just magically morph from swinging monkey to human."

"The Earth hasn't been around that long. The Bible gives us the entire genealogy from Adam on down. We're not quite at six thousand years yet."

"Dad, that's ridiculous. There are cultures all over the world older than that. There's the fossil record."

"Old bones don't disprove the Bible."

"I don't know what it says about the Bible. But they have bones from hominids tens and hundreds of thousands of years old."

"Who says they're that old?"

"Archeologists, paleontologists. Scientists of all kinds."

"In other words, man says it."

"Men yes, some women. Who else?"

Zeke walked over to the end table and picked up his well-worn Bible. "See this. This is what God tells me. God tells me the age of the earth. Now why should I believe your scientists over God?"

"God wrote that? How do you know? It looks like it was written by humans to me. It's not even one book, it's quite a few, around sixty-six as I recall. Some of it even contradicts itself."

"The Bible does *not* contradict itself." Now, Zeke was beginning to turn red. Not the deep, almost plum shade that entered his face when he was completely worked up, but already, it was a mid-level cherry.

Andrew put his pencil down and grasped the Bible from his father. "Look here in the first chapter of Genesis. It says that God created man and woman both on the sixth day, right? Then, here in the very next chapter, it says that women didn't exist yet. He created Eve on the eighth day."

"So?"

"So, it contradicts itself."

"That's just two parts of the same story."

"That's not what it says. It says clearly that the first part occurred on the sixth day and the other part, which the writer . . . ."

"You mean God."

"You think God sat down and wrote this whole thing?"

"Humans may have written it, but God inspired them and told them what to write."

"Whatever. Whoever wrote it put the creation of women in an entirely different chapter and on an entirely different day. It can't be accidental."

"You're saying you don't believe the Bible?"

"I don't know. I don't believe that story. It doesn't make sense. And, it couldn't have happened just six thousand years ago when the earth is so much older than that."

"You believe your scientists when they say that the earth is older, but you don't believe God."

"The scientists don't just make up stories that don't make sense. They have a lot of evidence. Fossils, carbon dating, DNA, all kinds of things."

"Things man made up."

"Made up? They didn't just pull these things out of their asses."

"You watch your language."

"Sorry. But, do you really think they invented the bones in a lab? That they're making up all of these skeletons and bone fragments?"

"I don't know what they're doing, but I trust the good book more than them. Maybe the bones just aren't as old as they think they are."

"Some of these bones have been buried in rock for hundreds of thousands of years."

"They say." Cherry had given way to crimson.

"Are they mistaken? Are you smarter than all of them? Or are they lying?"

"Watch your tone boy. You aren't too old to go out and cut a switch. I may not be as smart as your scientists, but I know what God tells me to believe."

"How do you know the Bible isn't mistaken?"

"Because it's the Word of God. God is not mistaken, cannot be mistaken."

"But how do you know? Who told you? Your parents? The pastor? What about all of the people in other countries who grow up with other religions? Are they all going to hell?" Andrew's left eyebrow was lifted nearly an inch higher than his right. His voice was calm, but unmistakably dismissive. One did not speak to Zeke Grey this way.

"I didn't need anyone to tell me. I have this book right here that tells me everything I need to know."

Crimson had by now given way to plum, but this time, it wasn't just the regular plum, it was the deep purple of the small Avalons. Janice was always scared when her father got worked up, but this color was beyond any she'd yet witnessed. She worried that he was going to have a heart attack or stroke. She was certain that one of his blood vessels would pop at any moment.

She would have liked to leave the room, but no chance. First, Zeke would have called her back, told her that she needed to hear this too. She knew that from experience. Plus, her parents insisted that both siblings do their homework in the living room. Zeke thought it important to monitor their work, though he usually wasn't home at the time, and Olivia simply liked having them around.

Janice was shaking. She knew she should say something, but

there were no words that would slow down this train. The big worry was that she'd just make it worse.

Liquid dropped on her essay. She thought there were tears in his eyes, but mostly, it was sweat. There was perspiration all over Zeke's face and neck. "I'll tell you how I know," he told Andrew, shaking himself as he spoke. "I know the Word of the Lord. I know because He told me."

"God spoke to you? Directly? Did he just show up and . . . "

"It doesn't work that way!" Zeke was shouting now; Janice dropped her pencil.

"It does in your bible." Dismissive again, and in Zeke's mind, blasphemous. This kid of hers was now openly defiant of both him and the Lord.

"The Bible says that children are to be seen and not heard," he began.

"Actually, I don't think it does."

"So, I'm saying it. I talk, you listen." Zeke had stopped turning colors now, but he was panting. I know the Bible's true. I know it because I feel it. I feel the power and the glory of the Lord right here in my heart." Zeke pounded his closed fist into his chest. Janice was weeping by now. "Your scientists can say whatever they want. They can't change what God put in my heart. They can't take it away."

"Well, I can't argue with your heart." Andrew was still dismissive, almost mocking, but Zeke's eyes were so filled with tears, his face and ears so full of blood that he seemed not to recognize it.

"No, you certainly cannot." With that, their father left the room, mistakenly triumphant and completely exhausted.

A full minute passed, maybe two. Janice used the back of her hand to flatten out the pages of her essay, which were covered in the salty water that had dropped from her father's face. Once she got her own breath back, she quietly asked her brother, "Why did you have to do that?"

"Do what?" The look on his face was not in the least challenging. It was inquisitive. He really didn't know.

Days later, at the dinner table, Zeke made it a point to address the issue with Janice. She would not be taking honors biology, he declared. And should evolution be a part of her regular biology class, she was to inform him, so that he could pull her out of that section. She could study in the library while her fellow students got corrupted with the devil's garbage.

Janice pinched her brother's leg as hard as she could to keep him from speaking up. She didn't need to hear the argument again. Of course, she had no intention of telling her father about the content of her biology class. Unlike her brother, she knew when to keep quiet. She didn't have to air out every disagreement.

That ability to roll with the punches stood her in good stead in the emergency room. She handled patients with great skill and was rarely rattled, even in the most stressful moments. Still, it was authority figures that made her nervous. And now, she had to find the charge nurse and had been told she was in the chapel of all places. Just that morning, she'd handled two open fractures and a moderate heart attack without skipping a beat, but stepping into the chapel, her breath quickened. She hadn't been inside a church in years, except on visits home, which were becoming increasingly rare.

She needed to get a form signed for the doctor, something about overtime for one of her colleagues, which she had surmised was this particular doctor's favorite nurse. Whatever; not her problem.

And surprisingly enough, Debbie was not only in the chapel, but she was sitting in the front pew, seemingly in prayer. Janice walked up the aisle as quietly as she could and took the seat behind her boss.

"What do you need Janice?"

"It can wait until you're done."

"I'm done. And, there's no time like the present. What is it?"

"Dr. Salazar needs your signature on this. He wants Carol to stay late again."

"Again huh. Let me ask you a question. Would you sign this?" Janice was hesitant. "I don't know. I just started here."

"But, I'm guessing you have an opinion on Carol and Dr. Salazar."

"I've heard the rumors."

"And?"

"I don't know if they're true. None of my business if they are."

"Walk with me." With that, she took the form from Janice, gave it a quick glance, and signed it. "I could be wrong, but I'm fairly certain that those rumors about Carol and Dr. Salazar are untrue. I'd appreciate it if you didn't repeat them."

"I'm not one to gossip."

"That's what I thought. You don't seem the type." Debbie glanced over her. Janice hated the sensation; she felt like a goldfish in a bowl. "Here's what I do know. While the rumors about their extracurricular relationship are probably exaggerated, I've seen them work together. Carol's a good nurse anyway, but she has a special rapport with Dr. Salazar. She's like a third arm for him, seems to anticipate what he needs before he does. I can say with some certainty that there are at least a few patients who are alive today because those two work together so well."

Janice nodded. She saw the point, just not why it was being shared with her.

Apparently, as usual, Debbie had more on her mind. "You were cool as a cucumber during that MI this morning."

"It's just the training, I guess."

"It's more than that. There are lots of good nurses here, dozens. But the majority of them aren't fit for the ER. It's a whole different ballgame, with the stress and all. The cancer ward, the NICU, they have their own challenges, big emotional ones, but the ER, that's a special skill set. You've got it."

Janice had no idea what to say. She'd never been comfortable with compliments; she always suspected an ulterior motive. "Thank you," she said, nervously waiting for the form to be handed back to her.

"Look, I'm not forever in this job. I've got at least fifteen more years before retirement, but I'll be damned if I spend all of them with my heart racing beyond its comfort zone. Two, maybe three more years, and I'm going to want to move on to another area. I'm going to need someone to take over as charge nurse."

Janice was incredulous. "You can't mean me. There are at least five nurses with more experience."

"Oh, there are twice that and more. But experience isn't everything. You need the right combination of book smarts, and the ability to think quickly. I've seen today, and earlier this week, that you have the latter. Your grades and license test scores suggest you've got the former." Debbie paused, seeming almost to rethink herself. "Look, I'm not exactly offering you the job. And keep this whole conversation to yourself, if you don't mind. I just want you to be thinking of these kinds of management decisions you might have to make if, and I do mean if, that day comes. See, Carol's overtime is going to hurt my budget. It's probably also going to piss off a couple of other nurses, one of whom has already been somewhat vocal about it. But, if you believe, as I do, that bending the rules might save a life or two, you bend them and you take the necessary heat. Got it?"

"I think so."

"No promises, just keep thinking. I'll be watching you, could still change my mind. But, I was impressed this morning, I really was. I've seen a couple dozen of those since I've been down there and every time, I get the shakes. Usually, thankfully, not during the crisis itself, but after. Funny how things work that way."

"Is that why you're here? In the chapel, I mean?" They were halfway down the hall, but Janice was still in quiet reverence mode. Too many years with Zeke had her gun-shy about places of worship.

"I just need a few minutes to myself after a case like that. The chapel is the quietest room in the hospital."

"I thought you were praying. Sorry, I don't mean to pry. I just didn't think you were religious."

"I'm not; not at all. I wasn't praying. Well, maybe I was, just not to any God you might recognize. Silence is its own kind of prayer I suppose."

Janice nodded, not that she understood.

**

A different kind of nervousness enveloped Tina as she climbed the steps of the St. Paul's United Methodist church in central San Jose. It was her first time attending with Andre and his family and afterward came their first session with the pastor for premarital counseling. *First session*, she thought, still with some surprise. She had expected it to be a formality, just one meeting to get a lecture about what marriage means and to plan for the ceremony. But the packet of information Andre had handed her included plans for four scheduled meetings with the pastor, along with a three-page questionnaire they'd both had to fill out, separately, about future plans and compatibility. Now, she worried that if their answers didn't match, they'd have to find a new officiant for the ceremony. (She had no doubt however, of the wedding's inevitability).

Andre took her elbow and greeted the pastor as they went in. "Morning Pastor. I'd like you to meet my fiancé, Tina. Tina, this is Pastor Isaac Davis."

"Nice to meet you."

"It's good to meet you too Tina. I'm looking forward to our discussion after church."

"Me too," she said, though it came out a bit more meekly than she was used to feeling.

"Now miss, the first thing to learn is it's a sin to lie in church." Noticing the stricken look on her face, he chuckled. "I just mean to say, I know that the premarital discussions are not what people look forward to most in marriage. There are other things couples usually anticipate with far greater joy in their hearts." *Did he just glance down at my belly*, she wondered. It mattered little as the pastor was already going on. "We consider it necessary nonetheless. I'll try to keep things as painless as possible."

**

"Deke Zeke! Deke Zeke!" Now it wasn't just the Selmy kids chanting; they'd gotten several other of the young people into their little game. He was not amused. "Are you staying after church? For the dinner?"

"Of course we are."

"And did you bring the olive loaf?"

"Yes, we did," Olivia replied for him. She was happy they'd remembered; it was good to be known for something.

The couple separated at the entryway, Zeke stepping onto the platform with the other deacons and Olivia walking down to the second pew in the sanctuary. She greeted several of the other women with warm hugs and a few kind words. The church wasn't segregated by sex; most families sat together. But the deacons always sat in the upper level facing the audience, behind the pastor. She missed sitting with her husband, especially now that the children were gone, but his term as deacon wouldn't be up for another year. And, she suspected he'd like to serve another term.

Tabitha Selmy was the only woman on the upper level, tinkling at the piano as the parishioners took their seats. She nodded to Olivia as she launched into a rollicking version of "One More River to Cross." Olivia wished she knew an instrument like Tabby, but Zeke complained that Tabby played too fast, "almost worldly" he called it.

Her mind drifted as the service proceeded. She tended to look to her left as the music washed over her. The seats next to her had been empty until recently when a new family had joined her. The similarity of these two new children, a boy and a girl, to her own were too striking not to notice. It wasn't that they looked much like Andrew and Janice, but she still saw the reflection of her own kids in them nonetheless.

This girl was older, about five or six, with braids in her hair and a pink ribbon at the end of each braid. It was similar to the way she used to dress Janice, only her ribbons had been yellow and the braids much looser for some time. Maybe she could ask that woman for her technique. After all, she'd have grandchildren one day, hopefully soon.

Someone had started singing "Where We'll Never Grow Old" and Olivia stood with the others. She watched the little girl play with her doll. In her mind's eye, the girl morphed into a four-year-old version of Janice, but no, the doll wasn't right. Zeke hadn't allowed his children to play with toys at church, he wanted them focused on the service. Janice had pulled out a Betsy-Wetsy once and her father had taken it from her and handed it to Olivia. Olivia had spent much of the service that day struggling with the reaching toddler who could not be consoled.

Now, Pastor Cartwright was talking, was it time for the sermon already?

"I'd like to speak with you all today about the church. You know what the people say out there. You know how they refer to us.

'Plenty-crossed' they call us. Too many things offend us. We forbid too many things in the church. Our standards are too strict." He paused for effect. Isaiah Cartwright knew how to deliver a sermon; even Zeke thought so. "Do you think our standards are too strict?"

"No."

"No sir!"

"Neither do I, and I will tell you another thing. Neither does the Lord."

Amens abounded. He was just getting started. Olivia's mind drifted further. The little boy in this new family was young, probably not quite two. He rocked back and forth to the cadence of the sermon, just as he had with the music.

Momentarily, he was Andrew, not much older and no longer rocking, but in fact standing perfectly straight. Almost from the beginning, Andrew knew when to stand and when to sit. He sang when the rest of the church sang, not loudly, but with a determined focus even before he could follow the words. Those hymnals were likely some of the first words he ever read. In those days, he'd stood next to his father, a thin, lanky version of Zeke himself, seemingly mimicking Zeke's seriousness and, for a time, his piety.

Zeke's own voice startled her out of her daydream. Reciting from Romans, his voice rose in timbre as he moved through the passage from Romans, ". . . God gave them up unto vile affections. . . ".

Olivia purposely stopped listening. She often felt bad about doing that, but there were some passages she didn't enjoy hearing and "vile" anything certainly was one. She tuned out the sermon at times as well, a source of continual guilt. She'd rather fill her mind with positive thoughts instead.

"So it doesn't matter how they see you," the pastor continued. "It doesn't matter how they speak to you, how they speak about you. We are here to uphold a standard for our community. For our reward is not of this world, but of the next. For while those who are out enjoying these worldly delights may laugh at you, we'll have the last laugh. When they are engaged in the weeping and the gnashing of teeth, we'll be enjoying our eternal reward, resting in the arms of the savior, living in the everlasting joy. So let them enjoy their vices.

KNOW MY NAME

Let them talk about changing with the times. We worship a God who doesn't change with the times, but whose love for us endures forever."

There were more amens and at least two people encouraged "Preach on." This particular comment was one Olivia disliked. Sermons were often too long for her taste; why would they want it to go longer?

She looked over at the children again. The little boy was kneeling on the pew, making faces with the teenagers behind them. Janice had done some of the same things as a child until Zeke put a stop to it. He expected the children to face forward and pay attention in the house of the Lord. She knew he was right, he usually was, but sometimes, she wondered what the harm was with kids just being kids.

The boy's shoes were untied. This brought to mind another memory, one of Andrew, reaching down to tie his shoes. He must have been about six or seven and he couldn't quite reach the shoe sitting on the pew. Zeke wasn't a deacon then, so he was sitting there with him. Each time Andrew knelt down to tie his shoe, Zeke would grab his shoulder and pull him back up. "But I need to tie . . . " he started before Zeke shushed him. Finally, Zeke gently, but firmly grasped him by both shoulders and positioned his body in the reverent position, facing forward. He put his finger to his lips with the expression that brooked no dissent.

Little Andrew seethed until the end of the service. As the last piano note sounded, he turned to his mother. "Mom, Dad wouldn't let me tie my shoes." His expression was full of weightiness, and he seemed certain of the justice of his cause.

She'd always enjoyed playing with her children, but she'd never joked with them, or poked fun. It wasn't her personality. Except this time, he just seemed far too serious for someone so young. So for the first and only time, Olivia had tried a bit of levity. "Sorry honey. First Timothy says I am not to usurp authority over a man."

Her son didn't speak to her for three weeks.

**

Still, Andrew had no prayers.

Lest one be tempted to oversimplify, as is so common, he was not unmoored because he wasn't a Christian or the right type of one. Disjointedness is not an endemic characteristic of atheists.

Nor is it easy to say that family dysfunction was the wellspring of his condition. After all, his mother was more than loving; she was devoted. And Zeke, for all his rigidity, was there for his family in every way he was capable. And his sister did her best to keep the strings from unraveling.

Nonetheless, for reasons beyond easy comprehension, some strings unraveled. Some roads led in circles or simply moved from pavement to gravel to dirt to wilderness indistinguishable from their surroundings. Some kōans just exist for the asking, not for the understanding.

So he paced. In those moments when the pain had subsided, driven from his ribs and joints down into someplace deeper, swallowed like a ball of coagulated and condensed toxin, undigested, yet unexcretable, he paced the apartment, unsure what to do, where to go. He checked his temperature yet again: 100.2, still not a concern. He should go out, get the mail, replace his cell phone, pick up his prescription, yet, he didn't want to do any of those things. It wasn't fear exactly, more like recalcitrance. The world didn't need him it seemed, so why should he extend himself to it? A world of solitude held the greatest appeal. There was no one for whom he had such respect, such undiluted approbation that he needed to re-establish contact with the world for them, or them for him. Only his own intellect had earned such consideration and he hadn't the arrogance to impose it on others.

So, let the world come to him. Until they did, he'd wait right here.

**

Tina looked in admiration at her fiancé. His baritone resonated as he sang. "Kyrie eleison, on our love and on our way." She wondered what the lyrics meant; she'd have to ask later. It reminded her that she loved his voice. He didn't sing often, and never like this. A couple of weeks ago, when back pain was keeping her awake, he'd held her close to steady her breathing and sang an old Otis Redding song softly into her ear until she fell asleep. It was a precious moment, though she'd forgotten it by morning. Right now, if anything, his voice was even more sonorous. She almost envied God, to whom she assumed he was singing.

Now, she was surprised, both at him and the service, which she'd enjoyed more than she'd expected. She tried keeping her mind in the moment, focused on the song and Andre's voice rather than the upcoming discussion. But, this was the sending song, so as their turn came, Andre steered her out toward the back of the church. After shaking hands with the pastor and greeting a few of the congregation, all of whom Andre seemed to know, they moved toward the church office. Momentarily, Pastor Davis joined them and sat across the desk. "So, you two want to get married, huh?"

Andre replied for them, "Well, we'd like to pastor, only if you think it's OK."

Tina's whole body tensed and she looked over in alarm, but both men burst out laughing.

Pastor Davis reached out and took her hand in both of his. "I worry that you've come here expecting an interrogation. Did Andre here tell you I was an ogre?"

"No, it's just that, well, I didn't really know what to expect. And . . ." Her hand had gone instinctively to her belly. That seemed to happen often lately.

"Oh, you're afraid I'm going to judge you? That I might see that you've, well, jumped the gun a bit on the whole marriage thing?"

Tina had no idea what to say, so the pastor continued. "Well, let's start with the obvious since it is right there in front of us. It would seem that you've reversed our preferred order of things a bit. So, do you think getting married will improve your situation?"

"Well, yes. Don't you prefer that people get married?"

"The church is very much in favor of marriage. And though we'd rather a couple make their relationship permanent before having children, we don't necessarily endorse every pregnant couple getting married."

"You don't think . . . "

"Let's hold off a minute. I don't think much of anything at the moment. I'm just saying that an unexpected pregnancy is not of itself a reason to get married. Typically, it's a recipe for a quick divorce."

"Oh, but that's not why we're getting married."

"Yes, Andre has told me as much. I've known Andre for quite a few years now, so I know he makes good choices, of which I am sure you are one. And I've looked over your questionnaires. For today, I just want to get you started thinking about a few things. Often, I'd start by asking if you're planning to have children, but I guess the cat's out of the bag on that one."

Tina could do nothing but nod and give a nervous laugh. Andre seemed more relaxed, so she tried to draw comfort from his certainty. But the pastor was going on. "Have you discussed how many children you'll have?"

"Not really. I think it came up a couple of times." She looked over at her fiancé for help; he was being too quiet.

"No, I think on one of our first dates, you mentioned wanting two, but we haven't come back to it." It was about time he chimed in.

"And, how about finances? Have you discussed how the bills will be paid? Are you planning to merge your accounts or keep things separate?"

"Well, we're on the same cell phone plan now. And we're li . . . " She stopped short, sure that she shouldn't discuss the fact that she'd practically moved in with Andre three months ago and was in the process of giving up her apartment altogether.

"You're not going to shock me with your living situation. I've been around far too long to be offended. Perhaps that brings us to a key theological question. When will you consider yourself married?"

Andre piped up, "Well, if you're available, we've set the date for . . . "

"You misunderstand young man. I didn't ask when you will have your wedding. The ceremony is just that, ceremony. I'll be happy to perform that service for you and I already am aware of the date you've chosen. What I asked was not when you'll have a wedding, but when you'll be married."

The couple looked at each other. Tina took some comfort in the fact that Andre was also confused.

Pastor Davis looked at them for a few moments, seemingly

enjoying their anxiety. Finally, he broke the tension. "Marriage is not words or ceremony. It is commitment, actions, and communication. If you've made the commitment, you're married in the eyes of God whether you've said the words or not. So, are you committed to be married?" He put his hand up as they were both about to interject emphatically. "Are you committed to one another, not just for now, not just for the good days, but for the bad ones, and" with that he looked directly at Tina's belly, "and, very soon, the sleepless nights? Are you committed to working through problems with one another? Are you determined to stick it out through meddling in-laws, health problems, joblessness, differences of opinion, philosophies on life, on how to divide responsibilities, on how to raise your child, or children?"

Before they could interrupt, he went on "Don't answer now, and don't answer me. This question is for the two of you to consider. Answer it in your own hearts and be honest with yourselves. There's a reason why we say marriage is not an institution to be entered into lightly." After a momentary pause, he went on, "I don't believe couples often do enter into it lightly. But sometimes, they enter into it for the wrong reasons. Out of fear of being alone, fear of what might happen if they start over, many other fears."

Andre's voice was quiet. "I believe we are committed."

"I believe you are too. There are just a few things I want you to think about during the next few weeks. We'll get into some of the specifics later. For now, I have just one other question. Do you know what the prophet Lyle said?"

Tina looked at her husband-to-be. Now, Andre was smiling, and visibly more relaxed. Apparently, he'd heard this one before.

"Well, the good prophet Lyle Lovett said it this way. The pastor paused for effect before reciting, with exaggerated reverence: 'To the Lord let praises be. It's time for dinner now, let's go eat.' That's just another way of saying I'm hungry and you have enough to think about until next week. So let's all clasp hands in a moment of prayer."

Tina bowed her head, taking Andre's hand in her left and the pastor's in her right. She did have a lot to think about, but she was no longer nervous. Maybe it was just the power of suggestion, but suddenly, she was indeed hungry.

On her way down the road, Lucinda was hungry as well. More importantly, she was late. Lunch at her mother's was a weekly ritual, at least most Sundays, unless she could find a good excuse.

Her excuse for being late today wasn't going to cut it. She'd spent the morning with the last set of boxes, carting each up from the storage room and unloading them meticulously into the new bookcases. Each case was now just over half full, with space left over for what she calculated would be at least three years worth of new books. From Abbey to Zettel, it was a collection to be envied.

Now, though physically exhausted, she was as happy as she could remember. Her mother's house would be chaos, she well knew, but she was ready. She loved her nieces and nephews dearly, but the level of noise and general commotion was always a source of fatigue. This time however, she was determined to maintain serenity throughout the afternoon and despite her tardiness, get out in time to stop at the bookstore for the latest Diana Gabaldon paperback.

"You're late" Alma chimed in, the moment she opened the door.

"I know, I know. How mad is mom?"

"Quietly fuming, as usual. She says you need to get married so your husband can keep you on track."

"Not that again. Save me."

"You're on your own on this one. I'm already on her shit list. I had to move back in for a few weeks."

"You and Sal didn't work out?"

"Now you don't ask. Let's just say I'm here until I get a couple of paychecks. That is, unless you want a roommate."

Lucy was spared answering by a tornado of rampaging children, two boys and three girls, tied together with bedsheets. The youngest member of the little train, trailing the others, was little Ignacio, blindfolded by a pillow sham. He was stumbling along, trying to follow the others, but mostly getting dragged by his siblings and cousins. This might have been comical, but perhaps more problematic, the oldest, Lupe, was also blindfolded, and she was in the lead.

"Watch out!" Alma shouted.

Lucinda was more practical, saving baby Carlos from getting trampled. The child cooed at her, always happy to see his aunt. She cooed back and made faces at him until she noticed where the train was now heading. "Alma!"

Her sister had already seen and was redirecting the train just before it crashed into the 22 by 28 inch framed portrait of their father. She also grasped hold of the train's engine and pulled its blindfold off. Lupe's feet were still chugging along, prepared to restart the locomotive once her mother let go of her shoulders. Taking a cue, the other children, all except Ignacio, also started chugging their feet. "What did I tell you about blindfolds?" Alma chided. "Now get this train down the hall and watch where you're going."

"Aye Aye, captain" was the retort as the train restarted and made its way down the hall. The other children repeated their own "Aye Ayes" and the parade moved on.

Lucinda was still trying to catch her breath. As her sister reached for Carlos, she turned and handed her the bag of groceries and took the photograph instead. At that moment, their mother called from the kitchen. "Lucy, I know you're here. Where are my tortillas?"

"I'm bringing them mom. Remember, I'm the good daughter." Alma gave a smile to Lucinda, but she wasn't looking. Instead, she set her nephew down on the floor where he fussed for the lack of attention. She needed both hands to lift her father's portrait above the fireplace.

"I've told Mom several times. You have to be up high to be safe from these kids." Her eyes were glistening as she touched her fingers to her lips, then to her father's. Turning her attention back to Carlos, she lifted him high. "Come with me little man. Mom can't yell at me if you're with me." The boy giggled conspiratorially and settled into her arms as they headed together to the kitchen.

At lunch, her punishment was silence, though Lucinda knew it wouldn't last. Jaime came to her rescue with a reminder about the upcoming election. "Lucy, you saw who we recommended for city council, right?"

"Yes, I got the flyer. I might even vote for them."

"Who else would you vote for? Cervantes and Baker are the best of the lot."

"Why should I vote for someone just because they're Latino?"

"Baker is not Latino. And, the point of our group isn't to elect Latinos, at least not primarily. It's to elect people who will further the interests of the Latino community."

"And those differ from the rest of the community?"

"Not really. It's not about race, but about those who understand the needs of everyone and take all of our interests to heart. Some candidates are better . . . "

Ramira Fuentes broke the silence by dropping a rice spoon with a loud clang. "I'm sorry, I do believe we've forgotten to say grace. Lucinda, since you couldn't see fit to make it to mass this morning, perhaps you could do the honors?"

If a little sarcasm was the worst she'd have to deal with, she was getting off easy. "Of course, *mami*" she said, putting down her napkin and bowed her head reverently. "Bless you O Lord, and thank you for this day that we are able to be together and for these thy gifts we are here to receive. Amen."

"Amen," several voices repeated. Lucy could recite most of the prayers in her sleep, this one included. She hoped that this would put an end to her penalty, but no such luck. The prayer request was just her mother's opening serve.

"*Mija*, you know I would understand if you miss once in a while for something important, like if you had *a date*, or if you needed to do something for a friend, but to skip mass and be late for dinner just to put away some books, well, that just says something about your priorities. And it seems your family is not high enough on the list."

"I've already apologized *mami*. I just got caught up in things and wanted to finish. I didn't mean to be late."

"And then," her mother continued, apparently not having heard and just continuing with her own thought, "and then, you show up all sweaty and looking like you just got up."

"If I'd taken the time to shower, I would have been even later."

Lucinda didn't mean to whine; she just wanted out of this conversation.

"How do you ever expect to attract a *novio* if you don't fix yourself up? A shower, a little makeup, just a little effort, *mija*."

"Well, I don't come to family dinners to meet men anyway. Unless you want me to marry little Carlos here" she said, patting the back of the child on her knee. "Or Jaime."

Her brother was quick to pick up the cue. "I love you baby sister, just not that way" he interjected.

His wife took the bait as well. Netia was always nervous around any family conflict, and tried to deflect it with levity. "You stay away from my husband," she intoned with mock anger.

"Well, she may have to start looking under rocks soon if she doesn't get started."

Now, it was Lucinda's turn to drop a utensil. She looked at her mother, who remained defiant, then around the room for support. Her eyes landed on her sister's, but Alma looked away, almost smirking. Clearly, she was happy that her mother's anger had been deflected from her own situation. She got up quietly, handed Carlos to his father and stepped back from the table. Remembering her manners, she asked coldly, "May I be excused?"

"I'm sorry *mija*, I didn't mean it. Sit down please."

"No thank you. I'm not really hungry," she lied as she exited the dining room and stepped out to the patio.

"She's so sensitive," Alma piped in casually.

Her mother cut her off. "You haven't much room to talk yourself about maintaining relationships." After a short pause, she continued, "I'm not sure what I did wrong with you two girls. You've gone to opposite extremes and it won't serve either of you well." After another moment of silence, it was back to wounded mother mode, "Well, I suppose I should go after her."

It was Jaime's turn to step in. "No, let me. I think you've said enough." His mother only glared, but let him alone.

Jaime was a man of few words, much like his father. As he stepped onto the patio, he said nothing, but just slipped his arms around his sister's shoulders and waited, both of them staring out into the yard and watching the dogs mark the fences.

After a full minute, she finally spoke. "Why is this so important to her? Why can't she just leave me alone?"

"Would it sound like too much of a cliché if I said she worried about you?"

"Yes, and condescending to boot. I can take care of myself."

"Of course you can. Do you want to get married some day?"

"Maybe, someday, but not now, not today."

"Don't you get lonely?"

"Not you too," Lucinda stepped away, but only a few inches, and turned back to look at her brother.

"You know me better than that. I'm on your side. I just want to understand."

"Try understanding this and see if you can get her to: there is a difference between alone and lonely."

"And you're saying you like being alone and you're not lonely?"

"Yes. For now at least, that's exactly what I'm saying."

"Good enough for me."

With that, they both relaxed, and watched the dogs play.

**

Andrew did not play, and still, he could not pray.

Praying over food was not something he'd have done. Food came from the grocery store, and before that, from farmers. He was thankful for farmers in an abstract way, but would not have prayed to or for them, much less to a God of whom he saw no evidence.

He'd have been on the same page as Lucinda in terms of the difference between being alone and lonely. Andrew would never have called himself lonely. The solitude of his apartment was a haven, though that word was too close to heaven for him to actually use it. Refuge might be the term he'd have preferred.

Determined to stay in the apartment until he recovered or someone noticed his absence, he marked the time. The time between bouts of pain was valuable. And, it was getting shorter. He'd tried taking three pills every three hours, but that was going to drain his supply. Going into the mid-afternoon, the pain was returning, now moving up his body like ripples, calves, thighs, abdomen, on up. He was no longer experiencing sharp spasms that knocked him to his knees; now, the waves sent slow shudders of discomfort through every part of him. He was shivering now, partly from pain, but also, seemingly, cold for no reason.

He had hoped a nap might help, but he couldn't sleep. Between the pain and his lack of exercise, his body was confused and seemed to be working against him. By mid-afternoon, he remembered a recent dental appointment. The dentist had given him something for pain when he pulled his tooth; what had that been?

Rummaging through his medicine chest, he finally located the bottle. Tylenol with codeine, almost full. After that first day, there hadn't been much pain from the filling and he'd nearly forgotten about those pills. What a luxury! This would give him several more days to recover. He put two pills in his mouth and followed them with a swig of water. Staggering toward the bed, he paused, took one more pill and swallowed it dry.

Now, there was definitely no need to leave this apartment. Not for weeks. Maybe, he thought, settling under the covers, he wouldn't leave this room, this bed. *The world doesn't need me; I don't need the world.*

**

The newest nurses always work weekends, something Janice didn't mind, usually. But a double shift on a Sunday had her physically and anticipatorily exhausted. The walk home though was always relaxing, just as it was tonight. She was happy to take these shifts for those with spouses and kids and might take them the rest of her career, as she never expected to be in their category. Plus, she got to live vicariously through them on Mondays, hearing the stories of late night partying or middle of the night fevers, depending on who was doing the telling. It's possible that could be her life someday but for now, she was happy just to listen in.

The walk to work was only seven blocks, and she found it invigorating. It cleared her mind for the day. As often as not, there was no time to think during a busy shift, which was just fine by Janice; it made the day go by faster, or the night, as the case may be. And that same walk refreshed her mind on the way home, calming her nerves from whatever calamities the ER had afforded.

Distance had been on her mind a great deal lately. She realized tonight that she hadn't been more than two miles from her apartment in more than three months. It was nothing intentional, just that she'd been busy and there had been no need. It was nice to be able to keep the same place after college. The hospital was just a mile from WSU and her apartment almost halfway in between, almost as if planned to maximize practicality. The grocery store, the park where she stopped sometimes to feed the ducks, the hospital, and everything she needed were within a pretty small radius. She knew she should get out more, meet people perhaps, maybe even travel, but on a daily basis, the thought just didn't cross her mind.

With the summer over and the weather cooling, she pulled her sweater over her shoulders. Those seven blocks would seem longer when the snow started, farther than she'd want to walk when it got really deep. Having lived in Kansas her entire life, she was mostly unfazed by the weather, but did find it interesting how the same distance seems so different with the passage of a little time and the drop of a few degrees.

Salina was a little ways to the north, less than an hour and a half up the 135 when things were clear. Debbie had mentioned the other day that it was the perfect distance to be from your parents, "close enough if you need them, but far enough away that they'll never pop in without calling first, right?"

Janice had nodded because she still found the boss intimidating, but she found the whole idea ridiculous. The idea that her parents would pop in was laughable. In all her time in Wichita, they'd made the trip exactly once, for her nursing school graduation. They both looked like fish out of water the whole time, with Zeke standing around with his shoulders hunched most of the time and Olivia gawking at everything. She'd offered to take them some place nice for dinner, her treat, but after several suggestions, Zeke had insisted on going to Arby's, the same place he had his men's prayer group back home. Olivia had still seemed out of place, surprised that the floor plan was reversed from the one in Salina.

She supposed she'd call her parents if there was an emergency, like if she needed her appendix out or something. They were on emergency forms because she couldn't leave the spaces blank. But she couldn't really imagine they'd be much help. What would they do after all, sit by her bedside and pray? They might even bring Pastor Cartwright with them; what an embarrassment that would be.

The weather would be a good excuse not to go home for Christmas, but her mother was insistent. She knew she'd have to work Christmas day, and probably, hopefully, the days before and after, but she'd find a way to make an appearance some time that week, like it or not. Even if the roads were good, it would probably take twice as long as usual to get there, what with the snow and the holiday traffic.

She wished Andrew would come, but that would probably never happen again. She doubted he'd ever set foot back in Kansas. She'd visit him in California, but he'd never invited her. Janice still found it hard to imagine him there, stick-up-his-butt Andrew in sunny and relaxed California? She still couldn't picture it even though he been there for several years. He never talked about what he did there and maybe he didn't do much of anything. He mentioned a girlfriend a while back, but the next time she'd talked to him, he said they'd broken up, but didn't want to talk about it. She couldn't really blame him, she supposed. It wasn't like she shared the details of her dating life with him either, such as it was, or wasn't, if she was really being honest.

So, Andrew was less than three hours away by air, but he might as well be on Mars. Once more, distance is relative.

She wondered why she wanted him around at the holidays anyway. They were supposed to be a buffer for each other from parental nosiness, but it never really worked out that way. Somehow a fight always broke out, usually between Dad and Andrew. Those two couldn't be any different or any more the same, though if she said that to either of them it would start another argument.

Olivia was another story, she just wanted them all to be at home and she couldn't take a hint. During her last visit, just a few weeks after graduation, Olivia had given her job listings for Salina Regional Health Center. Janice tried to remind her that she'd already had taken a job in Wichita, but when she got home, she found the ad, right there in her suitcase, tucked between her underwear and bras so she couldn't miss it.

Distance must always be the same for Olivia. She probably had an even shorter radius than Janice, home, church, library, maybe the grocery store once a week. Like Zeke and Andrew, they were probably more alike than Janice liked to think. Maybe she should do something about that, change her patterns, but she'd have no idea where to start.

But for now, she didn't have to. It seemed she'd just left the ER and already her apartment door was within sight. Placing the key in the lock just under the door for 3F, she yawned and walked through, another day complete.

**

Each time the waiting room door opened, all three of their heads turned. But, it was never the doctor, or even a nurse to report progress, as had been promised. It was just other patients and their waiting families, or orderlies on breaks getting candy from the vending machine. Two nurses had walked by once, laughing and talking, but that had been so early into the surgery, they knew not to take any meaning from it. Four hours later, another nurse had walked out of the operating room, her face grave but noncommittal. Harry and his father were talking at the time, so they didn't see. Ashlynn said nothing.

The operation had been going on for well over six hours and though none of them expressed it, worry was in all of their minds. As the door opened once more, a small man with a beard walked through, looking around. He bore a hospital name badge that said 'Clergy' and the look on his face was inquisitive. "Jamison?" he asked.

"Yes?" they all three piped up at once. If the hospital was sending a minister, that couldn't be a good sign, could it?

"Good afternoon. I am Imam Javed. I am so sorry it has taken so long for me to reach you. There was a mix-up and I just found out about Kevin's operation. May I sit with you?"

"Of course" Kevin Senior replied. "What did you say your role was at the hospital?"

"I am an Imam at the local mosque in town. An Imam is like the Muslim equivalent of a pastor or minister if you are a Christian or a Rabbi if you are Jewish." His tone was patient and quiet as though he'd been through this explanation many times before. "May I ask if your family has a religious faith?"

"We're not really church-goers" Kevin Senior replied, almost apologetically.

"That is quite alright. There is a lot of variety in this community of course. There are several Christian ministers who spend time at the hospital, of various denominations, and members of several other faiths as well. For those without an affiliation, whoever happens to be present at the time usually tries to stop by and visit with the family and tend to their needs. If you'd prefer, I could call someone closer to your own preference?"

"I don't think that is necessary. We appreciate you stopping by Imam. Do you have any news of my son?"

"Most likely, I don't know much more than you do, but I will check with the nurse's station in a few minutes to see if I can get an update. I was told his procedure began at about 2:30 and was expected to take a few hours. I don't have a prognosis, but they did say his condition was very serious."

"They said at least three or four hours, but it's been five hours and forty-two minutes," Harry piped in.

"I wouldn't worry just yet. Often, these things take longer than originally thought. And sometimes, they wait until they have the patient in the recovery room and the doctor has had a chance to make a few notes before they inform the family." After a moment's pause, he continued. "Would you like me to pray with you?"

"We don't really . . . " Harry started, but his father broke him off.

"It would be just fine. We haven't much religious faith, but it certainly couldn't hurt. I don't really know your procedures. Do we lean forward or?"

"I appreciate your kindness, but it is I who will adapt to your traditions—even if you do not have a particular faith. Perhaps we could just hold hands and have a moment of silent prayer, each in our own manner."

Ashlynn reached to her sides and took Kevin Senior's hand in her left, Harry's in her right. The Jamisons each clasped hands with the Imam. Her eyes closed, she could hear him whispering a silent prayer. Harry clenched her hands more tightly and she felt Kevin Senior shuddering with quiet sobs. The small circle became a haven of sorts, a refuge like none she'd experienced. Her own tears flowed, silently and painlessly down her cheeks. She felt her breaths lengthen and the tension she'd been holding gradually dissipate. For a moment, she thought she might fall asleep.

Finally, with a motion, Imam Javed broke the prayer circle and pulled up a chair from the next aisle. Kevin Senior was wiping tears from his eyes and seemed embarrassed. Harry still clutched Ashlynn's hand and moved closer. She clenched back and gave him a reassuring smile.

"Thank you for praying with me," the Imam said. "Sometimes, I think I get as much out of this experience as the families I work with. I will check on your son in just a few minutes, but for the moment, my concern is with you. Can you tell me if there is anything I can get for you, anyone I could call? I do want to be of service if I can."

"We thank you, but I think we have all we need. We're just anxious for news."

"Of course. In a while, I can bring some food up from the cafeteria if you like. Many families neglect to eat at times like this and do not want to leave this room. But nourishment is still important. Do you mind if I ask how Kevin Junior came to be here? I understand there was some kind of accident."

There was quiet for a moment, so Ashlynn tried to make herself useful. "Yes, it was a bike accident. Well, bike and car actually. My car." She added that last part not sure if she could be heard or if she wanted to be.

"Motorcycle actually." Harry had found his voice. "It was not far from here, actually. He was turning left from Bascom onto Hedding and the other driver . . . " Harry looked at Ashlynn apologetically, not noticing the shock on her face. "Well, I guess she didn't see him."

"I see," the Imam noted. "I'm afraid these things happen all too often, especially with motorcycles."

"Kevin loved, loves that bike," Kevin Senior said. "He always said he used it because it got better mileage, but I think it was the closest he ever was to feeling rebellious."

"Wait," Ashlynn's voice was a whisper, her throat tight. She couldn't get any more words out for several moments. "Mo . . ." was all that came out. Harry put his arms around her shoulders and she took two deep, long breaths, then a third. "I hit a bicycle." This time the words came out flatly and she looked around waiting for the expressions of accusation.

The Imam was considering his words. Kevin Senior and Harry didn't have any, though Harry's arms hadn't left Ashlynn. She was sobbing.

"It wasn't me, not me, but then who did I?" The rest was gibberish and Kevin Senior took her hand while Harry continued to hold her. Imam Javed knelt in front of the family, giving them a moment to process.

Several minutes passed this way. Ashlynn's sobs subsided and she gradually caught her breath, then hugged first Kevin Senior, then Harry. The Imam stepped back to his seat, giving them a respectful distance. Ashlynn clutched herself together and shuddered, tears giving way to a nervous kind of half laugh-half cry.

After another minute, Harry stiffened suddenly and looked at her. "You don't have to be here," he said quietly, the first hint of fear she'd seen in his eyes yet.

Ashlynn took his hand again and looked at him. "Where else would I be?"

With that, the small family circle closed tightly again and their advisor went off in search of information.

DREAMS

As Andrew's determination slipped into intransigence, and his world narrowed from his adopted city of acquaintances and strangers, to his small apartment, to his bed, days turned into nights into days, bleeding into indecipherable combinations of the two. But just, as has been said, as fenced yards aren't hole cards, neither are bedrooms sanctuaries. For once eyes are closed and consciousness given up, willingly or not, dreams come. And dreams have no respect for boundaries, doors or fortresses, either of mind or body. They come to all. They came to Andrew in those next days as they came to those he knew or had crossed his path or been affected in some peripheral way by his seemingly ineffectual life.

**

The wind blew softly through Lucinda's room as she drifted off. Andrew was with her, as he often was. The two of them lazed quietly in a sailboat, and the seas were clear. It was a common and enjoyable dream for Lucinda, whether it came to her at night, as now, or during her work day.

When it was a daydream, she often wondered if she should name the boat. In dreams, she had on occasion seen the name Dawn Treader on the side and mast, though the physical attributes of the boat bore next to no resemblance to those of the C.S. Lewis classic. This was a small schooner, if it could even be called that. From time to time, Andrew got up and adjusted the sails, though the details of exactly how he did so did not concern Lucinda.

Though the waters were calm, the wind began to pick up slightly, just enough to ease the warmth of the sun. Lucy was reading in her deck chair on the right, Andrew with his book on the left. The pages were blowing and though it made it tough to read, she wasn't bothered. In fact, she laughed at the adventure. Andrew did the same.

Shortly, she finished her book, called out "trade," and laughing together, the couple tossed their books to each other. Andrew found himself with Paoilini's *Brisingr* while Lucy took *East of Eden*. Lucinda was thrilled that she'd found a mate who was so generous. He traded whenever she finished, regardless of how much he'd read of his book. And, in truth, he was never finished. She read almost twice as fast as he did. Occasionally, he teased her about it, but there was always pride in his eyes.

Generally though, Andrew spoke little in her dreams. His presence was quiet, a companion with whom she could speak or not, as she chose. Lucy, on the other hand, and unlike in her conscious life, was a chatterbox. Not all of the time, not even most of the time, but most nights, at least part of the evening was spent with her regaling her love with all of her hopes and fears, telling him of the books she read, the unexpected plot twists, what she thought was coming next. Her dreams were busiest when she was in the middle of a series as she turned over each possible next step the characters could take. *The Hunger Games* had been a fertile example as she'd picked up each book just after they came out, the second and third of the trilogy the minute the store opened, so she'd had months to wait in between each, months in which she could and did contemplate each possible scenario for how the storyline would resolve itself. With each of these, Andrew was her sounding board, listening patiently, asking few questions, but always interested.

These were no lovers riding off into the sunset. While romance was certainly in the air, it was of a mild, comforting sort. What's more, this sailboat always seemed to be heading east. Whether it was morning or evening in her dream, the sun at their backs or in their eyes, they headed east. There was never talk of a destination, just delight in the journey and the glorious setting.

The weather was always good, though today there were a few clouds to be seen, the genteel kind, of a vaguely non-threatening sort, the type that one stared at as they went by and imagined the various shapes as creatures, both real and mythical.

Lucinda rarely looked back. Her view went directly ahead, sometimes off to the sides at landmarks , but most often, her thoughts and her eyes were focused on the spare contents of the boat itself, its simple sails, the chairs, her companion, and the cooler of drinks between them, piled with her books and Andrew's.

Today, the clouds were particularly well defined. She laughed as her eyes moved south and counted off the creatures she saw: a Chinese dragon complete with a flaming pearl and lengthy tail, a unicorn slowly transforming itself into a turtle, a gorgon that should have frightened her, but which, she found silly. Then there was a child angel, similar to those stone ones her mother collected for her garden; that she did find a bit creepy.

As she continued to turn her head south, following the clouds, Lucy let out a soft gasp. The next cloud was the clearest yet, its image unmistakable. Her father stared at her, his eyes warm as always. As the surprise of seeing him again gave way, she was amazed at the detail in the layered nimbostratus cloud. There were more than a dozen shades to be seen, varying between opaque white and ashen grey. Her father's mustache, deep black when she was a child, salt and pepper by the time he passed, was perfectly outlined somewhere in between. His smile gazed down at her as though welcoming her into his lap as he had when she was a toddler, reading from *Go Dog Go*, then she reading back to him at the age of three and a half.

Lucinda thought of grabbing Andrew's hand, but kept the moment to herself. Her father noticed and gave a slight nod in Andrew's direction and winked at his daughter. The nod might have been one of approval, or perhaps simply of acknowledgement. His face slowly began to dissolve, the features still visible, but less sharp. But just before fading away completely, he winked again, puffed up his lips, and blew. He wasn't blowing her a kiss as she first thought. No, she soon realized, the boat was picking up speed. He'd blown a puff of air in their direction, one what was turning the gentle breeze into a constant wind, one which moved the boat unmistakably eastward. She raised her hand for a moment, a tear in her eye and the word *no* on her lips, then she dropped the hand, as the tear fell to the deck, leaving her cheek dry, and said nothing. Quietly, but resolutely, she turned around, faced the morning sun, reached to her left and grasped her companion's hand. He smiled, she knew, though she did not turn to see it. No words need be spoken.

**

Calm was not the word you'd have used to describe Andrew in these days. Though his room was as quiet as Lucinda's, and though he was as alone as she was, perhaps more so and more intentionally, he was restless. Sleep achieved through the continual use of medication tends to be of the fitful sort. As he drifted in and out of his uneasy reverie, his dreams did the same. He had come to the certainty that he was never leaving the apartment again. That is, he would not leave unless someone, somehow intervened. His experiment would continue until such time as his absence, or at least his existence, was noticed.

But it wasn't noticed, or so it would seem. So, he drifted. He suppressed the pain, stayed in bed, and drifted. The body within his mind floated, not that kind of floating from those in near-death experiences who leave their bodies and return, but rather a leaving that brooks no return, a float that does not go into the light, but into a darkness. He didn't float above his bed and body and into the ceiling, but instead just floated into a nothingness, not away from the particular setting of his apartment and into another location, but rather away from any connection with his fellow humans.

But, there were humans in this new place, after a moment, he saw them. There were a dozen of them, men and women both, then two dozen, then three. Floating into the nameless space with no boundaries or walls, but somehow small and shrinking, he looked into the faces of the nameless. They looked as well, vaguely in his direction. They neither smiled nor frowned, evinced no recognition or acknowledgement. Their faces were grey, almost melting into the walls. In fact, one could not identify an ethnicity among them, a cultural background, an accent, nationality, or region. Each had their hands at their sides, not moving, looking through him or just to one side or the other. Gradually, they began to look more like one another, the men and women indistinguishable, even their eyes misting over with a similarly-shaded grey haze, preventing visual penetration. He thought of reaching out, but his hands were heavy and getting heavier. So, he closed his eyes and spun. Revolving slowly, he assumed for a while that his velocity would increase, like clothes in a washing machine, but it didn't. Instead, he rotated slowly like the second hand of a clock, but counter-clockwise. He counted off one minute, two, three, seventeen. He should open his eyes before losing count, but no, he wouldn't. He felt, rather than saw, the absence of his new companions, those strangers he'd never know. When they were gone, perhaps he would be as well.

**

Pete was floating and spinning as well, but for different reasons. He usually had only three or four beers each evening, six at most, unless it was the weekend. On a Friday night, he'd usually have found some friends to hang out with. But he didn't like to go to bars by himself. Sykes had been avoiding him and Gil Ballard was turning into a family man, hardly wanting to party at all.

He tried a few college buddies he hadn't seen in a while, but no dice there either. To a man, they were either busy or had moved on from the frat lifestyle. Pete was beginning to think he'd been little more than a hanger-on, someone they tolerated, but neither needed nor truly enjoyed. This worsened his melancholia, so he opened a tenth beer.

There was nothing but crap on TV. He was rarely home on Friday nights, so he was not familiar with any of the programs. He tried a couple of sitcom reruns, but they couldn't hold his attention. Eventually, he amused himself as he had as a child, holding down the channel button and watching the shows flicker by at lightning speed. For a moment, he thought he might be able to make a story of the rapidly flashing images, but he simply didn't have the energy, or at this point, the coherence of thought.

Pete's bachelor apartment was furnished simply. He thought of himself as a throwback, a man from an earlier time. Posters adorning the wall included one of the Joe Montana-led 49er Super Bowl team from 1984, a movie poster from Fight Club and a Tremors poster, signed personally by Kevin Bacon. On one wall was the classic babe poster of all time, the Farrah Fawcett swimsuit photo from 1976. This had adorned his father's dorm wall and had been given to him when he was accepted to college. It was worn by time and touch, but a treasure.

As he drifted off, the beer dribbling down his shirt and drool dripping from the side of his lip, the Farrah image flashed before him, moving his way, no, she was swimming toward him like Phoebe Cates in *Fast Times at Ridgemont High*, his favorite movie. As she emerged from the pool, he saw with horror that the look on her face wasn't the sultry smile Cates had shown in the film, but a smirk, gradually moving toward a derisive laugh. Soon, she was pointing, pointing at Pete, his Barcalounger, his stained shirt and his cooler of beer. Pete knew he was in an alcohol haze, but still, he was confused. The signs of young bachelorhood should be a source of pride, not ridicule.

But now it wasn't just Phoebe Cates laughing, it was Farrah as well. He was in a bar, the one down the street from campus that had been a second home during the frat days. It wasn't just the two famed actresses either, but a gauntlet of women stood between him and the bathroom. Suddenly, he had to go, and badly. Crossing his legs, he walked slowly toward the men's room door, Fawcett on his left and Cates on his right. As he passed them, he saw he knew the other women as well, old girlfriends mostly, the short blond he'd had a one night stand with several months back, the sorority girl he'd convinced that he was a member of the mayor's staff, the dark-eyed single mother who'd slapped him when he called her a MILF. Behind the rows of women were rows, two or three deep, of men. All of his old frat buddies were there, some hooting and shaking their heads, others bent over in laughter or talking and pointing. Gil Ballard had one of his sons on his shoulders, the other in his arms. He was talking to the latter, who looked in Pete's direction and nodded with knowing disapproval. Duane Sykes was there, his arm around a young woman at least six inches taller than himself. He gave Pete a knowing look, pulled a condom out of his pocket and winked. *Even you, Sykes?* he thought, his mood sinking a bit further.

He turned away as quickly as he could when he saw Aimee, his first college girlfriend, the one who'd kicked him out of her dorm room when he came too soon. His high school prom date was there, the one he'd fallen in love with, but had turned him down when he asked her to forgo Berkeley so they could go to college together. After several moments of talking with her friends, none of whom he could name, but all of whom reminded him of high school classmates, she met his eyes, lifted up her hand and showed him the sapphire engagement ring. An arrogant smile spread across her face as she lowered her hand and turned back to her friends.

He finally made it through the bathroom door and made his way to the urinal. He was surprised, considering how packed the bar was, that the bathroom was empty. Unbuttoning his pants, he reveled in the luxuriousness of his urinary relief, his embarrassment waning as his bladder emptied.

Looking up, he saw that above the urinal was a photo cut from a magazine of a topless woman, her breasts large and high. But it wasn't just any woman; it was Ellie Davenport. Pete knew this photo couldn't be real. He'd never seen Ellie's breasts, though he'd always wanted to, but he knew they weren't this large unless she wore sports bras every day, and she didn't. Ellie was smiling down at him, her eyes alluring. In the space of a minute, a new series of images flashed in front of him, Ellie rolling her chair over to his cubicle, patting him on the shoulder, manipulating him into buying her coffee. How had he missed the signs? In short order, his reinterpretation of her every behavior became his new reality. Filled with confidence, Pete flushed, then stepped over to the sink and turned on the faucet.

The cold washed over him as Pete awoke, finding himself shivering in a puddle of urine and beer. He was embarrassed for a moment, then remembered he was alone. *But I won't be for long*, he thought as he walked over for a towel to wipe the chair. Grabbing the last beer from the cooler on his way, he stumbled at first, then slowed down, realizing it hadn't been as long as he'd thought and he wasn't quite sober. Skipping the towel, he grabbed his phone instead.

Ellie's voice was groggy when she picked up, but her annoyance came through loud and clear. "Pete, what the hell? It's 2:30 in the morning."

"Elsie . . . " he began, then remembering, "sorry, I mean Ellie, Eleanor Davenport, will you go out with me?"

"What? Pete, no. It's the middle of the night."

He sat down again, and, realizing this called for seriousness, tried to gather his wits. "I don't mean now. How about Friday?"

"It is Friday, or at least it was until a couple of hours ago. Pete, just go to bed, you're obviously drunk. Don't embarrass yourself anymore."

"I'm just a little drunk, but I know what I want. I want you. It doesn't have to be Friday. You name the day." He paused to burp, turning his head, hoping (vainly) that she couldn't hear. Noticing the odor, he tried to remember if smell travelled through the phone. As Ellie fell silent, Pete searched his mind for the right words. He settled on what he hoped was somber formality. "Ellie Davenport, I'd like to take you to dinner one night. I'll wear a jacket and tie, take you to some place nice, maybe Mannesser."

Manresa was a place Ellie talked about often, but she hadn't been able to afford. She'd tried to get G-dub to have the annual bonus party there, but no dice. "We need a place where we can cut loose" he'd told her, "not some snooty place with $200 bottles of wine. We'd get thrown out of there inside of ten minutes, especially with Sykes and Massey around."

Ellie was speechless for a moment, touched at least, by the gesture. "Pete. Let's talk about this another time when we're both sober and awake."

"Promise me Ellie. Promise you'll go out with me."

"You're not helping your case. We'll talk about it another day. Frankly though, I don't think you're my type."

"You're exactly my type though. You're the one; I know you are. Ellie . . . I think I'm in love with you."

"Pete, you can't be serious."

"Serious as a heart attack. Which I'm going to have by the way if you don't agree to go out with me."

"Pete, threats don't work unless you threaten something I actually care about." Ellie paused; that sounded callous even for her. "Pete, if you'll hang up right now and get some sleep, I promise we can talk about a lunch date, maybe in a month or two if you're still sure it's what you want." *Am I really giving up Manresa* she asked herself? It didn't matter; this was the right thing to do. Besides, Pete couldn't afford Manresa any more than she could. She'd seen the books and he made at least six thousand less than she did.

"I'll wait," Pete said, his intensity coming through despite the slur. "I'll wait exactly one month and then I'm going to ask you out again Ellie. You can mark it on your calendar. One month."

"I'll mark it Pete," she replied patiently, wondering if he'd even remember this conversation in the morning. It would probably be less awkward if he didn't. "Good night Petey."

"Good night Elsie," he replied. Then he put the phone down and ran to the bathroom to throw up.

**

Olivia had been sitting in her own Barcalounger for as long as she could remember. She must have rocked, forward and back, at least a million times in that chair. It was her comfort spot. She looked down in her lap; Andrew had finally gone to sleep some time ago and was beginning to stir again. He opened his eyes, raised the left brow as though curious then turned to look at the wall. She hummed as she kept rocking and soon he was asleep again.

It seemed just minutes later that she was rocking again; maybe she'd never stopped. Now, it was Janice in her arms, her hands and elbows thrashing in vain to get out of the swaddling blanket. It was something Olivia insisted upon; the doctor had said that babies sleep better swaddled and she took his advice seriously. Andrew was on the floor, intently studying his Davey and Goliath coloring book. She just knew her little boy was a smart one. He stayed within the lines already and he wasn't quite three years old. He switched back and forth between the page he was coloring and the cover of the book, making sure he was using the right colors for each character and scene fixture. It was easy for the little boy and dog character; he colored them the same as the cover. But the parents weren't on the cover, nor were some of the other characters. Each time he started a new page, he paused for a moment, trying to remember from the television show which colors should be used.

Janice stirred briefly and Olivia looked down. It was no longer Janice, but Mitzy, her Pomeranian puppy, who yipped each day about this time until the kids came through the door. Olivia looked out the window and sure enough, here they came, Andrew dutifully holding his sister's hand just as she had instructed. Her first week of kindergarten had gone well, though Olivia had cried as she dropped her daughter off on Monday, as much from the fact that her daughter didn't cry as from the separation itself. "Better let them in," she told Mitzy, but the dog just curled up and went back to sleep.

Sleep was all Mitzy seemed to do lately, but that's just because she's getting older. Seventeen is pretty old for any dog, isn't it? The vet had said that a year or two more was about as long as she could expect to hold on and that had been last year, but Olivia couldn't imagine putting her down, especially because Zeke had said he didn't want another dog. This saddened her, but she really couldn't blame him given how Mitzy had nipped on the heels of his pants almost every day until recently. Now, she spent most of her day in Olivia's lap, right here in this chair.

The door opened quietly as Janice came in, with another load of college catalogs peeking out of her suitcase. This made her nervous; there must be thirty or forty of those catalogs stacked up on the desk in Janice's room. What was worse, she seemed to be only looking at the ones from far away. Andrew had sent her ones from San Jose State and Stanford, which he said was nearby, but Olivia had looked it up and the two colleges were at least 25 miles apart. Andrew said her grades were good enough, but she couldn't imagine visiting such a fancy college or why anyone would pay so much. Her friends had sent her information from Oklahoma and Missouri and one friend who'd graduated the previous year, one of whom Zeke had never approved, had even sent two from Buffalo, New York. Imagine her little girl in such a big city!

She'd tried to be subtle and had moved the Kansas brochures to the top of the stack, but they always seemed to end up on the floor. The Kansas Wesleyan catalog was now being used as a doorstop and Janice had broken out in laughter when Zeke had brought home a pamphlet from Salina Area Technical College, as though such a school were beneath her status. Lately, Olivia had given up on the idea of keeping her daughter at home or even in Salina, but was still hoping to convince her to stay within the state.

As Janice went to study the catalogs, Mitzy jumped awkwardly down to follow and seemed to vanish in thin air. Janice was gone too now, she knew. The Barcalounger itself was getting older; she could tell by the squeak. Still, she continued to rock, closing her eyes to the empty room around her. But, as the darkness invaded her senses, the squeak got louder. It was now present on both the up and down-swings of the chair. She dared not open her eyes, yet the longer she kept them closed, the louder the rocker squeaked. She gripped the chair's arms, just where cloth and wood met, holding so tightly, she thought her knuckles would pop. Still, the volume of the squeak increased, and it became constant, just changing tone as she rocked up and then down. Squeak might be the wrong word now, it was a screech almost, one unlike any animal she'd ever heard; no living thing expressed itself this loudly or constantly. Her hands were trembling and she thought for a moment her eardrums would burst.

Finally, there was a pop and her grip loosened. She thought at first that she'd broken a finger bone, but it was actually the arm of the chair that had splintered in her arms. Opening her eyes, Olivia saw, not the splintered chair arms, nor the open window through which she'd been staring seemingly just moments before. It wasn't the living room at all, but rather the ceiling of her bedroom that met her gaze. Looking to her right, she noted the comforting sight of flannel pajamas and a balding head, her husband's body curled into the fetal position in which he often slept. Breathing a bit more deeply, Olivia wondered if she'd be able to get back to sleep. She reached over and grasped Zeke's hand. He muttered something not quite intelligible as she curled up next to him, untwined her hand from his, but kept it on his upper arm. She was not sleeping, but clutching tightly to the comforting silence of the room.

KNOW MY NAME

**

Zeke was alone is his dream, and it was the day he'd been preparing for. He stood before the throne, awaiting word. There were two other chairs, perhaps they were thrones as well, to the right and left. He peered to each side, trying to look around the obstacles, to get a better view. No living man had seen the face of God, he knew, but if he were here, that would mean he was no longer living. Certainly, he'd now have the opportunity to gaze upon his good Lord's face, assuming he had proved himself worthy.

As he waited, he went over his own mental tally book. He'd done as well as he thought he could, certainly better than most. He had lived an honest and truthful life. Yes, there was that one exception, but it was just the one, and surely it wouldn't be considered a continuing or ongoing sin. He'd served the Lord, attended church, and done all he could to support the congregation and hold to the highest of standards. He'd remained faithful to his wife, as had she since that first day. He'd worked hard all of his life, without complaint. His children, he'd raised as best he could in this corrupt world. If they'd varied some from the path he'd laid out, he hoped that would not be laid at his feet. He'd done what he could.

Awaiting word, he tried again to get a glimpse of the face of his Lord. The Greek pillars lining the backdrop seemed to be in the way, although this was strange as they weren't between Zeke and the godhead before him. Beyond the pillars though, clouds, puffy white and grey, seemed always to be in the wrong place, though again, it hardly seemed there were enough clouds to prove an obstacle.

The most he could see were hands, white and perfect, three sets of hands. The pair on the left was obscure, mysterious, barely recognizable as hands. The pair on the right was familiar, holding to the sides of the throne, the holes were visible even from this distance, the scar on his side sill prominent.

But in the middle, the hands were holding the famed Book of Judgment. The hands paused on a page, then scrolled through, the occupant of the chair seeming to pause only for a moment on each page, satisfied with what He saw. Page after page went like that, with Zeke allowing himself some hope. At the end though, the hands scrolled back to that earlier page at which they'd paused, the one less than halfway through the book. Surely that one thing wouldn't prevent . . .

The book was closed now and the verdict seemed to be in. Surely, he'd get the view he'd been searching for now and the sound. Zeke had always wondered what the Lord's voice would sound like. He presumed the tone would be baritone, or perhaps even bass, though a gentle one.

But as the hands closed over the top of the book, they seemed to be rising, or was the throne itself rising? Or, was Zeke falling? He couldn't tell; all he knew was that the distance between himself and his Lord was increasing. He reached out, he reached up, but to no avail. He began to feel a crackling beneath his feet, then a warmth, though the rest of his body was suddenly cold. His descent was slow, but that Zeke was falling was now certain. His thoughts went now from confusion and worry over what decisions he could have made differently to the permanence of his fate. He tried to resign himself, but eternity was . . . eternal. His knees buckled, but he locked them, the muscles of his calves and thighs tightening to the point of cramping. Zeke worried that he would fall, and finally he did, tumbling backward head over heels in a way a man of his age never should. Strange that he would think about his dignity when his eternal soul was damned, damned forever.

Zeke woke with a start, which wasn't unusual as that's how he usually woke. He took several breaths to calm himself, removed Olivia's hand from his arm and shoulder, then patted hers affectionately. In a few minutes, he'd need to get up. Perhaps he'd have a bit of time for prayer this morning.

**

Andrew wondered how long he'd slept, though maybe sleep was the wrong word. He'd been in bed the whole time, but he was sure he'd drifted away somehow and for some unknown amount of time, minutes, hours, maybe days. He was dropping now, no longer spinning, but falling at an accelerating rate. The walls had closed in, but they weren't really walls, just a vague blackness that was somehow solid despite its haziness. He heard the same crackling noise his father had, began feeling the same increasing warmth. His reaction was different though.

Surprising himself, Andrew began to laugh. It wasn't just a laugh, but an uproarious whoop, loud and exuberant. No one in his life would have recognized this Andrew. He giggled like a schoolchild, guffawed like his coworkers after several drinks, and continued to laugh until his body ached. *Old Zeke turned out to be right after all, he thought*, the irony strangely delicious. As he fell faster and faster, the paradox that had been his life became only more hilarious. His eternal damnation had been inevitable all along, he realized.

As he continued to fall, he shrieked with laughter, his sides aching, cramps forming along them, rippling through his oblique abdominal muscles, through his back and legs, traveling up, through his pectoral muscles, then the deep group along the middle of his back, through the traversospinalis, the erector spinae, to the splenius near the base of his neck, sharpening there and pulsing along his brain stem like a parasite from a Heinlein novel. Yet still he laughed, boisterously and without pretense, laughed until the pulses formed in various symmetrical points in his body, two along his sides, two more in his calves, two in the pectorals, two in the lower back, and the strongest, the one that seemed to be the source of it all, even if it was the last to develop, fixed at the back of his head.

His acceleration continued, the wind blowing by, sourceless, but continuous, it was as though there were a vacuum below him, perhaps he was being sucked down, being pulled as much as falling. Then, he stopped. It was sudden, a slam almost, though there wasn't an impact or an increase in the pain, just continued throbs, rhythmic and steady. Andrew opened his eyes, saw only blackness around him, no source of the pain, nor a solid substance that might have prompted an end to his descent. He tried to determine if the warmth he'd been feeling had increased. It certainly should have if he was falling to where he thought. But he could tell nothing. Not that the heat hadn't increased; the pain was simply obscuring his ability to sense anything. He looked around again, simple nothingness. He closed his eyes once more and resumed laughing.

This time though, his laugh seemed to break the silence and he felt a warm, dampness beneath him. He opened his eyes again and saw his bedroom. The pain had returned, more palpable now in its actuality. He needed more sleep he knew, though he feared it. Yet he wouldn't get it with spasms rolling through his body, up from his feet to his calves to every part of his body, such that he couldn't relax enough to turn to his side for several minutes. Summoning what seemed to be his last remaining reserves of strength, he leaned over to find the two pill bottles on the nightstand. There was no water, so he gulped down the last four codeine tablets dry. Knocking over the other bottle, he was thankful the lid hadn't been on it as he hadn't the strength to get past a childproof cap. But three pills fell out on the nightstand, maybe the last of his Vicodin, and he grasped them and brought them to his mouth, but two of the three dropped on the pillow. Andrew left them. He could get more medication in a minute. For now, he just needed to rest. So, without further ado, much less laughter, he turned over and went back to sleep.

**

This teacher was dreamy. All of the girls thought so. When she could break her gaze away from his face and look around the classroom, she saw that every student, not just the girls, was captivated. Every eye in the room was glued to Mr. Jamison as he lectured. His style was interactive, and he was calling on students each time he raised a question. Today's discussion was about Roosevelt, Keynes and the economic policies of the Great Depression. With any other teacher, that would be boring, not to mention over the heads of middle-schoolers, but not with Mr. Jamison. He made tough issues seem easy, explaining sometimes, but usually letting things become clear with discussion. When he asked a question, at least half the hands in the room went up.

The one he posed had to do with the goals of the Works Progress Administration. He wanted the students to list a few of the projects the agency had completed. It was a test of whether they'd done the reading, and the students were eager to prove themselves. Ashlynn raised her hand along with several others, but Mr. Jamison called on the boy two rows to her right. He hadn't even seen her. The boy named off four or five projects when Mr. Jamison had only asked for three. Show off!

He walked back up the aisle again, challenging the students on the constitutionality of the Social Security Act of 1935. They knew he was playing devil's advocate, but he played it from both sides. Most times, when political topics like this came up, the students could not figure out which side he was on. In one minute, he was arguing the need for the program, the next, he pushed them to figure out where exactly in the constitution such a thing was allowed. Ashlynn raised her hand several times, but he was on the other side of the room and didn't notice.

He took that constitutional argument to the next issue, Keynes and government spending. Most of the students took the side of John Maynard in these arguments, but Mr. Jamison asked them again, where did the constitution allow this? One of her classmates piped up, "Are you an originalist or a textualist on the constitution, Mr. Jamison?" Another show off!

"There are good arguments for both of those, as well as for those who say that the constitution is a living document. I'm more concerned with what you think."

"You're the teacher. Tell us what we're supposed to think."

"Wrong." Mr. Jamison was at the front of the room and hit his buzzer, which always got a laugh out of the students. He did it so good naturedly; they never felt insulted. "My job is not to tell you what to think. I'm here to help you learn how to think. I'm not interested in whether you agree with me, but how you construct your arguments."

When he got to the "how you construct your arguments" part, several students recited it with him. They'd heard all of this before.

"Now," he continued, "moving on from constitutionality, who can tell me how the Keynesian programs are *economically* justified?"

With this, Ashlynn's hand shot up. She had studied this on her own, not just in the book, but on the Internet. She could really impress Mr. Jamison with her knowledge of Keynes and his theories, even how they might apply to the current economic situation. There weren't as many hands up this time; the issue was a bit complex for middle school. Still, Mr. Jamison didn't seem to see her. She was waving her left hand right in front of him and he seemed to be looking right through her toward the back of the room. None of them had her enthusiasm and this was the issue she'd been waiting for. Ashlynn waved both hands in the air as he came down her aisle, almost right in his face. Still, he looked past her. "Javier, maybe you can enlighten us."

Javier did OK on the question she supposed, but she was barely listening. How could she get his attention? Ashlynn looked down at her outfit, the designer camisole over the striped skirt, calf-length boots lined with cashmere, and a diamond pendant dangling between her still-forming breasts. Was that why he didn't call on her? Did he prefer girls more developed? That didn't make sense, the last one he'd called on had smaller boobs than she did, and Javier. . . . Was that it? Was Mr. Jamison gay? No, she was sure he was not. He called on boys and girls equally.

Shaking her head, she tried to push these thoughts away. Though she did have a slight crush on him, as did most of the girls in class, Ashlynn was not delusional. She knew he'd never be inappropriate and anyway, it was the question she really wanted. She wanted to impress him with her intellect, not her boobs.

Then she looked at Mr. Jamison's clothes. He was dressed simply as always, khaki pants today and a loose hanging polo shirt. A couple of times a week at least, he came to school in jeans. The more lurid of her classmates had commented on how his butt looked in those. Suddenly, Ashlynn felt overdressed, especially for a discussion of the Great Depression.

This mood was exacerbated because during her reverie, the discussion had moved on. Mr. Jamison was showing them photographs of men standing in soup lines. Welfare was always a hot topic. "Do they look lazy to you?" he challenged. "See the shame on their faces. It's important to remember that there were no jobs for these men to get. Men were leaving their families and taking whatever work they could find. Even dangerous work." The room had taken on a somber tone and, sensing it, Mr. Jamison immediately determined to liven things up. "Pop quiz, boys against girls. How many people died during the construction of the Hoover dam?"

"Over a hundred," several voices piped in.

"That was almost a tie, but I think LaVonne was first. Two points for the girls. LaVonne, for one point extra, add something extra your classmates might not know."

The voices were fading, but Ashlynn could still hear LaVonne's confident voice. "Ninety-six of those deaths were considered industrial fatalities, meaning the families of the workers got some benefits. The rest were from diseases, mostly pneumonia from the carbon monoxide exposure."

"Very good. Three points girls. Next question. . . .

The tears were almost dry on her down pillow as Ashlynn woke up. She looked down at the expensive sham and wanted to rip it apart. Instead, she tossed it to the side of the bed. It was time to move from grief to action. Kevin Jamison would never teach, would never lead a classroom. There was so much he wouldn't do, but now, it was more about what Ashlynn would do. Stepping over to her desk, she pulled out a small, yellow notepad. Time to make a list.

**

Tina's sleep was fitful. The pain in her back wasn't labor, not for a few weeks yet, but her growing belly had made it increasingly difficult to find a good sleeping position. Andre had bought her a long pregnancy pillow, but their full bed seemed too crowded and it always seemed to end up on the floor.

She had managed to drift off by now, but the baby was crying. It seemed as if the baby was always crying, had always been crying. She rocked her, cooed to her, placed a breast in her mouth, nothing seemed to work. Tina hadn't slept in what seemed like days. Her hair was a tangled black mess and she couldn't remember when she'd last showered. She bounced her daughter on her knees, but the crying moved to screaming and the look on the little girl's face showed she had no confidence in her mother. Tina bounced her more, faster, higher, continuing until her legs took on a life of their own, the muscles clenched and rigid. She was sure by now that this constituted abuse, but couldn't seem to stop. Now, though the crying had only increased in volume, she couldn't hear it anymore, at least not distinctly. The child was bouncing in her arms, actually leaving her hands for an inch, maybe two before dropping back down. Finally, the baby flew into the air and over her mother's head; Tina awoke with a start.

Andre was rubbing her back in his sleep, kneading the muscles just the way she liked. Tina managed to relax and breathe normally after a few moments, giving in to his touch so she could get some rest. Now, her daughter was older, two or three at least, and she was adorable. Her curls were up in a bow and she was playing in the street, riding her tricycle. But wait, she wasn't old enough to be in the street, was she? Tina called out from the front step, but there was no sound. Cars drove by, none of them seeing the little girl and the girl not noticing them. Tina tried to call again to her daughter, but couldn't remember her name. What kind of mother didn't know her daughter's name? She looked down in shame and when she looked back up, there were more vehicles, only now they all were Fed-Ex trucks. This would be OK, she thought, her colleagues were all good drivers. They had experience delivering in residential neighborhoods and none had ever come close to hitting a child. But, looking closer, it seemed that the trucks were coming closer and closer to the little girl, who remained oblivious. Tina raised her voice, confident that even if she didn't know her daughter's name, she could get her fellow drivers' attention. A glance into the cab of the next truck made her heart jump. The woman at the wheel looked like Tina herself. She looked to the next one, coming from the other direction, and saw the same thing. She was driving each of the delivery trucks and each one came closer to the cycling toddler and neither the driving Tinas nor her daughter had any idea that anything was wrong. She opened her mouth to scream, to get the attention of anyone, if not the child or the drivers, perhaps one of her neighbors would come to her aid. But again no sound came out. Again and again she attempted and again the silent screams. Each driver came closer to the tricycle than the one before until Tina could no longer look. She heard the brakes and the swerving screech of the wheels, then gasped aloud again.

Again her fiancé was a comforting presence, his arms around her body from behind, his left hand holding her breast and his right stroking her aching legs. Andre mumbled in his sleep, "Bad dream hon'?"

Tina just whispered "Uh huh," willing herself not to wake him and more importantly, to relax enough to get some rest. It took longer this time, but after several minutes, exhaustion took over.

Her daughter was older again, maybe five or six and wanted her hair combed. She wanted it something easier to manage than the expanding volume of curls growing on her head. But no matter what Tina did with the comb, the mass of hair just expanded. "Mommy, I don't want an afro," her daughter complained.

"I'm trying sweetie. What do you want?"

"Give me braids."

Tina paused for a moment. "I don't know how to do braids," she concluded.

"But Grandma says you always had braids when you were little. She says you did them yourself as soon as you were seven."

Tina looked closer at her daughter's hair as though it were a foreign object. "Yes, that's true. But I don't remember." After another pause, she tried another tack "Maybe we should get your hair cut."

"I don't want shorter hair. I just want it easier. Why can't you give me braids?"

Now the little girl was older again, at least seven or eight. She was sitting at the table, seven braids dangling from the back of her head, with multicolored bows tied to each. But she needed help with her homework. But the numbers on the page seemed foreign. The problem should have been simple: 14+8, but she couldn't seem to manage it. Feeling like a little girl herself again, she tried counting on her fingers, but quickly ran out of fingers. She looked down, considering including her toes in the count, but realized there still weren't enough. Her daughter began to laugh. "It's easy Mommy."

She jumped ahead again and the teenage girl in front of her had a demanding look on her face. "Which one Mom?" she asked holding out two dresses, one red and one blue. Tina couldn't decide, both were beautiful.

"Either one would be fine honey."

"But I need your advice. Which one, yellow or green?" Tina looked again. Indeed the dresses were now yellow and green. Both were beautiful and she simply couldn't decide between them. "I don't know."

The teenager stamped her feet. "You're no help at all!" she exclaimed, tossing both dresses to the floor. "I guess I just won't go to prom."

The car was moving way too fast, Tina knew, and her daughter was in the passenger seat. She was filled with outrage as the driver tipped the beer to his lips, draining the last of it. Tina screamed for him to slow down, to pull over, let her drive, but he only laughed, as did her teen daughter. Scoffing at the worrisome nature of adults, they ignored her. The girl reached to the floor for the six-pack of beer, but her purse spilled. Tina saw condoms spill out. "Oh no, you're too young!" she exclaimed, but her daughter only laughed again, looking conspiratorially at her boyfriend.

"Here you go," the girl said, handing the beer to the boy and taking one herself. Both tipped the bottles to their mouths for what seemed like a long time, ignoring the road. Tina wanted to warn them, wanted to take the wheel, but they heard nothing she said. She looked up as the horn blared and screamed as the glare of the headlights filled her view.

She was gasping now, and crying uncontrollably. Still only halfway awake, Andre pulled her to him, their faces touching now. He said nothing for several minutes, just holding her close. Reaching up, he gently brushed the tears from her face. Though it was awkward given her extended belly, he reached under her and pulled her body across his, maximizing contact. Tina sobbed and he let her. Still holding her with his left arm, he stroked her hair with his right. "Shhh, shhh, I'm here. I'll always be here. Shh."

**

Andrew was no longer falling; instead, he seemed to be floating. He thought for some time that he was floating upward, but eventually, it seemed more like he'd stopped, motionless, statusless, decisionless. Where was he going to go from here? He'd have to just wait.

And wait he did, for what seemed like hours, but perhaps was only minutes. At first he was patient, or at least he told himself so. But as time went on, his anxiety increased. He was no longer spinning, but floating, unable to determine for some time whether he was moving up or down, or perhaps remaining in the same place. It was not clear what this place was. There were no landmarks, only dim fog extended for some distance.

He wasn't in pain; there were no spasms, but worry flowed through his body. He gripped the sides of, what was it?—it wasn't his bed, but a platform keeping him from falling. He couldn't see anything around him. Instead of spinning, his body rotated clockwise, then back. He held on even tighter hoping he could stop the movement, but he couldn't change it. He continued to move, tick-tock clockwise, then tock-tick, counter-clockwise like, time moving forward one second, then back. He braced his feet and tried desperately to stop the motion, but he was jolted as his muscles tightened and he moved back and forth, tick-tock, tick-tock, tick-tock. Giving up on changing the motion, he loosened his grip and reached for his ears, hoping to muffle the sound. But, as he did, his body felt loose on the platform, as though he would fall from whatever platform was holding him, and he retook his grip. The clock sound only increased, TICK-TOCK, TOCK-TICK, TICK-TOCK, TOCK-TICK. Andrew tightened his hold as his body moved back and forth with more force, rocking as his hold was challenged. He feared he would spill over the side. If he did, would he fall or would he wake up? Was he still sleeping? TICK-TOCK, TOCK-TICK, TICK-TOCK, TOCK-TICK. He reached again for his ears, but the sound only increased in both volume and tempo. TICK-TOCK, TOCK-TICK, TICK-TOCK, TOCK-TICK. Though he finally managed to reach his ears, it did no good as the sound simply came through and the clock movement continued his body almost sliding again and again. He thought perhaps he'd now identified what he was lying on. It must be the minute hand of the clock, solid and narrow, just capable of holding him up. He couldn't decide what to do with his hands, to try to cover his ears or grab the sides of the clock hand; both had proven ineffectual.

His body tensed, his spine grasping the sweep hand as his hands had been unable to. Most of Andrew was now off the hand of the clock, only his feet and upper back were still connected as the rigidity increased, a rod seeming to have slipped up through his body, up his spine about to emerge through his neck if he allowed it. Opening his eyes, he gazed upward into the dark, shadowy void. There was nothing to see, no one to help, no object to grasp onto. His arms flailed, reaching for he knew not what, and Andrew's silent scream filled the darkness with its non-sound.

His mouth was open, but he was no longer screaming; there was no sound at all. Something had broken, though he knew not what. His jaw ached, his throat was dry, but his body felt nothing. Only silence, deafening silence as Andrew's mind slowly came back to him, and he, back to the room in his apartment. His body felt like viscous liquid.

The bed was not just sweaty; there was blood on the sheets where he'd banged his legs against the footboards. The panic rose through him as Andrew awoke, partly jumping, partly falling down from the bed. He knew he'd been wrong. He crawled through the dusky bedroom, reaching for the doorknob. Andrew ignored the spasms of pain racking his body, they would stop when he reached the pharmacy. He'd go to the cell-phone store as well, replace his phone and call the doctor for an appointment. Maybe he'd call his mother as well.

He rapped his knuckles as it took four attempts to open the bedroom door and banged his head rushing through it. Crawling through the living room, he made his way to the front door, reached up and unlatched the deadbolt. His hands scraped the wall again as it took three more attempts to get a grip on the doorknob. Grasping it firmly, he pulled himself to his knees, then used both hands to open the door wide.

Andrew fell backwards as the shock of the sunlight hit him. He hadn't considered the time, hadn't imagined it could be daytime; there had only been darkness for, how many days? He had no idea. He wasn't prepared for the San Jose sun, glaring at him like an enemy, glistening off the balcony railings, blinding him.

"No, No, NO!" he screamed out to the afternoon, to no one present to hear. In his fall, the door had remained open wide, the sun gleaming at him, reflecting from the hoods of cars in the carport, from the rooftop solar panels on the next building, from the windows off the office building across the street. The sun came through, glistening, relentless, attacking.

Summoning his last reserves of energy, Andrew used his foot to push the door to and began his long slow crawl back to his room. He was defeated and like a soldier who did not recognize the enemy, or who saw in him a force too great to engage, much less conquer, he retreated, retreated to his room one last time.

DISCOVERY

The truck was loaded and ready to go when Lucinda's phone rang. "What's going on Jaime?"

"Hey little sister, how's it going?"

He could never just get to the point. "I'm at work, remember? Heading out on my route right now."

"I just wanted to remind you that it is Election Day. Did you vote before going in?"

"No, didn't have time. I'll have to stop on my way home." Actually, she'd forgotten. She'd been up late finishing the newest edition in the Magicians trilogy. Tuesday was her day to return library books, so she had wanted to finish the last one.

"Do you remember who we're voting for?"

"Who do you mean 'we' bro? Don't I get to make up my own mind?"

"Have you even looked at the candidate statements, read your sample ballot?"

She hadn't of course. The sample ballot and pamphlet were both sitting on the kitchen counter, right where she'd dropped them. The only thing she could think of that day was how heavy they were to lug around as she was delivering, so it was just about the last thing she wanted to look at in her apartment. But she certainly wasn't going to share this with her brother, who already thought she was apathetic. "I looked before, but I'm going to give them another

KNOW MY NAME

glance before I go. Especially the um, propositions."

"There aren't any state propositions this time, but you need to vote for that school bond. They really need it. And vote "no" on city measure C. It's not what it looks like on the surface."

"Remember that part about deciding for myself?"

"I'm just sharing my opinion, little sis. You are voting for Cervantes and Baker aren't you?"

"Probably. There were a couple of others I was looking at."

"I don't want to be pushy, but I doubt the others are as good. By the way, do you want to come to the victory party tonight? Cervantes has a suite at the Hilton."

"Isn't a victory party a bit premature?"

"It's in the bag. Plus, regardless of the outcome, it's just a way of saying thanks to all of us who've been working so hard on the campaign the last six months. But guests are welcome. You know how many hours I've put in?"

"Yes I do. Your wife and kids have forgotten what you look like."

"Well, I'll be correcting that soon. I'm going to take a couple of weeks off after the campaign, though he may want a couple of us on his staff." Jaime trailed off as he often did when musing about the future.

"You're daydreaming again Jaime. And I gotta go. I'm running late for work."

"OK, but I can count on you to vote tonight, right?"

"Of course."

"And will you come to the party?"

"I don't know. Let me think about it."

"You need to get out more *hermanita*. Come on, it will be fun."

"Maybe. Gotta go. See you soon big brother."

"*Orale* sis."

With that, Lucy stepped back into the cab of her truck. She wasn't going to bother going home for that sample ballot; she'd just wing it when she got there. But she would try to remember: Vote today.

**

The phone rang just once and went to voicemail again. Olivia paused and left her fourth message of the past three days.

"Andrew. It's your mother. Please call me back. I'm getting a bit worried. I think I told you before, but just in case, your dad and I want to come out and visit. We were hoping you could take off a few days to spend with us. Maybe you could show us around. You know, the sights, where you work, maybe the Golden Gate Bridge. Do you live close to Yosemite? It looks close on the map, but it's hard to be sure. I've never been to the ocean; that will be so exciting. Andrew, please call me back. Andrew . . . "

The machine cut her off as it had the last couple of times. Olivia put the phone down on the nightstand and stepped down from the bed, plodding disconsolately to the kitchen. Zeke had finished his breakfast and was tying his shoes. "I'm getting worried. He still hasn't called me back."

"He will eventually," Zeke grunted as he stood, placing his wallet in his pocket and picking up his Bible and his keys. "Besides, it's early. Remember the time difference? It's not even six o'clock where he lives.

Olivia looked up hopefully. "Yes, I always forget the time difference. Maybe he's just not up yet. Still, I've left messages before."

Zeke was becoming impatient; he needed to leave for work and he was loathe to indulge his wife's fantasies. Still, he made an effort to be gentle. "Liv, this trip will either happen or it won't. It may be best not to get your hopes up."

"Well, maybe we can go even if he doesn't call back. It could be he lost his cell phone and didn't have our number. You know how unreliable those things are. Maybe we can surprise him. Just show up on his doorstep and knock. Wouldn't that be a hoot?"

"We've had the same telephone number and lived in the same house since Andrew was three months old. I'm quite certain he knows how to dial it. Even if he didn't, there's a phone book and that Internet thing. He could look it up. No, if that boy can't be bothered to return a call, we're not going to traipse halfway across the country to find out if he wants to be a part of the family. For all we know, he might have moved."

"But what if he doesn't call?"

"He probably will. But if he doesn't, maybe we'll wait and make the trip next year. There's plenty of other things we can do right here in Kansas."

Olivia tried to hide her dejection. She handed Zeke his coat as he stepped toward the door. "It's getting cold outside, don't forget your jacket hon'."

"Thank you dear," he replied sincerely as he walked out, leaving her to her worries. Olivia walked back to her room and picked up the phone to dial again. It took Janice to the third ring to pick up.

"Mom, what is it?"

"I'm sorry, did I wake you?"

"Yes, but it's ok."

"No, I'll call back."

"Mom, I'm already awake now. What do you need?"

"Have you heard from your brother?"

"Not recently."

"How long has it been?"

Janice paused for a moment, thinking. "I guess two, maybe three months. Why? Didn't his boss tell you he'd been in an accident or something?"

"That was more than three weeks ago. It was the office manager." Lillian had given her the information after Olivia called back asking if they'd heard from Andrew. She'd been very apologetic at the time, though she'd wondered why Andrew hadn't called his family himself. "They said he was home resting and was supposed to be back at work in a week or two."

"Well, there's your answer. If he's back at work and missed time, he's probably got a lot to catch up on. After all, those papers don't push themselves around."

"Now Janice . . . "

"Sorry Mom. Couldn't help it. But you see what I mean? He's just busy. I'm sure he'll call you eventually."

"Maybe you could try."

"Why would he return my call if he isn't returning yours? You did leave a message this time didn't you?"

"Yes, I left him a message. More than one actually." She wasn't going to admit the actual number of messages because she didn't need another lecture from her daughter. "I tried calling him just a little while ago."

"Mom, you know about the time difference. It's early there."

Now Olivia was getting peeved. She wasn't an idiot and didn't like being treated like one. "Yes, I know. I just forgot this morning. I'll call him back later this afternoon."

"I'd wait until the evening. He may not be able to talk while he's at work. I don't think he gets off until five or six, and he has to drive home. That would mean seven or eight our time."

Olivia decided to ignore the mini-lecture. She could add and subtract two hours to the time. But she wasn't going to wait so late. If Andrew didn't answer again, she'd go to bed worrying and not be able to sleep. Plus, she would rather not make the call while Zeke was at home. No, she'd wait until lunchtime. At home, Andrew had always been very punctual, just like his father. Lunch was at 12:00 exactly. She'd give him a few minutes to unpack his lunch and start eating. Maybe 12:15. That would be 2:15 Kansas time.

"Mom, you there?"

"Yes, sorry honey, I just dropped the phone for a second. I'll call him later, just like you suggested. Oh, I just remembered the other reason I called. Your father and I were hoping you'd join us for a trip."

A vacation with her parents was just about the last thing Janice wanted, even if she had any time built up, but she had to be cautious. "A trip where?"

"To California!" Olivia couldn't hide her excitement. "We're going to visit Andrew. Will you come?"

"And Dad approved of that?"

"Yes, of course he did. You father is not a stick in the mud, no matter what you kids think. We're going to visit and Andrew will show us the sights. Have you ever seen a California redwood?"

Janice hadn't, as her mother well knew. "When is this trip?"

"Hopefully soon, but it depends on Andrew. We have to find out when he can take some time off."

Janice chuckled softly as she imagined that conversation. She almost laughed out loud when she thought of her brother driving his astonished parents around California, showing them the sights. It

KNOW MY NAME

would be great payback. Especially since she had an excuse to get out of the trip.

"Thanks for thinking of me, Mom, but since I just started this job, I don't have any vacation time built up. It would be several months before I could really do anything like that."

"That's too bad. I'd like to go soon; I'm so anxious to see Andrew. But your father says we'll have to put off the trip if Andrew doesn't call back soon. But I so want to go now, I just can't wait."

"That's too bad. I hope it works out for you."

"I'm sure it will. Maybe if you can't come this time, you'll be able to the next time we go. I'm sure we'll want to do this often, at least if Andrew keeps living in California."

He will, Janice thought, *unless you chase him farther away with your visits*. "Sounds like a plan," she told her mother, hoping to get off the phone soon.

"Anyway, I should let you go. How is that job going?"

"It's going well." Janice looked at the clock—7:32. "I just got off an hour and a half ago."

"Oh, I didn't realize. You're working through the middle of the night?"

Janice had informed her mother of her shifts. She just couldn't be bothered to remember. "Yes Mom. I get off at 6:00 A.M. all this week. As the newbie, I get the least popular shifts."

"That's too bad. You be careful. You never know what could happen so late."

You have no idea, Janice thought. "I will Mom."

"Well, I guess I should let you go then, so you can get back to sleep." Olivia's voice sounded reluctant. "You still coming for Christmas?"

"I'll try Mom, but remember, I'll probably have to work."

"Oh yes, I remember now. Well, hopefully they'll be nice to the newbie—is that what you call it?" Olivia had learned a new word.

"Hopefully."

Hanging up the phone, Janice made a mental note to always use up her vacation days a little at a time. Reaching for her pillow she realized how much grief that would save her.

**

Everyone was already seated when G-dub walked into the room. He looked down at Lillian at the end of the table. "No Grey?" he asked.

"Nope," was her calm reply. Lillian had been worried until the phone call from that ditz in HR. Now, she just assumed that Andrew was taking a little extra time off. Her boss's opinion differed however. He'd already put off the project launch meeting by a day, hoping Andrew would return. He was clearly unhappy that he hadn't, but it appeared he'd prepared for that contingency.

"All right, looks like everyone is here who's going to be. Let's get this thing started. I'm afraid this one won't be quite as easy as the last. We've got a startup, a biotech company called *Cells of the Future Technologies*."

"Cute name," Gil chimed in.

"Cute is probably right. You know how it will be with a startup. We shouldn't make any assumptions, but you know that some of them use some rather creative accounting."

"If they keep any records at all," Sykes interrupted. "The last one had almost nothing, just handwritten notes on scraps of paper."

"Hopefully, it won't be quite that bad. But, be on your toes and watch out for anything. We get paid either way, but we'll need to walk the straight and narrow—and make sure they are."

"Where's Andrew?"

"Elsie, I'm afraid Mr. Grey's injuries will keep him out for another week or so."

Lillian gave him a look from the end of the table, but said nothing.

"We don't know exactly when he'll be back, but it's not today."

"But we need him on a project like this. How are we going to . . . " Pete broke off, realizing he'd said too much.

G-dub didn't care for the panicked look on his face. "Time to grow a pair of your own, Massey. You can't ride Grey's coattails forever." Pete looked abashed, at least momentarily, and G-dub noticed that Davenport was sitting a foot or so farther from him than usual. *The drama never ends here*, he thought. "I'm not going to belabor this; you all have your assignments, same as last time. Interview each and every key player, review every relevant document. No skipping steps on this one. They may well be on the up and up, but you have to be ready for anything. We'll head over there together in half an hour in my car, then split up for our tasks. Any questions?"

"Can I drive your convertible?" Ellie asked as they were picking up their folders.

"Sure, just as soon as you kiss enough asses to get my job and make the payments."

"Got you," Sykes teased.

"Bite me."

"Bare it and I will."

"Not in this lifetime."

"Let's go children. Thirty minutes. Lily—a moment."

Lillian had been expecting this. She stepped into the boss's office, pulling the door with her, but not quite closed. "You've heard nothing from Grey at all?"

"No, he should have been back last week. I tried calling him yesterday, but his phone is off. I left him a couple of messages to call me back."

"Pointed messages, I assume."

"The last was quite pointed. If he's getting his voice mail, he knows what he needs to do. Maybe he lost his cell phone in the accident, or he's decided to make his first attempt at irresponsibility."

"This is Andrew Grey we're talking about."

"Yes, it's Andrew, so . . . "

"So, the rest of the team and I are leaving in half an hour. I know you have some paperwork leftover from *San Jose Unified* to file. After lunch, I'd like you to stop by young Mr. Grey's apartment and check on him. If he's breathing and walking, you are to drag his sorry ass down here, sit him in his cube and tell him to wait for me. Send me an email to let me know what you find."

"Will do. You don't really think anything is wrong do you?"

"Andrew Grey would be here if that sorry Honda of his could get him here. Either he tried to call us and there's a glitch somewhere, or there's something wrong."

"I'll find out."

"I know you will."

MICHAEL CARLEY

**

"Bridget, come on, let's get this over with." Molly was beyond exasperated. She had four hours of homework and the last way she wanted to spend her time was with her little sister, especially when she couldn't keep her mind on the task.

"Why can't we just skip it? He's never going to answer the door."

"Because Mom said." Secretly, Molly agreed with her sister on this one. Mr. Grey hadn't been home the last three times they'd visited. But, their mother had insisted they be conscientious and try one last time.

"He only ordered one box. Why don't we just eat them ourselves?"

"Because then he'd complain that he never got his cookies. We're going to try one more time and then we'll give up. I promise."

Bridget was moving forward at least, stomp-walking her way along the second floor balcony toward apartment 2F. She was knocking on the door by the time Molly approached. "See, he's not answering. Let's go."

"Give him a minute. You just want to eat his cookies. Do I need to remind you that Mom already said we're sending them back?"

"It's just one box. I think she'll let me." Molly kept silent, though in this case, again, she agreed. Her mother probably would relent; she was never consistent. Bridget knocked again, louder this time.

"OK, he's not answering. Let's get home. You can tell Mom we tried." *And I can finally get to that homework*, she thought.

Molly was halfway down the balcony hallway when she realized her sister wasn't with her. "Bridget, come on!"

"I'm just closing the door. I almost forgot."

"What do you mean, closing the door? He's not at home."

"Yes, but the door came open when I knocked. If we leave it open, somebody might get in."

Molly was incensed. If this guy was home, hiding just to avoid them, he was going to get a piece of her mind. Had he forgotten that he'd already paid for the cookies? All he had to do now was take them. She stomped over to the door and opened it, first just a few inches, then wide.

Bridget was just on her heels as she stepped inside. "Ugh, it stinks in here."

"He's probably on vacation or something and left some food in the trash." Molly was speaking more to herself than her sister. If she got caught trespassing in someone's apartment, her mother would kill her twice, first for breaking the rules, then for putting her sister in danger. "Stay here," she told her firmly. No need for them both to get yelled at.

"Hello? Anyone home? Mr. Grey, we have your cookies." The irritation was sneaking back into her voice as she remembered the waste of time this guy had put her through.

Looking at the kitchen counters, she saw no evidence of leftover food. The counters were immaculate and everything seemed to be put away. She wasn't going to look into the trash or garbage disposal though because she'd have no explanation if he came out from the other room and found her. *Let's stick to the reason we're here.*

"Mr. Grey? Are you home?" By now, she really did suspect that he'd left without locking the door. But she wasn't going to leave without being sure. She opened the door facing the front of the apartment and it turned out to be a bathroom. Also, perfectly clean with everything in its place. Toothbrush and dental floss were on the counter at right angles to the counter. *This guy must be quite a stiff.* "Mr. Grey?"

The last door was on her left and it had to be the bedroom. She opened it tentatively. "Mr. Grey?"

Molly gasped as her hand moved to her mouth. She almost tripped as she stepped backwards from the door. Gathering her wits, she turned around, grasped her little sister's hand firmly in with her right and using the left hand to reach for the cell phone in her pocket. As the oxygen started flowing back into her brain, she realized reluctantly, *I'm never going to finish that homework.*

**

Lucy was quite satisfied with herself. She was ahead of schedule, arriving at the Bay Bridge Apartments at least a half hour earlier than usual. If the rest of the day went this smoothly, she could get off early enough to vote without wasting half of her evening.

She took her customary glance in the direction of apartment 2F, but the door was closed. Andrew Grey still wasn't home. The mail had been building up for a while now. This didn't really alarm her. It could be he'd been called away for his job. In truth, most people didn't stop their mail when they went on a trip these days.

There was a police car and an ambulance at the complex when she arrived. This wasn't especially surprising either as she was aware that quite a few older people lived there and emergency calls often intersected with her route. It appeared that the ambulance must have arrived first. The driver was sharing information with the police officer as she began sorting and distributing the mail. Lucy listened absently.

"So, who called it in?"

"Couple of kids, a teenager and her little sister were passing out Girl Scout cookies and apparently this guy bought a box. They found him." The EMT pointed to his left, toward Myrtle Street where Molly and Bridget sat, waiting to be interviewed.

The EMT's partner was finishing up some paperwork and Lucy saw the gurney in the back of the truck. Apparently, whatever old coot was in that apartment couldn't be revived. The body was covered and the paramedic was zipping something over his head.

"Guy had been gone for a while I guess."

"Hard to say. Coroner will have to determine that, but it's a few days at least. That wasn't a pretty sight those girls walked in on. The little one will be having nightmares. But, looked like he lived alone."

"No signs of foul play."

"Nah. The place was clean as could be. The door was open, but it looked like the guy just crawled up in his bed and died. Probably too stubborn to go see a doctor for whatever he had."

"Suicide?"

"Doubtful. There were a couple of empty pill bottles on the nightstand, some pain meds, but I doubt he took enough to kill him. We'll probably never know."

"Won't be an autopsy?"

KNOW MY NAME

"Not unless there's some reason to or the family wants to pay for one. If we find a family."

"You get a name?"

"Yeah, he had a wallet on the counter. Like I said, the place was clean, everything in its place. That is, except the body." The EMT pulled out a bag with the deceased man's personal effects. Lucy wondered briefly at how small it was. If she ever died in her apartment, what would she leave behind? She was closing up the mailbox group and getting ready to open the next as the young man pulled a driver's license out of the wallet. "Grey. The guy's name was Grey. Andrew Grey."

Her keys dropped to the ground. The handful of mail, mostly junk, but a few bills as well, met the same fate. The noise that came out of Lucinda's mouth startled both of the emergency workers and stopped them in their tracks. One of them would later describe it as the sound a banshee would make, but in reality, the scream, while it might have lasted as long, was more guttural. In fact, that might have been what startled them the most, not that she screamed, but that such a cute, petite young woman could make a sound that horrific, so utterly repellent and grotesque that it almost made the unsightly discovery they'd just made pale in comparison.

Lucinda's knees buckled, but somehow, she managed not to fall. Instead, she ran. Tears blinding her vision, she sprinted out of the complex, leaving her truck and its attendant mail behind. She ran past the hedges through the parking lot and toward the street. She couldn't see the road or the cars in front of her, but she was beyond caring. Lucy ran out into traffic, eliciting a cacophony of blowing horns and at least one unnoticed finger gesture.

Of the two screeching cars she ran in between, a white Prius travelling north, and a 1982 Oldsmobile Cutlass Supreme driving south, both managed to stop without hitting Lucinda as she tore through Myrtle street and down Emory disturbing the quaint little neighborhood with her wails, pausing only each time she ran short of breath. She didn't stop until the street ended, and not quite then. She brushed past several startled would be passengers and hopped aboard the Caltrain just as it was about to pull away from the station. As she gasped for breath and the other commuters stared, it finally occurred to her that she had no idea which direction this train was heading.

The problem with that Cutlass though, was not that it couldn't stop. Despite being built before anti-lock brakes became common, the car was sturdy and the man driving it, a tall gentleman in his mid-seventies, was quite proud of his driving skill, including his reflexes, which were much better than most his age. No, the problem for the Cutlass was that while its driver's reflexes were still quite good, the same could not be said of the driver of the Hostess truck driving behind him, who was looking at his clipboard for the address of his next stop. Just as he was catching his breath, the Cutlass was hit from behind with more force than one would have expected. As skilled as he was, his foot was reaching for the gas just as the impact occurred and the Oldsmobile, which he'd managed to own for thirty years and nearly four hundred thousand miles without an accident, went careening toward the curb of Myrtle street. The driver's eyes opened wider in their helplessness than they had in his nearly three quarters of a century on the planet as they met the equally astonished ones of the teenager and young girl who had been sitting on that curb and never had a chance to move.

**

Lillian listened with annoyance to the woman's voice over the GPS as she was directed to Andrew's apartment. She knew San Jose very well, so the instructions should not have been necessary. But this errand was important, so she was playing it by the book. She'd check on Andrew, see if he was home, and hopefully, drag his butt back to work. If she had to swear him to secrecy about the week she'd hidden from the boss, she now had the ammunition. He was indebted to her. Without her covering for him, he'd be in bigger trouble than he already was.

She wasn't really that worried though. Mostly, it was her nurturing instincts that had kicked in. Andrew lived alone, so probably he'd just been too sick or hurt to call. Nothing that couldn't be solved by Aunt Lillian and her famous chicken and white bean soup.

Turning off the Alameda onto Emory, she first saw the ambulances, two of them. Parking at the side of the road, she wondered aloud "Oh Andrew, all this fuss couldn't be for you, could it?"

RIPPLES

The first funeral was a modest one, but well-attended. As she knew the family was small, Ashlynn was surprised at how many people showed up. Looking out from the family viewing area where she sat in what had become her accustomed place, to the right of Kevin Senior and with Harry to her right, his left hand folded in both of hers, she marveled as the larger main room filled to capacity.

It shouldn't have been a surprise when the doctor came out of the operating room, his face somber, with a knowing look in his eyes. He never really got the words out, just began, "I'm sorry . . ." before the family, all three of them, broke down in tears, then fell into an impenetrable huddle, closed to the rest of the world, but bound tightly as if they always had been.

Imam Javed was a silent rock, ubiquitous, but nearly invisible. First, he brought the family tissues, and placed a second box on the table next to them. Half of that box was empty by the time they left the hospital.

The imam took out his notebook and with sober ease moved the nervous doctor to the corner of the room and took down the necessary logistical details. It was he who arranged with the funeral home and collected Kevin Junior's personal effects in a bag, handing them to Harry just as they left for the evening. Very few words were spoken after leaving the hospital. It just seemed to be understood that Ashlynn was going home with them. She spent that night at the Jamison house, then two at home, but stayed with them again the evening before the funeral.

Kevin Senior seemed to have aged a decade in the past few days. He nodded more than he spoke, and let Ashlynn and Harry make the decisions. There wasn't a lot of money to spend, but he wanted his son to have a respectable service. Ashlynn put the flowers on her credit card over his protests and quietly arranged to pay for the burial plot without his knowledge. When the funeral director presented Kevin Senior with the bill that only included the service and the coffin, he pulled out his checkbook and, his hands trembling, paid it without noticing the discrepancy.

When asked who the officiant would be, they all hesitated, but it was Harry who remembered Imam Javed and once the name was spoken, they all knew he was the right choice. Ashlynn contacted him through the hospital and the imam, for his part, was effusive with gratitude and told her he'd be honored. He pulled out that same little notebook and efficiently took down the details. Of course, he said, it was no problem to provide a simple secular service. He would include any kind of liturgy the family might wish.

As she peered through the curtain dividing the family room from the chapel, Ashlynn was struck by the discrepancy between the two rooms. Young Kevin had far more friends and acquaintances than family, the three of them being the only ones in the family room. The chapel was packed. When the imam called for people to say a few words about the recently departed, she had expected the customary awkward silence that usually took place in these moments. At her aunt's funeral, no one had spoken up at all.

But Kevin had apparently touched many lives in ways large and small. The moment Imam Javed spoke the words, a line formed in front of him, extending down the left walkway of the chapel. The first speakers were two high school friends who shared Kevin's impact on their lives since childhood. "He was peer pressure, but in a good way," one of them said, enlisting a bit of knowing laughter from the crowd.

The other speakers were mostly from the college. Ashlynn saw Professor Burke and made a mental note that she owed him an assignment. Her professor did not speak, but six others did, describing Kevin as one of their best, most inspiring students. "Young people like him are the reason we do this," one of them said.

Some of the others were students, including one young woman who clearly had an unrequited crush on Kevin, a regret she'd be carrying for some time. The one time Ashlynn felt her own muscles tense was when one of Kevin's classmates ended her speech by blurting out "that damn bike" just before bursting into tears and leaving the podium. The others were mainly from the school where he'd been doing his student teaching. Though he'd known these kids only a few months, their love for him was obvious. Three parents were among those who spoke. One father said that Kevin had turned his son's life around where he, as a parent, had floundered.

Nearly an hour passed before all of the speakers were through. Kevin Senior looked as though he might collapse and Harry cried so much his handkerchief was soaked as was the simple peasant blouse Ashlynn was wearing. As the mourners filed out, she pulled a stainless steel water bottle from her purse and handed it to him. "Drink" she told him after he'd first pushed it away. "I don't want you getting dehydrated." Her big sister instincts had kicked in without a thought.

Finally, it was their turn to pay their respects. Imam Javed greeted the last of the non-family mourners, explained quietly to someone who had come late that there would be no gravesite service. A brief reception would be held by the college's liberal studies department and food and drinks would be available there.

There seemed little to say as the family passed by the casket. Kevin Senior kissed his son on the forehead. Harry tried almost to hug him a move that would have been awkward anywhere else, but here, seemed almost normal. As she approached, Ashlynn bent down and took Kevin's hand. It was colder than she'd expected. "I finished *Everything Matters*. And it does; it really does." For just a moment, she felt almost guilty saying that, but not especially. She really did feel as though she knew him.

They did put in an appearance at the college reception, but just for a few minutes. Each time they thanked one of Kevin's professors, they received thanks in return as though they'd had the honor to have had him on loan for a short while and were now giving him back, spent though he was.

As they made their way back to the car, Harry stopped. "You are coming home with us, aren't you?" For the first time, it was actually a question.

"I am way behind on my homework and I have classes, but of course, I'm coming. Let me get my keys. You can ride with me if you want."

**

The walls were grey and the paint peeling as it is so often in government buildings, but since she was staring at her shoes, Lucinda hardly noticed. She was still half in a daze as she made her way into her supervisor's office.

"Sit down," came the terse command. Lucinda sat.

"I think we have the facts straight by now. You took off, leaving your truck with boxes of mail exposed, leaving a half-filled box standing wide open at the . . . " the local postmaster looked down at a sheet of paper listing Lucinda's crimes "at the Bay Bridge apartments. We didn't hear from you at all for six hours. Not until you texted me, saying, quote 'I have made a mistake'. Does that sound right?"

Lucy only nodded. The facts were the facts after all.

"OK, before we go any further, I want to remind you that you have the right to have your union rep here with you at this meeting or at any other that might result in disciplinary action. You want your rep?"

The shake of her head was just perceptible. Lucy had never bothered to join the union, though her brother had pestered her about doing so.

"All right, let's fill you in on what you may not know. We'd been looking for you for hours by the time you called. We got a call from the police that afternoon. The officer said he'd have called earlier, but there was an accident involving some pedestrians nearby and he got diverted. But as the officer tells us, you just up and screamed, rather loudly as he put it, and ran off. He had no idea why."

She finally spoke for the first time. "Andrew, it was Andrew."

"Who's Andrew?"

Lucy couldn't speak. The explanation would have been ridiculous even if she'd been able to summon the requisite energy.

"Is Andrew a friend, a family member? Did something happen to him?"

"Andrew's dead." Lucinda said flatly, her breath exhaling in a slow stream as though the same air had been in her lungs for a week.

The postmaster sat back in her chair, clasping her hands. "You lost someone close to you. Poor girl. What I still don't understand is why you ran off in the middle of your day. Did you just hear about it? Someone call you on your cell?"

"I just heard," Lucy replied meekly. She wasn't trying to hide information from her supervisor. She just had no idea how to explain, nor the capacity to do so.

A full minute passed as the postmaster studied her young employee. "OK. We have two issues here. I'm going to do you a favor. Clearly, you're not ready to come back to work." Pulling out a form from her desk drawer, she handed it to Lucinda. "Take the rest of the week off. If you need next week, or part of it, let me know and I'll figure out a way."

Lucinda took the form and said nothing.

"Unfortunately, that can't be the end of it. I'd already filled out your reprimand before you arrived, but I wanted to give you a chance to give me some information that might clarify things. I do have sympathy for your loss, but it doesn't really factor into this. Nothing would excuse you leaving your truck and mail unguarded."

Lucy nodded. Vaguely at least, she'd been expecting this.

"This can't happen again. Lucinda, look at me." With effort, Lucy looked up, a sharp intake of breath being necessary for the exertion. "This cannot ever happen again. Do you understand me?"

"Yes."

"I hope you do. I've always liked you. This job is getting tougher every year and I've got a couple more yet before I retire. I like employees who do their jobs and don't cause problems. Up until this week, you've always been on that list. I'm cutting you a break here. I hope you know that." She paused, but even if she'd been the type to need the affirmation, it wasn't forthcoming. "Look at this. You've probably never had cause to see this form. It's a 651.5, a letter of warning. I'm cutting you some slack by not suspending you. Anyway, read this, make sure it's accurate, and add any comments if you have any. If nothing else happens, this will just be a blip on your record after a while. But I'm going to be watching you."

Lucinda took the form and signed it, barely glancing at it. She had no defense.

"Lucinda? Lucinda?"

She finally looked up. "Yes?"

"You sure you're OK to drive home?"

Lucy's nod was just enough to be perceptible this time.

"All right. I know you're hurting. You're still young so maybe you haven't had to deal with this kind of loss before." She hesitated, wanting to ask about how Lucinda was related to Andrew. A boyfriend, she suspected. But it was clear Lucy didn't want to talk about it. "Spend time with your family. After a while, you'll only remember the good times. The rest will fade."

The irony of that statement had little impact. Lucy was a mental void. Without a word, she simply climbed into her car, drove absently back to her apartment and slept for two days.

**

It was only six in the morning, but the plane was nearly full as Zeke helped his wife into the window seat. He put their small bag into the overhead bin and found his way into the aisle seat of the Skywest aircraft. Fumbling around for the seat belts, he managed to get Olivia buckled before focusing on his own belt and settling in. Looking her way, all he saw was the blank stare she was giving the airliner's wing. She probably wasn't seeing even that.

This wasn't the trip she'd planned. There was none of the excitement of her first flight, only morose silence. She'd hardly spoken a word since they got the call two days ago. It had been that same office manager at Andrew's job and Olivia had dropped to the floor leaving her astonished husband to pick it up and collect the details. It hadn't been easy with the caller herself apparently stifling tears.

Arrangements such as these are never fun, but the logistics were made worse by the distance. A simple ceremony was all they could afford of course. They knew little of Andrew's friends in California, so it was impossible to know how many to expect. He'd been there several years by now, so surely there would be classmates from school, coworkers, and some other friends. It was probably too much to hope that he'd found a good church to attend, but Zeke knew it was best to maintain the possibility, at least for his wife's sake. The alternative was unthinkable.

The thing Zeke struggled with most was finding a pastor appropriate to preach the ceremony. Salina Free was an independent church, proudly unaffiliated with any of the major denominations. But the informal networks in which church leaders travelled proved valuable and Pastor Cartwright had been a workhorse, staying on the phone for hours until he found someone he believed suitable. The minister would be travelling up from a town called Madera, several hours to the south. Zeke had a check made out to him folded into his wallet that would hopefully cover at least his expenses.

While Zeke had been busy making arrangements, Olivia was a mess. She was nearly catatonic, not having eaten or showered since the call. She simply lay in bed twenty-four hours a day. He worried that they'd miss their flight as he'd been unable to get her to dress herself. After a while, he decided to dress her himself, but when he began lifting up her gown, she slapped his hand away. Finally, she took the clothes and absently put them on.

For once, he wished his daughter could have been there to help. That had been an even tougher call. Janice had been silent through most of it, though clearly choking back sobs she didn't want her father to hear. But, after taking several breaths he could hear quite clearly, her voice was even as she told him she wouldn't be able to make the trip with them. He had hoped she could get the time off, but Janice was sure asking would be useless. Zeke admired her work ethic, but wished in this case that family came first.

He managed to get his wife into the car and to the airport, but it was a struggle to get through security. Olivia didn't hear the TSA staff and Zeke had to help her remove her shoes and open her purse. The security officer gave him a sympathetic look as he took her arm and helped put her shoes back on and get their things together. The gaze suggested he was to be commended for taking care of his aging companion, though Zeke was in fact nearly a decade older than his wife. She'd never worn makeup, but until today, he'd never noticed how pale she was, or perhaps she hadn't been pale until today. For some reason, he couldn't remember. And, Olivia walked with such frailty, he suspected the officer thought she was his mother rather than his wife.

Now that they were seated, he patted her knee with some affection. He'd see that she got through the upcoming ordeal as he always did, with the help of the Lord. For more than twenty-five years now, he'd had the role of caretaker, one which he felt suited him. The husband cares for the wife just as Christ cares for the church. It was only natural.

**

An autumn breeze was flowing as they pulled out on the highway. The atmosphere seemed a bit lighthearted for the occasion, at least to Lillian. G-dub had meant to put the top up on the convertible, but he hadn't been able to that morning. Lillian had hoped they'd meet at the cemetery, but the boss insisted they come to the office and ride together. She was riding shotgun with Gil Ballard sitting in the back, expressionless behind his sunglasses. Massey, Davenport and Sykes were behind them in Duane's Volvo. Pete was going to drive, but, frustrated by his own car choice, G-dub insisted that Sykes' was the better vehicle for the occasion. "This is a somber day" he'd reminded them. "Our cars, just like our clothes, should reflect that."

As they pulled into the Oak Hill parking lot and got out of the car, G-dub looked them over once again, appraising his team as though he were showing them off to a new client. Ellie Davenport, like Ballard, was wearing shades. The boss was fine with that. If they got emotional, or if they didn't, it is better for the family not to know. She was dressed appropriately in black, though he'd already mentioned to Lillian that Ellie's skirt was a little short. That was something he'd never have complained about any other time. Sykes passed muster as well, his black sport coat and thin tie entirely appropriate. The only issue with him could be his easygoing mannerisms. But there was nothing to be done about that. Massey was the only one who couldn't be trusted. Pete hated wearing ties and he'd waited to tie his until he was in the car. It was a mess, not to mention he'd forgotten his handkerchief. His jacket was a bit undersized given Pete's expanding gut, but addressing that was pointless.

"Lily, can you help the dumbass over there," said G-dub, disgust dripping from his voice. "It seems he can't dress himself."

As she stepped toward Pete, Ellie Davenport beat her to the punch. "I got it," she called back to Lillian, retying Pete's tie, tucking in his shirt and pulling a blue silk scarf from her purse that would serve as a substitute for Pete's missing hanky. Ellie stepped back for a moment, looked him over, and remarked, "I guess that will have to do." More quietly to Pete, though still audible to Lillian, she whispered genially, "Do I have to dress you from now on?"

With everyone prepared, G-dub repeated his unnecessary lecture. "I know none of you knew Grey's family," after a pause, he added "or his friends. I just want you to remember where we are and why. His parents are rural and conservative, not to mention in mourning. None of that cut-up shit we have at the office."

"You can trust us." Sykes affirmed.

Giving Pete one last dismissive look, the boss replied, "I know I can."

The first row was reserved for family. G-dub led them to the third; a close, but respectable distance.. As they took their seats, Lillian looked around. She wondered if they were early, but the funeral was scheduled to begin about five minutes prior. There were only about thirty or forty chairs set up around the closed casket, and more than half were empty. She looked over and saw Tina, looking ready to pop. Andre was with her. Tina had said she'd try to come; Lillian appreciated it. Attending the funeral of an ex could be tricky, especially with your current fiancé, or was it husband by now? She wasn't sure. Lillian did a quick count of the months and calculated that Tina was due any day. She gave her an appreciative nod and got one back in return.

An older gentleman sat in the back row. Lillian had no idea who he was. With his goatee and tweed jacket, he reminded her of a stereotypical academic type. She'd encountered only a few in her two years at San Jose City College and they'd always amused her, the way they'd argued over the minutia of esoteric theories of no practical importance. Lillian wondered who he was, but after all, she hadn't expected to know everyone. Andrew had always been private about his personal life.

Just then, a couple walked over from a rental car parked some distance away. The man was short and seemed to walk with his teeth grinding together, his mouth pursed. His look was intense and determined. Next to him, his wife appeared to be barely hanging on, clutching his arm tightly and taking each step with begrudging effort as though walking against a stiff wind.

The pair sat in the front row, just in front of the pastor, the man patting his wife's shoulder as they settled in. *They must be Andrew's parents*, Lillian realized. She wasn't sure what she'd been expecting, but it wasn't these two. She'd imagined Andrew's parents as academics, not unlike the man to her left, but clean-shaven, uptight and a bit awkward like Andrew himself. *You never know*, she whispered quietly.

The minister approached the podium, a serious, tired-looking man wearing a long sleeve shirt with an open collar and a cheap sport jacket. Somehow, he made these clothes seem more serious than had he been in a three-piece suit. Suddenly, Lillian wondered if their group was overdressed. G-dub was wearing his best J. Press and at his insistence, all of the men were in jackets and neckties. There was no need for the microphone, so the minister set it aside.

Lillian found herself shivering, though the weather was pleasant. She continued to look around, thinking some of Andrew's college friends would arrive, or perhaps more family. None appeared and she was amazed to realize that more than half of the mourners were Maitland and Mason firm members, all G-dub's group.

She was pulled from her reverie when the minister's voice rose, before falling again quietly. Lillian realized she'd heard little of what he said so far, so she tried to listen.

" . . . know little about Andrew's last days, or even his life here over the past few years. We know that he had indeed strayed from the ways of the Lord." Lillian caught her breath, wondering where this was going. "I've spoken with Andrew's heartbroken parents. And while they do not know a great deal about his spiritual life over the past several months, they did teach him the way to heaven. Parents cannot control their children after they leave the nest, but they can, while they have them, teach them the about the righteous path and how to find it, how to walk it. So, we do have hope." Lillian sucked in her breath again and glanced over at her coworkers. Ellie was giving Pete a look of surprise, her eyebrows raised over the top of her sunglasses. Pete shrugged and took her hand in his. Ellie looked back toward the podium.

"We hope that Andrew found his way back to the path he was taught, the one and only straight and narrow road that leads to the pearly gates. We don't know what happened in his last days, what physical and mental pain he was in, but we do have hope. We have hope because his parents taught him well. Most of all, we have hope because the Lord Jesus saw fit to give us hope by giving us his life. He showed us the way; we have only to take it. And woe unto him who does not take heed. Woe to him who ignores the road the Lord God set before him. Woe to him who follows the ways of this world, for we are not of this world, but of the next. Woe to him who dares to create his own path rather than follow that one that the Lord set out before him. The very Lord God who has laid out a path of righteousness, leading to a city made of gold; that very same God will set before those who ignore that path a blazing hellfire that will burn them with brimstone day after lonesome day until the end of time. And as the gospel of Luke tells us, there will be weeping and gnashing of teeth."

Lillian exhaled, hoping this would be over soon for the sake of the family. Andrew's father was stoic; he even nodded a couple of times during this sermon. His mother looked like she might fall off her chair. She wasn't crying exactly, but it was likely because she was out of tears. Her shoulders shook and she kept blowing her nose.

"So I call on you sitting here today. You, who are Andrew's family, his friends and loved ones. If any of you have strayed from the path of the Lord. I should not say if, because I know, looking at each of you, that you have so strayed. Come, repent. God's wrath is incomprehensible, yet his love is boundless. If you will only return to him, or if you have never known the Lord, come to him. It is never too late to seek out the ways of God, to leave this sinful world behind and find that straight gate. Find that narrow way. For as God told us through Matthew, that is the way to life everlasting and so few, so very few will find it. Won't you be among those few? Won't you come to the path of the Lord?"

Now, it was the minister's turn to catch his breath. He paused for several moments and looked around at the crowd as if expecting one or all of them to walk up to him and proclaim their intention to repent and follow him. But he didn't seem surprised when no one did. His only remaining words were "Let us pray."

Lillian bowed her head, but looked around from the corner of her eyes while the minister said his prayer for Andrew's soul and the comfort of his family. Everyone in the small group had bowed heads. Pete fidgeted quietly. G-dub sat to Lillian's left, his face devoid of its usual joviality. In the next section, the professor also sat quietly, his head bowed and his hands clasped in his lap. Tina and Andre did the same, though Andre seemed to be whispering his own prayer along with the pastor.

As he ended his prayer, the minister nodded to a woman sitting at a small piano. The woman began playing and then sang with quiet emotion. Lillian wondered if she was the minister's wife. They had that similar look that couples get when they've been together for many years. The woman's voice nearly broke as she slipped into a high note she couldn't quite hit. "And I'll cherish the old rugged cross" she intoned, stretching the last word to nearly three syllables and with heavy emphasis on the word *cherish*. It was clear she'd sang this many times, probably more than a few of them at funerals.

As the song neared its end, the pastor motioned those who were not family members forward. The casket was closed, but they each walked by, paying their respects. The old gentleman was the first to pass and he stopped by and shook Andrew's father's hand, saying nothing Lillian could hear. Tina and Andre followed his lead, shaking the hand of Zeke Grey, who looked up dutifully and gave each person his thanks. Andrew's mother sat simply next to her husband, trembling with her hands folded in her lap.

G-dub motioned his group back, pausing until they had passed the casket and stepping to the lead, just in front of Gil Ballard, who looked like he'd like to get back to the car as soon as possible. In the silence, Lillian heard a page turn at the piano and the opening notes of *Softly and Tenderly* wafted in their direction.

G-dub stopped just in front of Andrew's parents and paused. Reaching out his hand, he introduced himself. "Mr. and Mrs. Grey, my name is Gerold Walker. I was Andrew's boss over at Maitland and Mason." Lillian heard one member of the team, it was either Pete or Duane, whisper "Gerold?" Apparently, they hadn't all known the boss's actual first name. G-dub continued "I want to say how sorry I am for your loss. How sorry we all are." It had taken a moment, but Zeke Grey eventually looked up and shook G-dub's hand. G-dub extended it to Andrew's mother as well, but withdrew after a moment when she made no gesture to reciprocate. G-dub looked back at his group, thinking to introduce his team, but deciding against it.

"I know today's got to be very hard for you," he continued. "I just wanted to let you know how important your Andrew was to all of us. He was a key member of our accounting team. Helped each of us out more times than we can remember. Hell, I'd probably have fired old Massey here if Andrew didn't always help him out." Lillian heard Pete shuffle his feet, but thankfully he said nothing.

G-dub was continuing, but was beginning to repeat himself. "Andrew was one of our best, our very best." Zeke Grey sat there, his lip trembling and said nothing. "We're going to miss him terribly. I just wanted you to know that. Andrew was a beloved member of our team. Quite beloved." Still hearing no response, G-dub withdrew with uncharacteristic awkwardness and gestured the team toward their cars. Following just behind him, Lillian heard both Gil and Ellie quietly tell Andrew's parents "I'm sorry for your loss," before moving on. She thought she heard the father whisper an even quieter "Thank you," after they passed.

As they were just beyond earshot, Massey spoke up. "Beloved? Really?"

G-dub and Ellie replied simultaneously. "Shut up, Pete."

KNOW MY NAME

**

Clark Mason sat at his desk and put down his pen. The paperwork was finished. He'd been the managing partner of Maitland and Mason for almost 38 years and today was the most somber he could remember. He'd been planning to stay to an even 40, but was now rethinking. As amazing as it was, he couldn't remember ever losing an employee. Grant Maitland, his longtime partner, had had a heart attack a few years ago, but had come through it fine and was back to working seventy hours a week shortly thereafter.

And this kid was so young. The firm was large enough now that he didn't really know everyone on all of the teams, but he did remember passing the intense young man in the hallway a few times. Seemed nice enough.

The paperwork had been easy and straightforward, especially for someone as meticulous as an accountant. Andrew had a retirement account invested in a target fund with the retirement date still 25 years away. And there was his company life insurance. Apparently, he'd been single with no kids, so he hadn't purchased any extra. Still, these two combined would provide a nice supplement to ease the family pain. Both listed his sister in Kansas as the beneficiary, so he had already composed a letter informing her, with two separate checks to follow. G-dub had said that the sister hadn't made it to the funeral, so no one had met her.

G-dub Walker was on his mind as well. One of the reasons he'd wanted to get to 40 years, other than it being a nice round number, was that G-dub was his preferred successor. The firm had a long-standing rule, one that had seemed quite sensible at the time. One had to have put in fifteen years before buying into partnership. It had kept many a good man out and at least one good woman, but he and Maitland had agreed that rewarding loyalty was a positive. G-dub had been loyal, but was still eleven months short of reaching his fifteen years.

There were at least two who'd been around longer, Chaplan and Rucker. He didn't have much faith in Chaplan, who seemed to be coasting. Maitland was fond of him though. Rucker was competent enough, but didn't have G-dub's networking ability. Anyone who became partner needed to be able to bring in business.

MICHAEL CARLEY

That's the way he'd always thought of it; after all, this firm was his legacy and he wanted to leave it in good hands. But, Andrew Grey's death had shaken him more than he'd have expected. *Life is short*, he thought, laughing at the cliché. He'd talk to Grant tomorrow and figure out his exit strategy, and he'd leave it to him to decide who got the partnership. Grabbing his jacket, he dropped the paperwork on his secretary's desk and left early for the first time he could remember. The firm could go screw itself, he had grandchildren to play with.

**

The south parking garage was nearly empty when Ashlynn pulled into her space. Friday afternoons were a quiet time on campus; she planned her trip this way. She had a bit of a walk as her two errands were in different buildings, so it didn't matter which garage she chose.

Her Ford Focus was three years old, but it looked like it was going to be a good choice, practical was her new mantra. She'd taken a bath on the Stingray, but she still came away with enough for the lesser car and the amount leftover was Harry's. She planned to wait several months before sending the paperwork, anonymously, to Kevin Senior with all the information about Harry's college savings plan. Still, they weren't stupid. They'd probably guess who it was from, but there was nothing she could do about that.

The money in that account, if spent well, should get Harry through four years of college, and hopefully bridge him to his next step, whatever it was. It was the least she could do for her little brother.

She didn't typically consult them about her life decisions, but somehow it seemed responsible to tell her parents about her plans. To their credit, they hadn't complained about the wasted money for the car. Her father had seemed to understand and even helped her narrow down the search for the used Focus.

Before walking up, she smoothed out her hair and pulled it into a rubber band. She hadn't colored it in several weeks and the blond was turning to a dusky light brown. She was thinking of leaving it that way. It seemed more natural.

It was almost four o'clock when she stepped through the doors to Clark Hall and found her way to the liberal studies department on the fourth floor. The receptionist looked up from her paperwork and asked what she needed.

"I'm here to change my major."

"To liberal studies?"

"Yes," she answered patiently.

"There's a form from admissions you need to . . . "

"I already have that right here." Ashlynn pulled out the form and handed it to the young woman.

"This looks OK, but you know liberal studies is an impacted major."

"Yes, I think my grades are good enough. If not, I'll get them there, whatever it takes. Here are my transcripts so far."

"Well, you're very on the ball. That's refreshing. Are you interested in the humanities option or . . ."

"No, the teacher prep. I'm going to be a teacher." Ashlynn's voice was definitive, perhaps more than it ever had been.

"Everything does seem to be in order, but you will need to meet with an advisor. Let me see when I can get you an appointment." While the receptionist was searching the computer, Ashlynn looked through her bag for her paper. She may as well prepare for the next errand, however futile it might be. "How's two weeks from yesterday, two o'clock?"

"That will work fine. Thank you so much." Ashlynn smiled as she took the appointment card and headed out the door and downstairs toward the faculty office building. One last assignment to turn in.

**

Solomon Burke stroked his graying goatee as he prepared to pack up his things. It was nearly six o'clock and time for a relaxing weekend. He was aware that he looked the part of the stereotypical college professor. It was even why he'd grown the beard, though it itched and irritated his wife. He enjoyed every bit of it, the discourse, the esotery, and even the image. His choice of disciplines even facilitated such feelings. What could be more useless in the minds of the public, yet essential in his own, than philosophy?

It had been quite a strange semester, especially recent weeks. He'd lost a few students during his career, but two in one semester was a record.

And, they could not have been more different. Kevin Jamison Junior had been everyone's favorite, including his own. Philosophy wasn't his subject, but he excelled and helped lead class discussions and clarify concepts for other students. Young, effervescent, and approachable, he'd been able to bridge the gap of knowledge between professor and student in a way few can. This kid would have been a great teacher at any level and not a few of the faculty were devastated at his loss.

It was at Kevin's funeral that he'd seen the notice about Andrew Grey. This surprised and disturbed him even more. He remembered the earnest young man from a few years ago. At first, he thought he might be someone he could work with, but his vision had been too narrow. He wanted to learn philosophy as a weapon, not as a method. Andrew's death had also surprised him and the scarcity of mourners at his service made him wonder if he should have, or could have done more for him.

He'd been teaching for more than a quarter of a century and every semester, at least one or two students managed to surprise him. It was what he liked about his job and it kept him feeling young. Like the young lady who'd visited earlier.

He'd pegged Ashlynn Parker as a flake from the first day. He tried not to judge, but she seemed like the type who'd do just enough to survive, maybe with a high C; competent, but never putting much real effort into her work. Her mind drifted in class, but she managed to fake her way through whenever he asked her a question. With such students, he hoped some little nugget of the intellectual might have an impact.

Ashlynn had completely blown off the religious exploration assignment, and then disappeared entirely. So when she'd shown up at his office with her paper this afternoon, he was skeptical. He normally didn't take assignments so late, he'd explained, expecting a

KNOW MY NAME

horde of excuses and explanations he'd never believe. But she said she understood, and if he had the time, she'd like his feedback anyway. She'd accept whatever points he thought appropriate and if it wasn't enough to pass, she'd repeat the course.

He'd almost tossed the paper in the trash, but he remembered seeing her at Kevin's funeral. It had surprised him at the time and he'd wondered if she had been a family friend. Perhaps he'd misjudged the girl.

Then he read the paper and was caught completely off guard. Thoroughly documented and more insightful than he'd ever seen from any undergraduate, he had trouble believing she wrote it. He checked the paper against his plagiarism database and came up with nothing. It was her work. He read it again and found even more to like. She'd visited the Vedanta society not once, but three times over a two-week period, asking more detailed questions with each visit. The discussion was nuanced and meticulous and she ended her work with a series of questions that might be explored further if someone wished to follow up on her research.

Professor Burke was flummoxed. Even penalizing her heavily for its tardiness, he couldn't give this paper anything less than a low A. He even thought about recommending she submit the paper, with minor modifications, to one of the academic journals. *Philo* might be a good choice; it was one of his favorites. Combined with her earlier work, she'd more than pass the course, despite having missed more than a quarter of the sessions.

Opening his battered briefcase, he tossed the paper in for a weekend read, this time for his own enjoyment. Picking up his tweed jacket from the hook on the door, he tapped twice on the picture of Einstein with his tongue sticking out and walked out of his office, his head high. It was a new world every day and he was damn happy to be in it.

**

Normally, the wheat fields would have been blowing in the light wind behind his fence, but at this time of year, all he saw was stubble tilled over with the sod. Zeke had always liked living in the country. Though they weren't farmers, and their own house was modest, the relative quiet usually provided some peace. Not today.

Today, he was staring out into what would have been his neighbors' farms, wheat on the left, corn to the right. Today, he saw neither. Today, the stillness wasn't peaceful; it was deafening and it made him jittery.

He'd managed to get Olivia home safely, though she still hadn't spoken ten words. In the days since their return, she had not eaten either. The first day, he'd done the cooking and her meals sat in front of her untouched before he'd put them in the refrigerator. Undeterred, he continued cooking, though he had rarely made meals during their marriage. "You gotta eat, hon" he said once, but she only got up and walked away. After that, she took her plate with her into the bedroom and closed the door. That had surprised him as well. They'd never eaten anywhere but the kitchen table.

There had been so much to do in the past few days, he hadn't had time to think. Now that it was the weekend and he was alone with his thoughts, they seemed to scream in his head, bouncing around like unwanted pinballs. He'd never even played pinball.

He'd never had cause to second guess himself as a husband and father. His role was to lead the family, teach them the path to God, and keep them from falling into the worldly traps that doom so many of today's young people. He'd done that with Andrew, he had. He'd consulted scripture every step of the way, yet the boy had run. Run from his father, run from his home, most of all, he'd run from God.

Zeke had never blamed himself for any of Andrew's mistakes, or his sister's. He knew somehow that he'd taught them correctly and hoped that they'd find their way back. Proverbs 22:6 had been his guiding principle. "Train up a child in the way he should go: and when he is old, he will not depart from it." The Bible never said children wouldn't falter along the way. He'd seen it often. But he'd always assumed they'd come back. So many seemed to need to try out worldly things, to sow their wild oats, but then, often upon marriage and children, they came back, realized that God and their parents had been right all along, and settled down.

It had never been that way for him. He'd been devoted to God from his teenage years. It hadn't been an easy thing from a dating point of view. He had been surprised that so many young women were intent on living lives of sin or as one had put it, "I need to have fun for a while." Eventually, his eyes fell on Olivia. He was aware of her mistakes, but there was something about her. She needed him, then, just as now. That day, when he professed his desire to take care of her, he meant it.

And that boy. He'd taken him in and . . . No! He wouldn't think this way. He'd promised Olivia, though not with words, so he'd actually promised himself, that Andrew would always be his son. The past was the past and it was behind them. Andrew was his son, his.

Zeke's hands trembled as he clutched the wooden fence. The fence shuddered and the decaying wood nearly cracked before he let go. And letting go might have been a mistake as he fell forward, scratching his forearms as he caught himself on the rail. Then, his shoulders began shaking. Zeke Grey didn't cry, not since he could remember, but for a moment, he gave in to grief, allowing the pain and anger to ripple through his body before, through slow and decisive control of his breathing, he calmed himself, swallowing with huge gulps, suppressing all sensation. "Help me Lord," he cried, daring to look heavenward in a way he rarely had.

After several more minutes, he turned around, resolved. *I will go on*, he thought. *I will take care of my family.*

**

The suitcase had lain open since their return and Olivia was finally dealing with it. She placed the bag carefully on the bed, opened it, and began withdrawing the contents. She pulled out Zeke's clothes, pants, shirts, underwear and socks and she carefully put them in the drawers. She moved his bag of toiletries over to the bathroom counter. Walking over to the closet, she pulled out three dresses, folded them carefully and placed them in the suitcase. From the dresser, she found an equal number of slips, underwear, bras and stockings and added them to the bag. She looked down and decided one pair of shoes would be enough. Pausing, she walked over to the bathroom and pulled the toothpaste out of Zeke's toiletry bag and added it to hers in the suitcase before zipping it up and pulling it down to the floor.

Zeke had done so much for her, and she'd always be grateful. He'd taken her in when few would have. She'd made many sacrifices over the years and had almost always viewed it as a fair trade. She'd had security and comfort and from time to time, even a bit of affection. She had two children whom she loved more than anything.

But now, how could she stay? How could she remain in a house, with a man who'd . . .

No, it wasn't really that she blamed Zeke for what happened to Andrew. The people in California weren't even clear what *had* happened to Andrew. He'd been just a phone call away one day and the next . . .

It wasn't Zeke's fault of course, but still, this house would be nothing but reminders and he was one of them. He'd taken care of her since it had happened, doing what he could in his awkward, gruff way. But Zeke was still Zeke and she just couldn't imagine staying with him.

She still had Janice of course and maybe she'd visit her. It could be that she could stay with her daughter for a few weeks while she found a job and got on her feet. She'd worked at the Jolly Kone as a teenager and volunteered with the library when the kids had been in grade school. Supposedly, the economy was improving. Surely something would be available. She wouldn't put Janice in the middle of things, just tell her they were taking some time away from each other and let that be that. The girl could be short with her sometimes, but she did love her mother. She wouldn't be turned away.

She stepped over to the window to look out one more time. Their house was modest, but it did have a second story, and she'd always enjoyed gazing over the desolate fields. The farmers near them had sizeable expanses. Their houses were on the opposite side, so it was usually quiet.

Zeke was standing at the fence, scrutinizing the overturned wheat stubs as if they would explain something to him. She strongly suspected they would not. And she no longer had the faith to wait and see.

As she grasped the suitcase handle and prepared to head down the stairs, her husband turned around. His eyes met hers and held. As he lifted his hand in a feeble wave, she could see it was trembling. Momentarily, he dropped his head and began the walk to the house. Though the distance should have been too great for such visual clarity, she was sure that she saw tears glistening in his eyes.

Her own shoulders shuddered and she turned around, slowly, but with determination. Lifting the bag to the bed, she unzipped it and lifted the flap. Her own tears slid freely down her face as one article of clothing by one, Olivia Grey finished her unpacking.

**

The bus was nearly full; she knew it was the wrong time of day. But this was the appointment she could get that didn't interfere with her school schedule. Molly pushed her chair up onto the ramp, then looked back to make sure her sister was close behind. Bridget was right there, but staring absently into space. "C'mon Bridge; they're all waiting on us."

She was sure by now that she could get around pretty well by herself, but her mother insisted that Bridget go with her for another week or two at least. "You need to get used to how that thing works" she'd said. "Until you do, I want one of us nearby."

Molly wasn't sure how much help the little brat would be if she got into a serious emergency or even if the kid would notice. Just now, her chair got stuck for a moment on the lip of the ramp and she'd backed it up and was across the aisle before her sister even noticed.

Physical therapy was important; she knew that, but she couldn't help feeling it was useless. There was no feeling there except the phantom pain the doctors had warned her about and that wasn't so bad. But the therapy was supposed to keep her remaining muscles active and who knew, maybe there would be some miracle medical advance. *Ha*, she thought bitterly.

Molly looked around the car. It was mostly full of older people, as she'd come to expect. There was, on this occasion, a young man just about her age. He looked at her, smiled briefly then looked away. *He's embarrassed*, she told herself, though maybe she was imagining it. She reached down, tucked the legs of her jeans under her stumps, making herself as comfortable as possible. It was only a couple of stops to the clinic.

Bridget was fidgeting as usual, shaking her head back and forth so that the hairclips at the bottom of her braids clicked on the pole she was standing next to. It didn't take long for one to strike one of the old ladies who leaned back and glared as if to say "Who's watching this kid?"

"Bridget! You just hit someone; be careful."

"Oops," the little girl said, moving to the second pole of the car right next to another old couple who looked wary.

"I'm sorry." Molly told the woman. "She has a lot of energy." The woman gave her a look that was nothing but pity and Molly turned away.

"C'mon Bridge," she called. "This is our stop." One thing she'd already learned was to be ready when the door opened or it would close on her unless the driver was on the ball. She was ready this time.

But Bridget was not. She was still staring into space, but now she closed her eyes and twirled her braids faster and faster.

"Bridget the Midget!" Molly called angrily; at least now she had her sister's attention. Skipping along the aisle, she walked up to Molly and put her hand on her shoulder as her mother had taught her.

"I'm not, you know" she intoned.

"What the heck are you talking about?"

"I'm not a midget. I've grown an inch and a half in the past month."

"Well, you're still a midget."

Bridget laughed. "Maybe I am, but this midget is taller than you now." With that, the little girl put her hand level at the top of her head and moved it over Molly's. Indeed, she was now four inches taller.

"I guess you are." Molly smiled to herself as she wheeled onto the ramp and waited for the lift to lower her to the ground. Whether that smile was one of amusement or bitterness, the other passengers could not tell.

KNOW MY NAME

**

The hospital room ceiling was a dingy white, almost yellow, and though her eyes were closed, the view was now burned into the back of her lids. Andre was on her right, her mother on her left, with the midwife at the end of the bed in what a comedian had once called the Johnny Bench position, ready to catch the baby lest it fall on the floor. She'd been pushing for close to an hour and the ordeal was nearing its end.

"Alright, we're getting close," the midwife said, "just a couple more pushes and you'll be a mom."

"I'm not sure I can."

"You can do anything baby," Andre encouraged, "we're almost there." Her mother was quiet, which was unusual, but she seemed to want to defer to Andre as Tina had requested. But the hand clutching hers told her all she needed to.

Her legs clenched and the midwife sensed it. "OK, here goes," she said, always Ms. Obvious. Tina reached up to grab Andre's collar and missed, ending up with a handful of tight curls near the back of his head. Andre screamed right along with her as she pushed, simultaneously pulling him down to the bed. Once the contraction was over, he gently dislodged her hand from his scalp and clutched it tightly.

"You're doing great, just great," he said, not knowing if she was hearing any more.

"We have a head," the midwife informed her. "Just one more big push and we'll be there."

Tina braced, encouraged by the nearness of the finish line. Andre and her mother had been squeezing her like an accordion for the past forty-five minutes and she was tired. But the baby would be worth it. She gave a last push, digging her fingernails into the hands of her husband and mother. After what seemed like a full two minutes, she heard a cry, faint at first, then quite robust.

"Congratulations. You have a beautiful baby."

"Is it . . . ?" Andre started.

"It's a boy," came the quick reply.

"I meant, is it OK? Everything look healthy?"

"Absolutely. You have nothing to worry about."

"You did it baby." He leaned over and kissed Tina on the lips.

"We did it," she replied.

Andre chuckled. "I think in this particular case, you get a bit more of the credit."

The next few minutes passed as a blur as the nurse cleaned off the crying child, weighed him and brought him back to her bed. "I understand you want to breastfeed. Do you need some help getting started?"

"Let me try on my own for a minute. I went to a class and I think I understand."

"I'll be right outside if you need me. The biggest thing to remember the first time is to press him firmly on your breast so that he latches on. Trust me, you're not going to smother him."

Tina smiled weakly in thanks and pulled her baby close. "We never finished talking about names" she reminded Andre.

Her mother kissed her forehead, then the top of the baby's head and quietly exited the room, muttering something about privacy. "No, I guess we didn't." Andre was entranced, both by the wonder of his new son and the almost equal miracle of breastfeeding, which Tina seemed already to have mastered. They hadn't wanted to talk about names, feeling as though it would jinx them. Plus, as the date grew closer, they'd both become convinced they were having a girl. Neither were disappointed though.

"You still don't like Andre Junior?" she asked.

"No, I don't think so. Too much confusion, too much pressure. He should get to pick his own path in life." Andre was stroking his son's head and holding his hand as he swallowed. The boy was staring at him, though surely he couldn't see much at this point. It didn't matter a bit.

"We have to pick something" Tina said as she switched him from her left breast to her right. She had a better view now. The baby's skin was light, almost pale, though that was common enough at this stage.

"You know, I really don't care what his name is. Any of the ones we talked about is fine. I'm just happy he's here and healthy."

Looking down at her son, she decided to give it some time. The right name would come to her, maybe as she got to know him over the next day or so. Just then, he opened his eyes and looked up at her, probably still not seeing, but somehow there was a question in those eyes. Unmistakably, the boy raised his left eyebrow a bit before drifting off to sleep.

Looking over at her husband, Tina said "Andrew. His name is Andrew."

**

The television shows always got it wrong. The ER dealt with a lot of crises, but only a handful each month were truly traumatic. Probably the biggest myth was how often they do CPR and pull out the paddles, shouting "clear" as they jump start someone's heart.

She'd never used the paddles to this point, except in practice, and this was her first time actually doing CPR on someone other than Resuscitation Annie, but Janice was a quick learner. Just like in the TV shows, she was atop the gurney as it bolted through the ER doors, pressing down on the patient's chest with rapid compressions.

The young man was a utility worker, but despite the precautions they take, he'd somehow been electrocuted. There were black and red burns on both of his arms stretching up above his elbows and another on the left side of his face. The paramedics had shocked him already with 200 joules, which worked, but they'd lost his pulse just after pulling him out of the ambulance. She was hoping to get to a room in time. Already, her arms were getting tired.

"Three hundred!" she yelled out as Carol handed her the paddles. "Clear!" she called, unnecessarily. The similarity to TV drama would have caused her to laugh if she had been conscious of it.

Debbie, the charge nurse, walked in and was standing in the corner. Janice looked over, expecting the boss to take charge, but she stood there, assessing. In her pocket, her cell phone buzzed; she ignored it.

"We have a rhythm!" Carol called out excitedly.

"Where are we?" Doctor Salazar asked as he walked in.

"We seem to be just fine," Debbie replied, nodding Janice's way as she walked out the door.

Janice was breathless, but managed to look over at the monitor. "Normal rhythm, but still a little weak."

It was another twenty-five minutes before she could get to the phone message, but that was fine with her as it gave her time to calm down. She had a cut to clean and dress and spent ten minutes explaining to a distraught mother that antibiotics would not help with her toddler's flu virus.

Eventually, she stepped out on the terrace for a break, exhilarating in the cool autumn air. She took a few breaths, then pulled the phone from her pocket, glanced at the log to see who had called, exhaling a quick sigh as she dialed up her voicemail.

"Janice hon, this is me, your mother. I hope you can hear me OK. I got one of those cellular phones. I thought you'd really like that." Janice was surprised. *There are miracles in this world.*

"Anyway, I was wanting to make sure you're going to be here for Christmas. You said you would talk to your boss about it." Her mother paused. "We'd really love to see you. I know it's been a tough year, for all of us it has." Another pause and Janice wondered if her mother didn't know how to end a call. "Anyway, I hope, we hope we can see you. If you can't get the day off, maybe you can make it that night, or the day after. Whatever you can work out. We love you sweetie. Call me back on my new phone."

Her mother left the number, apparently not realizing her own phone would capture it.

"Damn you Andrew" she said to no one in particular as she pulled out a cigarette and lit it. Janice took a long puff and held it. "Damn," she said again quietly as she put out the cigarette on the balcony rail.

Holding onto that same rail and leaning back, she gazed out into the expansive Kansas sky and took another deep breath, then another. Resigned, she turned, opened the door to the ER, and went back to work.

EPILOGUE

Lunardi's was busy at this time of day, but she didn't mind. Lucinda was on a mission, though you wouldn't have known from her demeanor. She was as relaxed as she had been in some time, just focused. The cold weather had probably driven people indoors.

She skipped the tortillas, but made her way over to the flour section. She'd make them herself; she had certainly seen her mother do it often enough. But she did choose whole wheat flour, which her mother would not have liked; Lucy figured she may as well live as long as possible.

In the speakers overhead, Ruthie Foster was singing "Set Fire to the Rain". Lucinda swayed sensually along with the music, letting it wash over her like a warm shower. If there was a hint of melancholy in her eyes, none of the other patrons were likely to have noticed.

She already had her staples, the yogurt was on sale this week, so she stocked up. Moving over to the refrigerator section, she picked up some *carne asada*. Black beans and rice were already in the cart. Pulling out the list, she checked off each item, one by one. Everything had a mark next to it, save one thing.

As she entered the produce section, it took a moment to find them. It was off season after all, so who knows where they had been shipped from. But holding a firm plum to her nose, she inhaled deeply and approved. What could be better than her Avalon plums? She'd thought about trying a new recipe for them, spicing them up with some cinnamon or chile or mixing them with another fruit, but decided against it. Maybe she'd serve them sliced, but nothing more. Simple is best.

Lucinda walked up to the express aisle and glanced around at the other checkout lines. Exhaling softly, she began putting her items on the conveyer belt. The cashier was a middle-aged woman she'd seen several times before, so she smiled and greeted her warmly. It only took a minute to ring up her items and she handed the cashier a twenty and a ten and waited briefly for her change. She gave her thanks upon receiving it and took the bag and receipt, along with another breath.

Lucinda walked along the rows of checkout lines toward the door. Stopping three aisles away, she tapped a bagboy on the shoulder. "Excuse me. Alex, isn't it? Could you help me out with my groceries?"

Alex waved for another bagboy to take over for him and hurried to catch up. Touching Lucinda's elbow, he pointed to her single bag. "Can I take this for you?"

She handed him the bag and made her way toward her car. Now, Alex took the initiative. "Lucinda, right?"

"Yes, Lucinda, Lucy. Lucy Fuentes." She stuck out her hand with a shy smile. Alex took it and held it for a moment, not quite shaking.

"My car is over here," she said, pointing toward the corner of the lot.

Alex paused for a moment, watching Lucinda's hair as it bounced softly on her shoulders. Regaining his senses, he rushed to keep up. His heart leapt into his throat as he walked along merrily. By the time he reached Lucy and her car, he was almost skipping.

ABOUT THE AUTHOR

Michael Carley is a writer, among a variety of other things, from central California. His non-fiction work has appeared in the web-zine No Depression, The Good Men Project, and The Andrew Goodman Foundation web site. He writes a weekly column for the *Porterville Recorder*. His short story, *People Like That*, was published on Kindle in 2013. Mr. Carley lives in Porterville California with his wife and son. *Know My Name* is his first novel.

Printed in Great Britain
by Amazon